D1499396

THE NEW FEMINIST LITERARY STUDIES

The New Feminist Literary Studies presents sixteen chapters by leading and emerging scholars that examine contemporary feminism and the most pressing issues of today. The book is divided into three sections. The first section, 'Frontiers', contains chapters on issues and phenomena that may be considered, if not new, then newly and sometimes uneasily prominent in the public eye: transfeminism, the sexual violence highlighted by #MeToo, Black motherhood, migration, sex worker rights and celebrity feminism. Chapters in the second section, 'Fields', specifically intervene into long-constituted or relatively new academic fields and areas of theory: disability studies, ecotheory, queer studies, and Marxist feminism. Finally, the third section, 'Forms', is dedicated to literary genres and tackles novels of domesticity, feminist dystopias, young adult fiction, feminist manuals and manifestos, memoir, and poetry. Together these chapters provide new interventions into the thinking and theorising of contemporary feminism.

JENNIFER COOKE is author of *Contemporary Feminist Life-Writing: The New Audacity* (Cambridge, 2020) and *Legacies of Plague in Literature, Theory, and Film* (2009) and edited *Scenes of Intimacy: Reading, Writing and Theorizing Contemporary Literature* (2013) and a special issue of *Textual Practice* (September 2013). She chairs the Gendered Lives Research Group.

TWENTY-FIRST-CENTURY CRITICAL REVISIONS

This series addresses two main themes across a range of key authors, genres and literary traditions. The first is the changing critical interpretations that have emerged since c. 2000. Radically new interpretations of writers, genres and literary periods have emerged from the application of new critical approaches. Substantial scholarly shifts have occurred too, through the emergence of new editions, editions of letters and competing biographical accounts. Books in this series collate and reflect this rich plurality of twenty-first-century literary critical energies, and wide varieties of revisionary scholarship, to summarise, analyse, and assess the impact of contemporary critical strategies. Designed to offer critical pathways and evaluations, and to establish new critical routes for research, this series collates and explains a dizzying array of criticism and scholarship in key areas of twenty-first-century literary studies.

Recent Titles in This Series

SUZANNE DEL GIZZO AND KIRK CURNUTT
The New Hemingway Studies
PAIGE REYNOLDS
The New Irish Studies
JENNIFER HAYTOCK AND LAURA RATTRAY
The New Edith Wharton Studies
MARK BYRON
The Ezra Pound Studies
MATT COHEN
The New Walt Whitman Studies

THE NEW FEMINIST
LITERARY STUDIES

EDITED BY

JENNIFER COOKE

Loughborough University

CAMBRIDGE
UNIVERSITY PRESS

CAMBRIDGE
UNIVERSITY PRESS

University Printing House, Cambridge CB2 8BS, United Kingdom

One Liberty Plaza, 20th Floor, New York, NY 10006, USA

477 Williamstown Road, Port Melbourne, VIC 3207, Australia

314–321, 3rd Floor, Plot 3, Splendor Forum, Jasola District Centre,
New Delhi – 110025, India

79 Anson Road, #06–04/06, Singapore 079906

Cambridge University Press is part of the University of Cambridge.

It furthers the University's mission by disseminating knowledge in the pursuit of
education, learning, and research at the highest international levels of excellence.

www.cambridge.org
Information on this title: www.cambridge.org/9781108471930
DOI: 10.1017/9781108599504

© Cambridge University Press 2020

First published 2020

A catalogue record for this publication is available from the British Library.

ISBN 978-1-108-47193-0 Hardback

Contents

List of Illustrations   *page* vii
List of Contributors   viii

Introduction   I
Jennifer Cooke

I. FRONTIERS   II

1. Radical Transfeminism: Trans as Anti-static Ethics Escaping
   Neoliberal Encapsulation   13
   Mijke van der Drift and Nat Raha

2. Graphic Witness: Visual and Verbal Testimony
   in the #MeToo Movement   25
   Leigh Gilmore

3. Trapped in the Political Real: Imagining Black Motherhood
   Beyond Pathology and Protest   41
   Candice Merritt

4. Feminism at the Borders: Migration and Representation   55
   Emily J. Hogg

5. Sex Work in a Postwork Imaginary: On Abolitionism,
   Careerism, and Respectability   69
   Helen Hester and Zahra Stardust

6. The New Plutocratic (Post)Feminism   83
   Diane Negra and Hannah Hamad

v

II. FIELDS   97

7. Feminism and Literary Disability Studies   99
    Susannah B. Mintz

8. Feminism's Critique of the Anthropocene   113
    Samantha Walton

9. Queer Feminism   129
    Sam McBean

10. Social Reproduction: New Questions for the Gender, Affect,
    and Substance of Value   143
    Marina Vishmidt and Zöe Sutherland

III. FORMS   155

11. Feminist Dwellings: Imagining the Domestic in the
    Twenty-first-century Literary Novel   157
    Karen Schaller

12. Who Rules the World? Reimagining the Contemporary
    Feminist Dystopia   169
    Sarah Dillon

13. Transnational Feminism and the Young Adult Novel   182
    Jill Richards

14. Feminist Manuals and Manifestos in the Twenty-first Century   194
    Jennifer Cooke

15. 'This is not a memoir': Feminist Writings from Life   208
    Kaye Mitchell

16. Feminist Poetries of the Open Wound   222
    Julie Carr

Bibliography   236
Index   254

Illustrations

1 *TIME Magazine* (17 December 2017)   *page* 30
2 Carson Ellis, "Killed by the Police" (2017)   32
3 Oliver Munday, *The New Yorker* (23 October 2017)   33
4 Paula Scher, 'Mixed Emotions'. (2017)   35

Contributors

JULIE CARR is Associate Professor at the University of Colorado in Boulder. She is the author of six books of poetry, including *100 Notes on Violence*, *RAG* and *Think Tank*, and the prose works *Surface Tension: Ruptural Time and the Poetics of Desire in Late Victorian Poetry*, *Objects from a Borrowed Confession* and *Someone Shot My Book*. Carr's co-translation of Leslie Kaplan's *Excess – The Factory* was published 2018, as was a mixed-genre work, *Real Life: An Installation*.

JENNIFER COOKE is Senior Lecturer in English at Loughborough University and Chair of the Gendered Lives Research Group. She is author of *Contemporary Feminist Life-Writing: The New Audacity* (Cambridge University Press, 2020) and *Legacies of Plague in Literature, Theory and Film* (2009), and editor of *Scenes of Intimacy: Reading, Writing and Theorizing Contemporary Literature* (2013) and a special issue of *Textual Practice* on challenging intimacies and psychoanalysis (September 2013).

SARAH DILLON is a feminist scholar of contemporary literature, film and philosophy at the University of Cambridge. She is author of *The Palimpsest: Literature, Criticism, Theory* (2007) and *Deconstruction, Feminism, Film* (2018), editor of *David Mitchell: Critical Essays* (2011) and co-editor of *Maggie Gee: Critical Essays* (2015) and *AI Narratives: A History of Imaginative Thinking About Intelligent Machines* (2020). She is General Editor of the Gylphi Contemporary Writers: Critical Essays series.

MIJKE VAN DER DRIFT lectures at Goldsmiths, University of London, the School for New Dance Development, The Royal Academy of Art, The Hague, and Sandberg Institute, Amsterdam. Their book *Nonnormative Ethics* is currently being prepared for publication.

LEIGH GILMORE is the author of *Tainted Witness: Why We Doubt What Women Say About Their Lives* (2017), *The Limits of Autobiography: Trauma and Testimony* (2001), *Autobiographics: A Feminist Theory of Women's Self-Representation* (1994), co-editor of *Autobiography and Postmodernism* (1994), and, with Elizabeth Marshall, co-author of *Witnessing Girlhood: Toward an Intersectional Tradition of Life Writing* (2019). She is writing a book on the MeToo movement.

HANNAH HAMAD is Senior Lecturer in Media and Communication in the School of Journalism, Media and Culture at Cardiff University. She is the author of *Postfeminism and Paternity in Contemporary US Film: Framing Fatherhood* (2014). She works principally in the area of feminist media studies and has published widely in this field, as well as on contemporary celebrity culture and the cultural politics of contemporary film and television. Her newest work is in the field of feminist media history.

HELEN HESTER is Associate Professor of Media and Communication at the University of West London. Her research interests include techno-feminism, gender and sexuality studies, and theories of work, and she is a member of the international feminist working group Laboria Cuboniks. Her books include *Beyond Explicit: Pornography and the Displacement of Sex* (2014), *Xenofeminism* (2018) and *After Work: The Fight of Free Time* (2021, with Nick Srnicek).

EMILY J. HOGG is Associate Professor in the Department for the Study of Culture, University of Southern Denmark, working on the Uses of Literature project led by Professor Rita Felski and funded by the Danish National Research Foundation. She researches literature and the contemporary, focusing particularly on precarious living, human rights and women's writing. Her work includes publications on Nadine Gordimer, Goretti Kyomuhendo, David Foster Wallace and feminism in the contemporary university.

SAM MCBEAN is Senior Lecturer in Gender, Sexuality and Contemporary Culture at Queen Mary University of London. She is the author of *Feminism's Queer Temporalities* (2016) and has published on contemporary literature and culture, and queer and feminist theory in journals including *Feminist Review, Camera Obscura* and *new formations*.

CANDICE J. MERRITT is currently pursuing a PhD in African American Studies, focusing on gender, sexuality and critical theory at

Northwestern University. She holds an MA in Women's, Gender and Sexuality Studies from Georgia State University and a BA in Women's Studies from Emory University. Her study on the race and class differences in visual representations of teenage pregnancy in popular US news media can be found in *Difficult Dialogues about Twenty-First Century Girls* (SUNY Press, 2015).

SUSANNAH B. MINTZ is a Professor of English and Chair of the Department at Skidmore College. She is the author of *Unruly Bodies: Life Writing by Women with Disabilities* (2007), *Hurt and Pain: Literature and the Suffering Body* (2014) and *The Disabled Detective: Sleuthing Disability in Contemporary Crime Fiction* (2019). She is co-editor of a critical anthology on Nancy Mairs, the Long Eighteenth Century volume of *Cultural History of Disability* (forthcoming) and a two-volume Gale-Cengage disability memoir encyclopaedia.

KAYE MITCHELL is Senior Lecturer in Contemporary Literature at the University of Manchester and Co-Director of the Centre for New Writing. She is the author of *A.L. Kennedy: New British Fiction* (2007), *Intention and Text* (2008), *Writing Shame: Contemporary Literature, Gender and Negative Affect* (2020), editor of *Sarah Waters: Contemporary Critical Perspectives* (2013) and co-editor of *British Avant-Garde Fiction of the 1960s* (2019).

DIANE NEGRA is Professor of Film Studies and Screen Culture at University College Dublin. A member of the Royal Irish Academy, she is the author, editor or co-editor of ten books, including *What a Girl Wants?: Fantasizing the Reclamation of Self in Postfeminism* (2008) and *Gendering the Recession: Media and Culture in an Age of Austerity* (with Yvonne Tasker, 2014). She serves as Co-Editor-in-Chief of *Television and New Media*.

NAT RAHA is currently a postdoctoral researcher on the 'Cruising the 70s: Unearthing Pre-HIV/AIDS Queer Sexual Cultures' project at the Edinburgh College of Art, having completed a PhD on queer Marxism and contemporary poetry at the University of Sussex. She is a poet and trans/queer activist, living in Edinburgh, Scotland, and the author of three collections of poetry: *of sirens, body & faultlines* (2018), *countersonnets* (2013), and *Octet* (2010).

JILL RICHARDS is an Assistant Professor in the English Department at Yale University. Her research focuses on comparative modernisms, postcolonial studies, transnational feminism, queer theory and the history of sexuality. She is working on two book projects: *The Fury Archives: Human Rights, and the International Avant-Gardes* and *The Ferrante Letters: An Experiment in Collective Criticism,* co-written with Sarah Chihaya, Merve Emre and Katherine Hill.

KAREN SCHALLER is Senior Lecturer in Literature at the University of East Anglia. She is a feminist scholar specialising in theory, politics and the intellectual history of emotion, feeling and affect. Her current research includes critically neglected twentieth-century writers and the affective economies of literary criticism, feeling and feminist literary practice in the contemporary university, and the domestic in twenty-first-century feminist work.

ZAHRA STARDUST is a sociolegal researcher interested in criminal law, queer sexuality, feminised labour and justice. She has chapters in *Orienting Feminisms* (2018) and *Queer Sex Work* (2015) and has taught in law, criminology, social policy and gender studies at the University of NSW and University of Sydney. She is a member of Australian Lawyers for Human Rights and a Mentor with Women's Justice Network.

ZÖE SUTHERLAND is a Senior Lecturer in Humanities at the University of Brighton and a writer. She has written on various aspects of feminist theory and history, as well as on contemporary art.

MARINA VISHMIDT teaches at Goldsmiths, University of London and is a writer and editor. Her work has appeared in *South Atlantic Quarterly*, *Ephemera*, *Afterall*, *Journal of Cultural Economy*, *Australian Feminist Studies* and *Radical Philosophy*, among others, as well as a number of edited volumes. She is the co-author of *Reproducing Autonomy* (with Kerstin Stakemeier) (2016), and *Speculation as a Mode of Production: Forms of Value Subjectivity in Art and Capital* (2018).

SAMANTHA WALTON is a Reader in Modern Literature at Bath Spa University. She co-edits the ASLE-UKI journal *Green Letters* and sits on the steering committee of BSU's Research Centre for Environmental Humanities. Book projects include a monograph on crime fiction and mental illness (2015), an ecocritical study of Nan Shepherd, and a cultural history of nature and well-being.

Introduction

Jennifer Cooke

This volume is timely. Right now, in the Anglo-American West, we need fresh and inclusive feminist thinking that engages with the twenty-first century's most pressing issues, including migration, racism, climate change, the results of austerity, and the pervasive sexual harassment that #MeToo highlights. *The New Feminist Literary Studies* steps up to this challenge, discussing these and other subjects relevant to contemporary western feminism. It contains work intervening in debates that shape the world we inhabit and contains urgent, important feminist scholarship. Each chapter was commissioned especially for this volume with the request both to reflect the field that its author is a specialist in and, crucially, to influence it. Thus, *The New Feminist Literary Studies* presents fresh directions for today's feminism across several disciplines and subdisciplines that intersect with literary studies, including environmental humanities, disability studies, and queer theory. It also fills a surprising gap. There are many guides to feminist literary analysis and companions or readers in feminism, primarily aimed at undergraduates, and there are a variety of edited collections in subfields that take a feminist approach.[1] There is also exciting contemporary feminist writing being produced by activists, often online and outside the academy.[2] However, literary studies lacks a volume of feminist essays concerned with addressing the twenty-first century and that presents established and emerging voices from different specialisms together, in one place, for an audience of academic peers.[3] *The New Feminist Literary Studies* rectifies this and will be of use both to feminists within the fields and subdisciplines represented here and to academics and their students working across literary studies more broadly.

The present moment for feminism is one of both great danger and great opportunity. On the one hand, the rise of populist leaders with a record of sexism and, in the case of Donald Trump, multiple accusations of sexual misconduct, legitimise a regressive political environment which denigrates women, objectifies us, and refuses to take our demands seriously.[4]

Evidence of threats to women's access to services, knowledge, and justice abound. One of Trump's first acts as US president was to sign a memo curtailing assistance to overseas abortion services.[5] Two years on and the banning of abortion in Alabama has cleared the way for several states to follow suit, making a Supreme Court challenge to *Roe v. Wade* likely.[6] Meanwhile, Viktor Orban, the far-right prime minister of Hungary, has abolished gender studies programmes from his nation's universities, and more generally the disturbing rise of the far-right across America and Europe signals a significant threat to women's rights and autonomy.[7] In the UK, as in many other countries, intractable problems remain: recent statistics demonstrate that the gender pay gap is endemic, women still undertake the majority of unpaid reproductive labour within households, and domestic violence against women and girls remains widespread. Since the global financial crisis of 2007–8, the UK and many other European countries have enacted swingeing cuts to publicly funded services in the name of austerity, measures that continue to have a more adverse impact upon women than men, especially women of colour.[8] As these and similar examples demonstrate, feminism still has significant battles to win, and in some worrying cases recently – as with the abrogation of abortion rights in some states of the USA – to re-win. It is difficult not to find these circumstances alarming; it is sobering to recognise that women's hard-won legal rights and positions in society are more fragile than we might have supposed. If it has become a staple in these seemingly darkening times to fear a future descent into conditions akin to those described in Margaret Atwood's *The Handmaid's Tale*, we should heed Sarah Dillon's warning about contemporary feminist dystopias in her chapter here: 'the imagined worlds we find in them are no longer so far removed from a potential reality for Western women in the twenty-first century as they might have seemed a few decades ago' and, indeed, that 'if one takes an international perspective, such worlds have never in fact been very different from the reality of life for many women across the globe' (p. 172).

At the same time, feminists have achieved so much. Women are at the forefront of social change movements: significant global protests and campaigns have been initiated and led by feminists, such as Black Lives Matter, #MeToo, and the Women's March.[9] Socially, attitudes are changing: people are more aware of the poisonous effects of racism, ableism, trans discrimination, and the inequalities of wealth distribution, and there is, broadly speaking, greater recognition and affirmation of minority voices than there historically has been. In terms of legal rights, there has been no better time to be a woman in the history of the West. The twenty-first century has even ushered in legalised abortion in the Catholic country of Ireland, which at the turn of the millennium appeared unachievable. Pop and film stars have aligned themselves with feminism in a manner that – while not unproblematic, as definitively demonstrated by Diane Negra and Hannah Hamad in their chapter here, criticising 'The New Plutocratic (Post)Feminism' – has nevertheless helped destigmatise self-identifying as a feminist for a generation of young girls. *The New Feminist Literary Studies*, then, is set amid and engages with this background of risks and achievements and, while this is a book concerned with feminism in relation to literary studies and the theories shaping that field, the political contexts of our times and their impact upon women's lives and their representation inform every chapter in this volume by necessity, and often explicitly, such as Leigh Gilmore's chapter on #MeToo.

There are, of course, different forms of feminism – political, theoretical, academic – and different forms of activism. A history of feminism can be told that emphasises its rifts and contortions, its arguments and divisions.[10] Knowledge of our history and of the different shapes feminism can take are crucial, not just to inform us of how far we have come and the mistakes that have been made but also to help us chart a better, more effective and collective feminist future. Certain chapters in *The New Feminist Literary Studies* are in dialogue with previous forms of feminist thinking, such as Marina Vishmidt and Zöe Sutherland's examination of social reproduction theory today and Candice Merritt's consideration of how ambivalent accounts of Black motherhood recounted in earlier feminist texts have not been the recipients of revival as frequently as other, more celebratory accounts have been, leading to a paucity of attention to the reality of Black parenting in the present. More frequently, though, the chapters featured in *The New Feminist Literary Studies* are critical of particular iterations of present feminism and call for feminist world-making aimed at radical structural change. Mijke van der Drift and Nat Raha castigate anti-trans and state forms of feminism, for instance, while Helen Hester and Zahra Stardust condemn anti-sex work feminists for the exclusions upon which their position relies. Both chapters argue against forms of feminism that reject the validity of the experience of other women, especially those women who are already stigmatised, in these cases, for being trans or sex workers. Several chapters – my own on feminist manuals and manifestos, Negra and Hamad on plutocratic (post)feminism, and Samantha Walton's important chapter on feminism and the Anthropocene – sharply criticise neoliberal, capitalist and 'lean in' versions of feminism which uphold the status quo.[11]

The aim of *The New Feminist Literary Studies* is not simply to berate, even while criticism of some of feminism's current incarnations is unavoidable, but instead to invigorate contemporary feminist thinking. The feminist commitments that emerge from the chapters in these pages are transaffirmative and intersectional, attentive to how classism, racism, ableism, geographical location, and other forms of discrimination and privilege differentially shape women's lives. The book deliberately opens with a chapter detailing new theorisations of transfeminism by van der Drift and Raha, and includes later chapters by Julie Carr, Jill Richards, and me that analyse trans writing. Literature by Black, Latina, Indian and British South-Asian writers is discussed across different chapters in *The New Feminist Literary Studies* and Jill Richards's chapter on young adult fiction, taking a transnational approach, discusses books from all over the world. The work of leading feminist scholars of colour, such as Sara Ahmed, Patricia Hill Collins, Inderpal Grewal, Audre Lorde, and Jennifer Nash, is drawn upon in the following chapters, showcasing the continued foundational position these thinkers hold within feminism. *The New Feminist Literary Studies* is particularly attentive to how certain women are othered in society, literature, politics, the media, and public discourse.

This book is divided into three sections: 'Frontiers', 'Fields' and 'Forms'. 'Frontiers' contains chapters on issues and phenomena that may be considered, if not new, then newly and sometimes uneasily prominent in the public eye: transfeminism, the sexual violence highlighted by #MeToo, Black motherhood, migration, sex worker rights, and celebrity feminism. In Chapter 1, 'Radical Transfeminism', van der Drift and Raha argue that trans people need to demand more than assimilation to a liberal political project which excludes the most vulnerable from its benefits because they are not compliantly profitable. They propose instead thorough structural social change borne out of an anti-normative trans agency that expresses solidarity with others threatened under the current system, such as undocumented migrants. Their vision of transfeminism is committed to producing new relational modes, future forms of living not determined by logics of extraction and exploitation. Leigh Gilmore's Chapter 2, 'Graphic Witness: Visual and Verbal Testimony in the #MeToo Movement', works with two senses of the graphic: one that names the intimate nature of #MeToo's multiple testimonies to sexual violence, and the other that allows Gilmore to carefully analyse images produced in response to #MeToo by artists and media outlets. In a memorable metaphor that captures #MeToo's illumination of what was already known, she likens it to 'flipping on a light switch in a darkened room' (p. 25). Aware of the risks of #MeToo, Gilmore is nevertheless optimistic that its sheer scale, its collective resonance and graphic significance, marks a promising watershed moment in feminist history. She notes that it was a Black woman, Tarana Burke, who started the #MeToo hashtag, and it is to Black motherhood that Candice Merritt turns in Chapter 3 to discuss the need for Black feminism to make space for the ambivalence encountered during the course of childcare. The Black mother has embodied various stereotypes within the public imaginary and within the discourses of Black liberation and feminism, Merritt demonstrates, from the pathologised 'bad', neglectful mother and the mother who loses her child to racism, through to the powerful but dangerous matriarch or exemplar of normative domestic heteropatriarchy. These tropes have their histories, as Merritt shows us, and the discourses they serve – even in certain forms of feminist thinking – tend to gloss over or ignore more complex accounts of motherhood that admit to the sacrifices of self it entails. Merritt thus calls for new space to articulate ambivalent experiences of Black motherhood.

Fittingly, for a chapter in a section called 'Frontiers', Emily J. Hogg's Chapter 4, 'Feminism at the Borders: Migration and Representation', is attentive to how actual borders and the differences between their enforcement shape subjectivity and the language used to represent it. She turns to the poetries of Warsan Shire and Vahni Capildeo and the life-writing of Valeria Luiselli, a Mexican migrant working as a translator in an immigration court for unaccompanied children who have crossed the border into the USA, in order to identify the counter-narratives to official and media reports of migration. These reveal the trauma of migration caused by sexual violence; searing experiences of racialisation; unrecognised connections between places usually considered on either side of a divide; and the creative potential as well as inevitable difficulties contained in the language used to describe those who migrate. Hogg's chapter ultimately highlights how feminist writers attest to the injustice of contemporary bordering practices. Another marginalised group, sex workers, is discussed by Hester and Stardust in their Chapter 5, 'Sex Work in a Postwork Imaginary', where they trace the trajectory of sex workers' rights campaigns within the wider context of work abolitionism. They note a lacuna in postwork theorising, which tends not to consider the crucial place of paid and unpaid social reproduction work in its visions of the future. For sex workers to advocate the end of sex work, however, sails dangerously close to the abolitionism of anti-sex work feminists. Hester and Stardust show how important it has been for sex workers to insist on what they do as work in order to launch campaigns and initiatives for better working conditions, yet also how the kernel of a promising postwork position is identifiable within sex work advocacy. The final chapter in this section is Negra and Hamad's Chapter 6 on 'The New Plutocratic (Post)Feminism'. Training their focus upon so-called celebrity feminists such as Emma Watson and Ivanka Trump, they demonstrate how flimsy these plutocratic feminist principles are in contrast to the commitment these celebrities have to themselves as brands. While most of the chapters in 'Frontiers' are broadly optimistic for feminism's potential to forge new relational and structural forms to help women's lives flourish, wherever they are and whatever they do, Negra and Hamad's analysis shows that in the most publicly recognisable form of feminism, as adopted by celebrity avatars, there is much to deplore.

The chapters in the 'Fields' section of *The New Feminist Literary Studies* are, in many respects, also contemporary frontiers for feminist thinking. Yet these contributions are more specifically interventions into long-constituted or relatively new academic fields and areas of theory: disability studies, eco-theory, queer studies, and Marxist feminism. In her Chapter 7, 'Feminism and Literary Disability Studies', Susannah B. Mintz offers analyses of Ana Castillo's *Peel My Love Like an Onion* (1999), Alison Bechdel's *Fun Home* (2006) and Octavia Butler's *The Parable of the Talents* (1998). She explores not simply how carefully disability is repre-sented in these books to avoid stereotypes, but also how these authors use disability to think through the creation of meaning, to open up creative possibilities for being that are so far underexplored. Such writers, Mintz demonstrates, offer new routes for the development of literary disability studies. Another field fertile for feminist intervention is tackled in Walton's Chapter 8, 'Feminism's Critique of the Anthropocene', the title of which indicates its scepticism of the dominant discourses that account for human impact upon the environment. Walton notes that alternative nomencla-ture for this period have been proposed – Plantationocene, Androcene and Corporatcene – to capture a more nuanced sense of blame and history than does the Anthropocene. Drawing upon Donna Haraway's recent work on the Chlthulucene, Robin Wall-Kimmerer's promotion of indigenous forms of knowledge, Stacey Alaimo's theory of transcorporeality, and Joanna Zylinksa's ethical critique of eco-theory's masculinist world-building, Walton provides an invigorating encounter with key contem-porary ecofeminist thinkers that demonstrates the importance of critical feminist appraisal of the assumptions unpinning the field of eco-theory.

A rather different process of enquiry is provided in Chapter 9 in Sam McBean's personalised account of being on sabbatical in the USA at the

Women's, Gender, and Sexuality Studies Department at Stony Brook University in New York. McBean listens to lectures, reads, and ponders the current state of women's studies in the USA. Charting her way through the debates between queer theory and feminism over the genesis and ownership of the study of sexuality, McBean draws upon a range of feminist thinkers, from Robyn Wiegman to Jennifer Nash, from Gayle Rubin to Judith Butler and more, to demonstrate that the queer/feminist divide continues to be a productive 'pairing that does a lot of work' (p. 139) in the contemporary. The final chapter in 'Fields', Marina Vishmidt and Zöe Sutherland's 'Social Reproduction: New Questions for the Gender, Affect, and Substance of Value', intervenes in debates within Marxist feminism. Providing a brief history of the theory of social reproduction and its relation to capitalist accumulation, Vishmidt and Sutherland then dissect recent theorisations to propose that value is a social form and that gendering itself should be put into question, thus indicating a new direction for theorists in this field.

The last section of *The New Feminist Literary Studies* is dedicated to how feminists use different literary forms. Karen Schaller's Chapter 11, 'Feminist Dwellings: Imagining the Domestic in the Twenty-first-century Literary Novel', is an appropriate chapter to follow Vishmidt and Sutherland's theoretical discussion of gendered labour. Schaller analyses the politics of domestic settings in Zadie Smith's *On Beauty* (2005), Deborah Levy's *Swimming Home* (2011), and Miranda July's *The First Bad Man* (2015). She gives a nuanced account of how these texts neither sustain the domestic as a site of uncomplicated happiness nor dismiss it or its continued importance within women's lives, highlighting the tensions and contradictions that emerge when the setting of these novels is brought to the fore. Staying with the novel, Sarah Dillon, in her Chapter 12, 'Who Rules the World? Reimagining the Contemporary Feminist Dystopia', uses Naomi Alderman's *The Power* (2017) as an exemplar of what she argues the genre sorely requires. For Dillon, feminist dystopias risk simply rehearsing or amplifying existing acts of violence against women. Instead, she argues, developing the work of Darko Suvin, feminist dystopias need to leverage a critical relation with the present. Novels, some of them dystopian, are also discussed in Jill Richards's Chapter 13 on 'Transnational Feminism and the Young Adult Novel'. Richards looks beyond the Anglo-American products in this genre, introducing readers instead to a range of texts from across the globe, including works set or published in Finland, Japan, France, Sweden, Nigeria, Denmark, and Canada. For Richards, these texts offer abundant opportunities to rethink gender and adolescence as sites which are mediated by local contexts, the globalisation of finance and information flows, and international policymakers. She makes a compelling argument for why the transnational young adult novel is a genre to which feminists should attend more closely.

The final three chapters of *The New Feminist Literary Studies* move away from novels and deal with feminist writing from life, manifestos, and lyric poetry. My Chapter 14, 'Feminist Manuals and Manifestos in the Twenty-first Century' contrasts the two forms of its title. Assessing the common-alities of feminist manuals by Laurie Penny, Roxanne Gay, Chimamanda Ngozi Adichie, Caitlin Moran, and Emer O'Toole, I show how these texts largely rely upon a forgetting of existing feminist knowledge and thus, while they may resonate or entertain, they fail to move feminist thought forward. By contrast, contemporary manifestos such as Sara Ahmed's 'Killjoy Manifesto', the Edinburgh Action for Trans Health manifesto, and the document 'Xenofeminism: A Politics for Alienation' all provide examples of galvanising demands for new, collective feminist futures. Feminist manuals frequently ground themselves in autobiographical dis-closures. Kaye Mitchell's chapter specifically addresses two forms of fem-inist autobiography: the recent memoirs of feminists Andrea Dworkin and Lynne Segal, who are looking back at their activism and the women's movement in the 1960s and 1970s, and deliberately innovative contempor-ary autobiographical writing by Chris Kraus and Kate Zambreno. Mitchell's comparison ultimately sides with Segal's collective memorialis-ing, suspicious of the lonely, angry individualism of Dworkin and cautious of the seeming self-absorption and appropriation of other women's states on display in Zambreno and Kraus, despite the exuberance and risks of their writing. The last chapter in the collection, Julie Carr's 'Feminist Poetries of the Open Wound', examines accounts of trauma and damaging gendered experiences in lyrical work by Serena Chopra, Khadijah Queen, Aditi Machado, Lisa Robertson, and Nat Raha, the latter also a contributor to this volume. Carr uses a Kristevan and Butlerian lens through which to frame her close readings of these poets' work. The analysis is attentive not only to language's ability to express trauma but also to provide creative avenues through it.

Commissioning for *The New Feminist Literary Studies* sometimes took me pleasurably outside of my own areas of expertise to read up on and contact leading and emerging feminist scholars working in the fields I had identified as absolutely necessary to include here. I initially approached individual feminists but was both surprised and gratified when four of my authors elected to co-author their chapters with others, a sign, I think, of heartening co-operation among feminist thinkers in the contemporary academy. Feminist commissioning is full of challenges, however. Women in academia routinely suffer from a range of structural inequalities and often bear the brunt of the workload burden, frequently having to take on far more of the affective labour of departmental life than their male peers.[12] Black and ethnic minority women, and trans and disabled women in the academy pay an even higher price for their place at the table. Mental health problems, overwork, stress, and exhaustion are common to women in academia, and not only because the workplace is white, cis, ableist, difficult to navigate for working-class women, and lacking in gender equality at senior levels. There are numerous structural problems within universities that disadvantage women, too many to list here. It is also the case that the under-representation of Black, ethnic minority, disabled, and trans women in the academy means that they receive more invitations to contribute to volumes such as these, to speak up as representatives for the scholarship they do, which is also sometimes scholarship about who they are. It is hard work for these academics, and so I am especially grateful to Mijke van der Drift, Hannah Hamad, Candice Merritt, and Nat Raha for writing for this volume. Many people have been involved in this book through its various stages, and I want to thank them all. May we all witness a better feminist future.

Notes

1. For examples of the former, see R. Robbins, *Literary Feminisms* (Basingstoke: Macmillan, 2000); E. Rooney (ed.), *The Cambridge Companion to Feminist Literary Theory* (Cambridge: Cambridge University Press, 2012). For feminist subdisciplines, see examples such as K. Q. Hall (ed.), *Feminist Disability Studies* (Bloomington, IN: Bloomington University Press, 2011) and C. J. Adams and L. Gruen, *Ecofeminism: Feminist Intersections with Other Animals and the Earth* (New York: Bloomsbury Academic, 2014).
2. For example, see *GUTS* magazine, available at: gutsmagazine.ca.
3. There are edited collections on different areas of cultural production. See C. Dale and R. Overell (eds.), *Orientating Feminism: Media, Activism, and Cultural Representation* (Basingstoke: Palgrave Macmillan, 2018).
4. M. Keneally, 'List of Trump's Accusers and their Allegations of Sexual Misconduct', *ABC News* (25 June 2019).
5. T. McCarthy, 'A Whirlwind Week: Trump's First 14 Official Presidential Actions', *The Guardian* (27 January 2017).
6. K. Reily, 'Alabama's Abortion Ban is Designed to Challenge *Roe v. Wade* at the Supreme Court. Here's What Happens Next', *Time* (15 May 2019), available at: Time.com.

7. M. Oppenheim, 'Hungarian Prime Minister Viktor Orban Bans Gender Studies Programmes', *Independent* (24 October 2018).
8. 'Gender Pay: Fewer Than Half UK Firms Narrow Gap', *BBC News* (5 April 2019); E. Akwugo and L. Bassell, 'Minority Women, Austerity and Activism', *Race and Class*, 57:2 (2015), 86–95.
9. Black Lives Matter was founded by Alicia Garza, Patrisse Cullors, and Opal Tometi. The #MeToo hashtag was first used by Tarana Burke, as Leigh Gilmore discusses in Chapter 2. All are women of colour.
10. For thorough accounts of rifts, difficulties and disagreements in feminism, see A. Phipps, *The Politics of the Body: Gender in a Neoliberal and Neoconservative Age* (Cambridge: Polity Press, 2014) and C. Hemmings, *Why Stories Matter: The Political Grammar of Feminist Theory* (Durham and London: Duke University Press, 2011).
11. Editorial note: I have chosen to use 'Black' in my chapter and this introduction to underscore that to be Black is not the same as to be white in the West: it is not a neutral racial designation and can be capitalised to recognise this and its political importance. However, I have retained in individual chapters whatever the author has chosen.
12. For a statistic-rich study with international examples, see T. Vettese, 'Sexism in the Academy: Women's Narrowing Path to Tenure', *n+1*, 35 (Spring 2019), nplusonemag.com. Women are frequently asked to be departmental diversity representatives (usually assigned to BAME and/or LGBTQ+ women) or made responsible for student welfare. The extensive paperwork for UK's Athena Swan programme, an award recognising work towards gender equality in HE, is nearly always completed by a team of women. See also S. Ahmed, *On Being Included: Racism and Diversity Work in Institutional Life* (Durham and London: Duke University Press, 2012).

I

Frontiers

Radical Transfeminism: Trans as Anti-static Ethics Escaping Neoliberal Encapsulation

Mijke van der Drift and Nat Raha

Introduction

Emerging in contrast to the falsehood of Dan Savage's popular claim and campaign that for LGBT people 'It Gets Better', radical transfeminism understands that there will be 'no inclusion'.[1] This understanding is practical, as we find ourselves living amid the future that liberalism has wanted for us – a future based in limited forms of social inclusion and legal rights, which operate as a mode of encapsulation. Inclusion as encapsulation entails an alignment into the body politics promoted by neoliberal and neocolonialist states, within which trans people must be content to have their documents (or their bodies) checked when requested, which normalises the violence enacted through such checks. Radical transfeminism embraces the necessity of a new futurity. We are: precarious and poor, trans and queer people, feminised although sometimes femme, of various genders, abilities and embodiments, brown, white and black, with different hirstories of migration, and with bodies that have necessarily enacted change.[2] Amid regimes of austerity, material dispossession through an upwards redistribution of wealth, governmental feminism, and the defence of borders in the name of a racist national security, radical transfeminist futurity embraces emergent relations which hold the potential for transforming material conditions through supporting different lives.

Radical transfeminism embraces trans as active and anti-normative, rather than defined as a stable form. We conceive of radical transfeminism in terms of agents and agency. The dynamism of the term 'trans' indicates that we must attend to questions of agency and structures of action, rather than the political-epistemological emphasis of critical theory's 'subjects' and 'subjectivity'. From this anti-normative trans agency emerges a feminism concerned with structural social change as futurity through a non-normative ethics.

Contemporary pluralist politics and normative social orderings remain overwhelmingly constrained in their conceptions of social forms. In a social ordering which is re-emerging as a visual ordering, diversity is primarily a spectacle, and hardly a practice. The norm constitutes itself by exclusion. A norm is either invisible and thus supports agents with a hidden presence or its terms become visible in the failure of the agent. Ultimately the norm exists to remove friction from some lives by transposing it to other lives in a hierarchy of duress. Not resisting this friction, and accepting the assigned position demanded of one – even in transition – constitutes social encapsulation. In the spirit of neoliberal multiculturalism, which as Jodi Melamed argues, 'sutures official anti-racism [as an official diversity politics] to state policy in a manner that hinders the calling into question of global capitalism', and thus 'produc[es] new privileged and stigmatized forms of humanity', we witness the incorporation of white, wealthy transgender people into the social order.³ In the political sphere, we have described this as 'trans liberalism' – a politics of inclusion extending 'queer liberalism', articulated at a moment when Western states are invested in neocolonial projects of capitalist accumulation through war in the Middle East and the fortification of European borders, coupled to Islamophobic and xenophobic rhetoric.⁴ These are administrative, juridical and military manoeuvres by states that buffer, but also have preceded, the rise of far-right populism and forms of neofascism across and beyond Europe.

The call for inclusion of differences into the social order, especially and currently heard loudly from liberal trans chorales, is a call to be *seen as part of* the order. It is the demand that switches trans agents from sonic presence calling for inclusion, to a visual presence – Caitlyn Jenner on the cover of *Vanity Fair* – a shift from the vocal to the visual, a shift towards 'capital-intensive forms of visibility'.⁵ This inclusion without structural change does not create much-needed protections for, and leads to increased violence against, women of colour, in particular trans women of colour, as Tourmaline, Eric Stanley, and Johanna Burton describe, because it opens up the faultline of political contestation over a pressured group.⁶ This visual spectacle of multiculturalism is itself relieved from the project of *substantive* equality, of social possibilities, safety and well-being, and material transformation, focusing instead on corporate (indeed capitalist) diversity and nominal legal equality through rights. In the context of freshly securitised nation states, corporate diversity, marketing and legal rights invite a 'fading into the population . . . but also the imperative to be "proper" in the eyes of the state: to reproduce, to find proper employment; to reorient one's "different" body into the flow of the nationalized aspiration for possessions, property [and] wealth'.⁷ We understand such imperatives as forms of social and material encapsulation, where the nominal equality of rights hides individualised forms of duress, administrative violence, divestment/disinvestment and dispossession, targeting and further marginalising people of colour, women, and disabled, queer, migrant and/or poor people.[8] Methods of encapsulation currently manifest as the rights of equality but without provision of the means to access them, as witnessed in the cuts for Legal Aid and the introduction of fees for Employment Tribunals by Conservative-led governments in the UK, while new regimes of security within nation states create fresh forms of biopolitical and necropolitical regulation and governmentality. Meanwhile, identity documents with 'correct' gender markers (where 'male' and 'female' remain the only correct markers) are issued at increased prices, and the state creates the demand to check passports while accessing public services (including healthcare), housing, and employment in addition to when crossing borders.

Encapsulation operates through institutional demands that trans people remain strategically invisible, demands that operate like norms. One can be who one wants to be, as long as one lays low and blends in within the workplace, the social space, is physically and psychologically healthy, does not challenge oppressions within these spaces, and 'celebrates' oneself when invited to do so in the name of diversity. Encapsulation is the licence to *be* but not a licentious being. To remove oneself from a prescribed position in the social order leads to further marginalisation. The demanded pay-off is a silencing, a becoming complicit in furthering the frictionless operation of the norm: do not protest, adapt, be still, or lose out even further. Cis is the power to protest *in* the norm, trans is the power to protest *against* the norm. To demand of trans to enact itself as 'cis' means to encapsulate trans in the forms of the dominant order, albeit in a subjugated position in terms of access. This means that trans people like us end up jobless, in precarious labour, doing dead-end jobs, with little means to continue developing our forms of life regardless of our volition. However, it should be noted that those born into money, or those who have made careers in the flows of capital's demands and its racial and gendered divisions of labour, can be trans without losing their material gains. Trans is not a singular descriptor of precarious lives.

Trans as Anti-static

In the context of social and bureaucratic norms, trans lives are conceived through clear forms of identity, which can be represented – even if in a multiplicity of representations – as a stable form, and which indeed *will be represented* if such representation is in the interests of the state and capital. However, transfeminism understands trans as departing from such encapsulation in normative contexts – as Paul Preciado elaborates through his experimentation with the techno-pharmaceutically mediated normality of genders.[9] Furthermore, Marquis Bey proposes transfeminism as a mode of fugitivity from the normative demands on trans and blackness.[10] Trans is thus conceptualised as a practice. This practice is, however, not neutral, but marked by a refusal of the current order, a negation of constraining demands of medicalised operational perfection, and an escape from the encapsulations in normative institutional demands.

Trans is thus a dynamic formation, which does not lay a claim to simply *be*, but which functions by disrupting static categories of being. As a form of refusal this entails claiming a difference of being, without necessarily leading to a separation with other forms of life.[11] There is no being left behind; indeed, the separation of categories is put in question. Trans emerges from its negation, its refusal, through a flight from the world of norms, as an indeterminate affirmation of life. This means, siding with Denise Ferreira da Silva, that trans formative practices do not need to lean on categorical differences, which imply and demand separability (p. 61). Thus the refusal of the current order need not lead to a practice of perpetual fluidity in which formlessness is hailed as the new regime. Trans as dynamic formation proposes a negation of the categorical separation of differences, and thus an affirmation of possible alignments, coalitions, and formations beyond the current static order of visual and capitalist dispossession. Trans is thus a claim to categorical change, which entails a change in the status of how categories are understood to operate. Trans is not only a practice, but, in its epistemic commitments, also a praxis of changing ethics and the analytics through which these operate.

Our praxis has been forged through the refusal of unliveable relations of gender – of the assimilative gender binary that privileges whiteness – coupled with the necessary claim to change. We, those who are not Caitlyn Jenner or Chaz Bono, intimately understand the forms of social and economic disenfranchisement of trans lives, especially for trans people of colour and trans sex workers, which is the 'price' of such refusal and such change. To refuse the over-determined positions of the gender binary, understood by María Lugones as a colonial technology that is in part enacted through forms of psychiatric, medical and state control, means economic and institutional marginality.[12] The 'price' that neoliberal capitalist society forces from us, offering 'deals' of inclusion, ensures cheap labour for society – labour which presents itself in its drive to inclusion as highly productive and thus good value for money.[13] This labour is extracted from bodies that have previously been neglected, refused nourishment and social support.

Through this claim to dynamism, to change, transfeminist action becomes a means for affirmation and building other worlds and futures. Affirmation of relations amid categorical change leads to the emergence of new forms of living not structured by the exploitation of difference. Dissolving borders spreads responsibility for relations while weakening categorical impositions of affect, thought, and patterns of power.

Navigating the norm, not every trans agent is *good* at finding loopholes, nor should they need to be: different people have different skills. However, within an environment that demands trans people make choices aggressively constrained by pathology, social and material pressure, affective extortion, and a withholding of sociality, trans agents find themselves needing to navigate fraught medical and social spaces often in isolation. Sometimes without the social skills or experience that could enable them to be successful or to maintain a liveable life, trans agents face particular forms of precarity. As witnessed in the UK, transspecific healthcare, and indeed the NHS in general, remain underfunded or freshly divested of funds, while psychiatrists and bureaucrats alike refuse to cede control of – or recognise the agency of – marginalised bodies (such as trans bodies, bodies of colour, migrant bodies, disabled bodies, HIV+ or bodies at risk of HIV infection, and working-class pregnant bodies).[14] Our access to healthcare is restricted on the grounds of 'cost effectiveness', while our physical and mental health is deemed a 'personal responsibility', rather than the responsibility of any institutions we interact with or which fail to provide us with healthcare. Furthermore, clinicians and psychologists guiding medical transitions want to see 'change' but remain reluctant to facilitate new directions, interrogating trans 'patients' to ensure they are leading conservative lives. In such contexts, where trans agents have little room to manoeuvre against these demands, some trans people end up sterilised against their will.[15]

Further Forces of Constraint and Their Refusal

Radical transfeminism necessarily aligns with penal abolition, works against societies of control, and objects to the extraction of labour and resources in both the personal sphere and globally. These tenets are rooted in an ethics that refuses disposability and punishment.[16] Instead of the criminalisation of deviance, whether by racist, gendered, or economic codifications, we understand transformative justice – interpersonal, communal, and social – to provide the tools to change the problems faced in the everyday. This means that the control of difference, as Luciana Parisi and Tiziana Terranova propose, needs to be surrendered in favour of an ethics of deviation, where change becomes an aspect of life in making new relations against disposability.[17] Surrendering control will enable new ethical relations, rather than preserving the exploitation of resources, labour, and ideas, with their concurrent aggressive protection of extraction and its attendant logistics.[18] The possibility of refusal undergirds our understanding of relationality.

In the context of what Ruth Wilson Gilmore describes as organised abandonment – the wilful and structural creation of social and economic marginalisation that transforms people and land into refuse by means of incarceration, the demolition of social support structures, and transformation of land into toxic dumping grounds – we understand that a refusal of current relations requires transformation.[19] Radical transfeminism thus entails an opening of space – of borders as well as social space, which means a sustained resistance against the encapsulations of capital and the policing of the limits of the nation state and overarching political projects. Radical transfeminism proposes a sustained transformative ethics that is needed to enable the modes of life of agents – an openness to categorical change rooted in trans leads agents to change their understanding of the world.[20]

Forces constraining trans practices and ultimately life are not only the material forces of finance departments, police forces, landlords, border guards, and medical authorities, but also include the submerged racist categorisations built into the algorithmic approaches streamlining arrests, bail, debt, zoning, and housing.[21] The algorithmic approach freezes categorisations for extraction and encapsulation, while mobilising 'diversity' to legitimise its epistemic existence and guarding its morality by keeping its constraining logics out of sight. The algorithmic politics of fiscal austerity, debt, and predictive policing, facilitating the redistribution of wealth from poor to rich, creates visible impoverishment, slowly creeping up to the middle classes, making life brutal for those below the line of inclusion. As the poet Verity Spott reminds us, austerity names a political practice of distributed death.[22] In conjunction with Brexit, as a phantasmic closure of the UK to outside influences and an imagined threat of migration, austerity politics has turned into a bureaucratic exercise of social and economic marginalisation.[23] Managerial politics that demand identification at the level of university enrolment, housing, medical care, education and job interviews turn what is presented as 'mere administration' into an everyday violence for precarious residents. Managerial activity is meanwhile contrasted by the unaccountability of omnipresent deaths.[24] This is primarily death distributed to Black and/or disabled people while these communities are the first targets for austerity logics of organised abandonment, which find expression in the retraction of social responsibility and practical support for those *made* to be worse off.

An example of a politics of control can be found in the resurgence of a forced frontline by anti-trans activists on the gendered use of toilets. This coerced debate on (gender neutral) toilets misses one key point: the space with the universally present gender-neutral toilet is indeed the site of the most gender-based violence: the family home. It is not the toilet that is to blame, but its placement in the capitalist enclosure of the nuclear family. Anti-trans activists meanwhile promote a further enclosure of space in a bid to defend the categorical innocence of the white woman.[25] The patriarchal violence of enclosure is ignored, because the gaze is as usual misdirected: it is the group under duress that is prompted to defend its existence against claims projected by the norm. Gender-based violence goes on in the family home, while the problematic of this violence is enhanced by material and normative enclosure structuring the impossibility of escape. Austerity measures ensure shelters for survivors/victims of domestic violence are closed due to a lack of funding. Being out of place becomes a trigger for social alarm, whether that is in public toilets, train stations, or the racialised surveillance of presumed terrorists.[26] The surveillance, with its racialised component, draws on images of the innocent white woman. The presumed categorical innocence of women, presented as the moral high ground levied against trans lives, makes it hard to adequately address this problem of violence. Carceral thinking – that proposes imprisonment and social exclusion – will not provide a solution to these problems of intimate duress because it is rooted in an understanding of innocence that is the problem of much normative feminism situated in *critical* approaches. Critical approaches, with their focus on limits and transgressions, fix innocence as a necessary category in order to situate a claim. Here, we can understand anti-trans violence as a defence of categorical innocence, so as not to lose voice. This categorical claim and its aggressive enactment show its violent structure as white innocence.[27] Categorical innocence is only possible to maintain by anti-trans activists with the complicity of not problematising normative enactments of racism, xenophobia, homophobia, and misogyny. A transfeminist understanding of the norm as exclusion provides a clarity of strategy. We need to change. Relations need to change and there is no recuperation of and in the norm, because violence needs to stop. Radical thinking with transformative justice and non-disposability upfront is, in our view, the only possibility to address these urgent issues. This is why we need to refuse the current order of binaries, innocence, and presumed neutralities of spaces.

Ethics for a Transfeminist Future

Radical transfeminism refuses participation in the dominant order and instead enacts a space elsewhere, through a refusal that structures an indeterminate affirmation of potentiality in action. As Bey lays out, 'Trans* is elsewhere, not here, because here is known, ontologically discernible, and circumscribable.'[28] Recalling our discussion of the need for ethical change with its attendant analytical change, this elsewhere is not a space beyond current categories and their borders; it is accessed by refusing categorical separation and embracing alternative futures. Against the exploitation of difference, radical transfeminism holds that no life is disposable in a feminist project of futurity.

Trans as an open, uncontrollable variable does not mean trans is individual. Trans agents can cluster and spread apart, find form and let go. Such practice can be discerned from historical shifts in naming-practices, which lead to shifting arrays of social alignments.[29] To name oneself *gay transvestites* or street queens as Marsha P. Johnson and Sylvia Rivera did, or gender bender, gender blender, genderqueer, non-binary, trans femme or simply trans leads to different social connections through tracing patterns of similarity and difference, what daniel brittany chávez and rolando vázquez call a 'mutually nurturing decolonial praxis' that challenges the hegemony of the gender binary.[30] Here, naming functions as finding form, experimenting in lieu of something that can be fully named, and not as a claim to new, stable categorisations. Trans, as a term of changing ethical formation, undertakes the work and play of relationality in the knowledge that belonging or community is not a given; instead, trans in its indeterminacy suggests belonging is created through openness. This is akin to Edouard Glissant's system of relation, whereby relation 'stretch[es] ... to the mass that bursts forth just from its energy, finding ourselves there along with others', such that life may be fashioned anew from solidarities and possibilities.[31] Trans as indeterminate affirmation is thus not a fleeting bourgeois plaything, because it entails the formation of shifting praxis emerging from the negation of dominant imageries.[32]

Transfeminist futures entail new forms of affective solidarity and commitment, the changing of orientations to ensure the support and nourishment of bodily life. This entails divesting from the relations and structures of feelings prescribed and mediated by hetero- and homonormativity (including their 'liberation' permitted in the form of the depoliticised Pride parade), which uphold standards of value and beauty rooted in whiteness, cissexism and ableism.[33] This divestment from normative relations aims to overcome the overwhelming negativity, isolation and disposability of neoliberal precarity and disenfranchisement for those marginalised. This is a praxis of feeling, as Anne Boyer formulates, 'not only of bodily articulation and modulation expressing material remedy but also of a modulation producing reparations of faces, lower backs, shoulders, genitals, and palms in accordance with the actual spectrum of who and what exists'.[34] Amid reparative affects towards all possible bodies, playfulness, foolishness, awkwardness, unease and surrealism's escapades find their way into trans as the aspects of emerging relationality, which may index new modalities of life.[35] Such a multiplication of affectivities and elaboration of relations entails embracing the unease of new desires as a necessary change towards the enrichment of life – to materialise this transfeminist future in the present.[36]

When we turn away from encapsulations of liberal inclusion to face disordering and embrace an ethics of transfeminist futurity, new forms of life emerge.[37] As we have argued, structured refusals can undermine the certainty of categorical encapsulations, and bring forth new relational modes. Projects of transformative justice, which address structures of agency, need commitment – because without a shift in praxis, the world, the social order as we know it, will not end.[38] Radical transfeminism claims that it is in this shift that modes of friction emerge and it is in these frictions that the possibilities and faultlines for radical change make themselves known. Through the refusal of current orders and logics of exploitation of difference and resources, indeterminate affirmations open the way for necessary futures to emerge.

Notes

1. See itgetsbetter.org for the full campaign.
2. In a definition of 'h/story / hirstory', Flo Brooks writes: '*noun*: an alternative spelling of history, some trans and queer folks spell the word with a "/" or with a "r" as a form of empowerment to move away from the "his" in the "traditional" spelling of history'. See F. Brooks (ed.), *Outskirts* (London and Exeter: Makina Books, 2017), 54.
3. J. Melamed, 'The Spirit of Neoliberalism: From Racial Liberalism to Neoliberal Multiculturalism', *Social Text*, 24:4 (2006), 14.
4. D. Spade, *Normal Life: Administrative Violence, Critical Trans Politics, and the Limits of Law* (Brooklyn, NY: South End Press, 2011); D. Eng, *The Feeling of Kinship: Queer Liberalism and the Racialization of Intimacy* (Durham and London: Duke University Press, 2010); J. K. Puar, *Terrorist Assemblages: Homonationalism in Queer Times* (Durham, NC: Duke University Press, 2007); N. Raha, 'The Limits of Trans Liberalism' (21 September 2015), www.versobooks.com/blogs//.
5. K. Floyd, *The Reification of Desire: Towards a Queer Marxism* (Minneapolis: University of Minnesota Press, 2009), 200.
6. R. Gossett [Tourmaline], E. A. Stanley, and J. Burton (eds.), *Trap Door: Trans Cultural Production and the Politics of Visibility* (Cambridge, MA and London: MIT Press, 2017), 1.
7. Aren Aizura in 2006, cited in M. Bey, 'The Trans*-ness of Blackness, the Blackness of Trans*-ness', *TSQ: Transgender Studies Quarterly*, 4:2 (2017), 277. For a discussion of trans legal rights and border enforcement in the context of Brexit and the policy of Theresa May in the UK, see N. Raha, 'Transfeminine Brokenness, Radical Transfeminism', *South Atlantic Quarterly*, 116:3 (2017), 633–7.
8. Spade, *Normal Life*.
9. S. Stryker, *Transgender History* (Berkeley: Seal Press, 2008); P. B. Preciado, *Testo Junkie: Sex, Drugs and Biopolitics in the Pharmacopornographic Era* (New York: Feminist Press, 2013).
10. Bey, 'The Trans*-ness of Blackness'.
11. D. F. da Silva, 'On Difference without Separability', in *Catalogue: Incerteza Viva* (Sao Paolo: 32a Sao Paolo Art Biennal, 2016), 57–65.
12. M. Lugones, *Pilgrimages/Peregrinajes: Theorizing Coalition against Multiple Oppressions* (Lanham, MD: Rowman & Littlefield, 2003).
13. D. Irving, 'Elusive Subjects: Notes on the Relationship between Critical Political Economy and Trans Studies', in A. Enke (ed.), *Transfeminist Perspectives* (Philadelphia: Temple University Press, 2012), 153–69; D. Irving, 'Normalized Transgressions: Legitimising the Transsexual Body as Productive', *Radical History Review*, 100 (Winter 2008), 38–60.
14. D. Roberts, *Killing the Black Body: Race, Reproduction and the Meaning of Liberty* (New York: Pantheon Books, 1997); *The People vs The NHS: Who Gets the Drugs?*, dir. M. Henderson, aired BBC2 (27 June 2018).

15. The requirement of sterilisation for the legal gender recognition of trans people is still practised in some European countries, including Belgium, Switzerland, the Czech Republic and Slovakia. There remains a lack of research on trans fertility, which adversely effects institutional provisions of reproductive technologies for trans people. The pathologisation of trans people remains the dominant medical paradigm in Europe in accessing treatment.

16. R. Wilson Gilmore, *Golden Gulag: Prisons, Surplus, Crisis, and Opposition in Globalizing California* (Berkeley and London: University of California Press, 2007).

17. A. M. Brown, *Emergent Strategy* (Chicago and Edinburgh: AK Press, 2017); M. van der Drift, 'Nonnormative Ethics: The Ensouled Formation of Trans Bodies', in R. Pearce and I. Moon (eds.), *The Emergence of Trans* (London: Routledge, forthcoming); Raha, 'Transfeminine Brokenness'; L. Parisi, and T. Terranova, 'Heat-Death: Emergence and Control in Genetic Engineering and Artificial Life', *CTheory* 5 (2000), n.p.

18. D. Cowen, *The Deadly Life of Logistics* (Minneapolis and London: University of Minnesota Press, 2014).

19. R. Wilson Gilmore, 'Fatal Couplings of Power and Difference: Notes on Racism and Geography', *The Professional Geographer*, 54:1 (2002), 16.

20. M. van der Drift, 'Radical Romanticism, Violent Cuteness, and the Destruction of the World', *Journal of Aesthetics and Culture*, 10:3 (2018), n.p.

21. J. Wang, *Carceral Capitalism* (Cambridge, MA and London: MIT Press, 2018), 228–52; E. Dixon-Román, 'Algo-Ritmo: More-than-Human Performative Acts and the Racializing Assemblages of Algorithmic Architectures', *Cultural Studies? Critical Methodologies*, 16:5 (2016), 482–90.

22. V. Spott and N. Raha, Queer Cultures Seminar, University of Cambridge (9 May 2018).

23. Wilson Gilmore, 'Fatal Couplings'.

24. A Freedom of Information request to the Department for Work and Pensions revealed that 111,450 people had their Employment Support Allowance – a social benefit payment that implies its recipient is fit for work – ended due to mortality between 2014 and 2017. The Department has refused to take responsibility for these deaths, in a climate that stigmatises people receiving welfare benefits. See S. Preece, 'DWP Forced to Admit More Than 111,000 Deaths', *Welfare Weekly* (13 August 2018), welfareweekly.com.

25. We are here referring to US state legislation which forces all people to use bathrooms according to their assigned gender within the gender binary, alongside similar extra-legal skirmishes by transphobic feminists in the UK.

26. Here we refer to the UK British Transport Police's 'See it, say it, sorted' campaign which promotes surveillance by members of the public of that which is deemed out of place, reinforcing a state of alarm.

27. G. Wekker, *White Innocence* (Durham: Duke University Press 2016); Wang, *Carceral Capitalism*, 260–95.

28. Bey, 'The Trans*-ness of Blackness', 285. A note on the asterisk: as Eva Hayward and Jami Weinstein write: 'In its prefixial state, trans* is prepositionally oriented – marking the *with, through, of, in,* and *across* that make life possible.' See E. Hayward and J. Weinstein, 'Introduction: Tranimalities in the Age of Trans* Life', *TSQ: Transgender Studies Quarterly,* 2:2 (2015), 196.

29. L. Feinberg, *Transgender Liberation: A Movement Whose Time Has Come* (New York: World View Forum, 1992).

30. d. b. chávez and r. vázquez, 'Precedence, Trans* and the Decolonial', *Angelaki,* 22 (2017), 39.

31. E. Glissant, *Poetics of Relation,* trans. B. Wing (Minneapolis: University of Michigan Press, 1997), 195.

32. N. Pieterse, 'Hybridity, So What? The Anti-Hybridity Backlash and the Riddles of Recognition', *Theory, Culture & Society,* 18:2–3 (2001), 219–45; van der Drift, 'Nonnormative Ethics'.

33. S. P. Holland, *The Erotic Life of Racism* (Durham, NC: Duke University Press, 2012); R. McRuer, *Crip Theory: Cultural Signs of Queerness and Disability* (New York and London: New York University Press, 2006).

34. A. Boyer, 'Formulary for a New Feeling', in *A Handbook of Disappointed Fate* (Brooklyn, NY: Ugly Duckling Presse, 2018), 108.

35. Wang, *Carceral Capitalism;* Wekker, *White Innocence;* Lugones, *Pilgrimages/Peregrinajes.*

36. J. E. Muñoz, *Cruising Utopia: The Then and There of Queer Futurity* (New York: New York University Press, 2009), 49–64.

37. van der Drift, '*Nonnormative Ethics*'.

38. D. F. da Silva, 'Towards a Black Feminist Poethics: The Quest(ion) of Blackness Towards the End of the World', *The Black Scholar,* 44:2 (2014), 81–97

CHAPTER 2

Graphic Witness: Visual and Verbal Testimony in the #MeToo Movement

Leigh Gilmore

During a twenty-four-hour period in October 2017, the status #MeToo was shared twelve million times on social media.[1] In response to allegations of sexual assault and rape directed at Hollywood producer Harvey Weinstein, an unprecedented virtual assembly emerged on social media that was public, voluntary, and global. By sharing the trending hashtag, anyone could add their presence to an emerging collective, thereby enabling it to grow through repetition across platforms and to visualise the scale of sexual violence. Like flipping on a light switch in a darkened room, #MeToo revealed what had always been there: sexual violence and abuse against women and girls (with men, non-binary, and trans survivors also sharing #MeToo). Yet because the scale of participation mapped anew the widespread, albeit widely known, existence of sexual abuse, what enabled #MeToo to transcend the impact of previous awareness-raising campaigns about the prevalence of sexual violence and translate internet virality into a new era of accountability? I will argue that accountability emerged through the verbal and visual representation of #MeToo as a *graphic witness*, which I define as testimony about sexual harassment, abuse, and violence rooted in feminist, intersectional activism by and on behalf of survivors. The #MeToo movement resonated within a long history of feminist activism and allied with other historical and contemporary social justice movements. As a practice of bearing witness, #MeToo is graphic in content because it concerns sexual violence, and graphic in form because images immediately became central to its uptake as justice-seeking rather than primarily awareness-raising, focused on accountability rather than exposing again a well-known problem, and connecting the dots from celebrity culture to everyday experiences of sexual abuse and histories of violence. Graphic witness makes these connections visible.

In 2006, #MeToo was founded by Tarana Burke as a grass-roots organisation. Burke chose those words in order to place shared experience and empathy among survivors at the centre of a movement to empower girls and women of colour. It interpolates survivors into an intersectional, feminist context of self-representation and community. It does not name a new problem, solicit for a specific campaign, or limit itself to a single abuser, form of violence, or location of harm. Instead, #MeToo distils an essential insight drawn from intersectional feminist knowledge about sexual violence: we need to centre survivors in order to create social change. It fills the blank space of non-representation with the opt-in of collective witness.

I attribute the prodigious spread of #MeToo to its dual histories: one #MeToo starts with actor and activist Alyssa Milano's tweet, the exposure of sexually predatory and abusive behaviour by powerful figures in Hollywood, and the ongoing reckoning as each new case emerges. This #MeToo focuses on famous men such as Weinstein, Woody Allen, and Roman Polanski who flout the testimony of #MeToo survivors with selfish stories of their own faux victimisation. Celebrity media play a shaping role in this #MeToo by training a spotlight on media figures such as Matt Lauer and Charlie Rose and the cultures of enablement in which they thrive. It is difficult to imagine how #MeToo might have gone viral outside the conditions created by celebrity, social media, and the fusion of entertainment and journalism. However, millions did not tweet #DumpWeinstein or #IStandWithRoseMcGowan or any other Hollywood-centric sentiment.

As much as #MeToo owes its rapid dissemination to the fusion of entertainment and journalism, the words that compelled survivors to identify draw upon a long tradition of feminist resistance and a network of organisations invested in that work. It calls out to other graphic witnesses to structural violence and to victims of police violence in communities of colour. As a *graphic witness*, #MeToo magnetises embodied protest, words, and images in a new testimonial assemblage that joins Black Lives Matter, I Can't Breathe, and Hands Up Don't Shoot to the explicitly feminist activism of #SayHerName, #MeToo, and #Time'sUp.[2] This #MeToo adapts #BlackLivesMatter's fusion of social media and embodied protest, leveraging a hashtag as an iconic signifier with the power to crystallise a long history of struggle in a concise form.

In contrast to single-focus awareness-raising campaigns or investigations into specific allegations of wrongdoing, #MeToo is decidedly multijurisdictional. There is no Department of #MeToo. No single institution or organisation is responsible for establishing rules of evidence, categories of harm, or penalties.[3] Yet, because inequalities and vulnerability persist across the institutions of home, work, education, and public space in relation to sexual violence, the new exposure of its pervasiveness also offers a key to understanding, broadly, who is most at risk and least likely to receive justice; who can be called to account and who is protected, excused, or even sympathised with; who can be sacrificed; and why. Histories of sexual violence intersect with histories of slavery and empire, placing women of colour and Indigenous women at the highest risk for both abuse and erasure.[4] Male elites in institutions such as education and religion exploit children and notoriously protect abusers. These histories of harm are linked. Here #MeToo represents a reckoning because it exposes the murkiness and inadequacy of civil and criminal procedures to address all sorts of sexual abuse. In so doing, it reveals how those in power benefit by hiding the costs to victims, traumatising and erasing them through abuse, and silencing and gaslighting them when they come forward to report it.

The #MeToo movement represents a new hearing as much as a telling. Both words and images carry graphic witness into hostile contexts of judgement characterised by what philosopher Kristie Dotson calls testimonial quieting, 'when an audience fails to identify a speaker as a knower', and 'testimonial smothering', which 'is the truncating of one's own testimony in order to insure that the testimony contains only content for which one's audience demonstrates testimonial competence'.[5] In developing a feminist critical language necessary to understand how bias favours powerful men, philosopher Kate Manne defines 'himpathy' as 'the inappropriate and disproportionate sympathy powerful men often enjoy in cases of sexual assault, intimate partner violence, homicide and other misogynistic behavior'.[6] I theorise the sticky judgements embedded within legal and popular jurisdictions – courts of law and courts of public opinion – that discredit speakers by attaching bias about race and gender to their testimony as it and they move through testimonial networks in search of an adequate witness.[7] For survivors of sexual violence, #MeToo represents that adequate witness: one who will not deform the terms in which survivors speak by freighting judgement with bias and doubt independent of the facts and even before a hearing in such a way that the need for a hearing is mooted because the testimony has already been discredited or the actual testimony is treated as if it did not happen.

Histories of exploitation, discrimination, abuse of power, and abuse of persons coil within the hashtag. The #MeToo discourse, therefore, has a lot of material to draw from, including the iconography of violated bodies *and* the iconography of resistance which fused in the production of a graphic witness to an epidemic problem appearing in the shape of a current event. Consider in this context the finding that sexual violence is so widespread that a recent study documents that 81 percent of women and 43 percent of men said they have experienced sexual harassment or sexual assault during their lifetimes.[8] Few filed complaints, and most reported multiple experiences of sexual harm in multiple locations (most reported four to five locations). Two-thirds of women experienced workplace sexual harassment. More than half of women and just under half of men experienced some form of sexual harassment or assault by the age of seventeen. Scale alone was not enough to catalyse a new conversation about sexual violence or generate a new framing of it as a problem demanding a response from a wide range of entities.

The #MeToo movement disrupted some mechanisms that silence survivors by conjuring a new witness in two temporalities: summoning the past, through memory, and the present, through testimony. Initially, the tweet appealed to many women as an invitation to see themselves and be seen by others as an emergent collective of truth-tellers and survivors, as silence breakers, and also as squeaky wheels making a demand. Accused of speaking out too late, but also of 'crying rape' whenever they speak, survivors are continuously troubled by accusations of bad timing: confounded by statutes of limitations, distrust of memory, and the seeming evidence of good behaviour by men accused of bad behaviour.[9] What is the good timing of graphic witness? Is there a propitious moment for survivor testimony? Or is it always too much, too soon, or too late? The silencing of victims is not neutral. It is designed to protect the accused, to insist on his right to due process, to defend his reputation from potential injury, often before any investigation has been undertaken. It is the principle around which reasonable people are invited to rally: defend the falsely accused man. Yet consider how #MeToo forced the bad timing accusation to malfunction. Initially, no one was asked to join a complaint or expose a particular abuser. Instead, people were asked to raise their hands and say, 'me too', rather than point a finger and say, 'he did it'. 'Too' transforms isolation into a new model of affiliation, one that addresses and includes others who choose to assemble for each other. A graphic witness is one whose testimony demands a context for interpretation as a means of securing justice. Thus #MeToo assembled that context by creating a collective witness to sexual violence, ensuring that the isolating strategy of 'he said/she said' and the insinuation of doubt would be offset by the visibility of millions through 'too'. The pattern of centring the discussion on a single act of sexual assault or harassment was replaced by a flow of allegations against numerous perpetrators, many of which have been reported in reliable and verifiably sourced stories in credible journalism.

Visual Testimony: #MeToo Iconography

The #MeToo movement was interpreted by illustrators, graphic designers, and comics artists who drew upon the visual iconography of both catastrophe and protest to picture #MeToo testimony.

In 2017, Tarana Burke, together with a group of women dubbed the 'silence breakers', became *Time Magazine's* person of the year (Figure 1). The visual display echoes the multiple box presentation that organises groups of people who, in this case, share a similar status. Survivors of disaster are often presented in this way to establish relation and preserve individuality. The uniformity of the grid and style of photograph (head shots) visually encodes people as sharing experience. In this case, the silence breakers have been styled to enhance their unity as a group, but also, through blending visual elements of documentary photorealism and fashion portraiture, to transform the women into iconic statues of grievance, uniting them across race and class, and lending to the activists the chic pallor of celebrity. As this visual display demonstrates, we are not only hearing survivors in a new way, we are also seeing them as part of an emergent iconography of graphic witness.

In the visual representation of graphic witness, images reference each other to create new identifications and pathways of empathy and affiliation. Media and journalism outlets, such as the *New York Times* and *Time Magazine*, often turn to a grid of faces as a conventional commemorative structure of representation of catastrophic loss – after an earthquake, hurricane, or 9/11, for example. This honours the singularity of each loss, and also marks a traumatic event as a moment in time experienced collectively. Because it also allows for the representation of scale, it has been adopted within reporting on #MeToo. Over 260 women testified during the victim impact phase of Larry Nassar's sentencing hearing and the *New York Times* created a visual grid of black and white portraits of the women: not posed, but candid shots as they testified. This presented them in the moment of bearing witness, reclaiming their power as individuals, collectively drawing strength from each other's courage and from the dawning knowledge that they were finally receiving justice.

The depiction of these three elements – scale, singularity, and collectivity – has been adapted and developed not only by the media in the representation of others, but also by those who are representing themselves. The use by #BlackLivesMatter and #SayHerName of portraits of beloved family members killed by police displaces mug shots or images of maimed bodies after death in order to rehumanise victims. Graphic artists, too, have

Figure 1 *TIME Magazine* (17 December 2017). Photographers: Billy & Hells. Permission granted by the artists and *TIME Magazine*.

adapted these three elements in works of memorialisation to endow names with the graphic power of image and to focus on the lives of victims of police violence. These replicate the structure of the grid – a representational strategy conferring value – used here as an oppositional strategy to assert dignity in the face of erasure.

In the drawing by Carson Ellis (Figure 2), the hand lettering conveys the human presence in a way that standard fonts do not. Some of the subjects smile, some are sombre, all face the viewer. The web of reference within the visual iconography of graphic witness represents a plurality of lives and voices, joined in violence and, through art, in testimonial memory in order to create tectonic shifts that disrupt the erasure of violence. The depiction of shared suffering visualises channels of identi-fication and affiliation that cut across divides of gender, race, class, or sexuality to enable many people to see, hear, and say – in other words, to witness – #MeToo in the context of #BlackLivesMatter, #SayHerName, I Can't Breathe, and Hands Up, Don't Shoot.

Structured initially as an utterance, #MeToo would seem to belong to the class of speech acts known as performatives, those oaths and other verbal acts that do what they say, such as 'I do' or 'You're fired.'[10] Performatives make change and when #MeToo named a pervasive and chronic problem, it sought to change it, as do the subsequent utterances that have followed in its wake such as #Time'sUp. They do so in the context of other citational practices that perform commemoration such as #SayHerName. These are part of a citational and collective intersectional feminist witness that gathers itself to oppose violence and erasure. Because graphic witness is performative of intersectional survivorship – it transforms victimisation, without erasing it, into a collective and political identity focused on justice and healing – its relation to the bodies of victims and to the circulation of images of bodies is fraught. The image of the dead black male body provides a powerful rallying point for protest and, at the same time, activists and people of colour cannot protect the dead or images of them from voyeurism or exploitation. These images painfully reveal whose bodies are seen as deserving of privacy and protection. Although the improvi-sational recording of evidence has exposed a reality previously managed into an invisibility that protects police, the voyeuristic – even pornographic – alliance of looking at vulnerable bodies and projecting social death onto them is also a risk for #MeToo visual culture.

Given the risk of representational vulnerability, of vulnerability to repre-sentation, it is important to observe how little #MeToo iconography draws on a pornographic imaginary of sexualised wounded women for its representa-tion of sexual violence. What makes graphic witness iconic of intersectional

Figure 2 Carson Ellis, 'Killed by the Police' (2017). Artwork copyright by Carson Ellis. Reprinted by permission of Writers House LLC acting as agent for the illustrator.

feminism is the use of words as images to represent survivors rather than to expose the body, while visual representations of abusers often feature the bodies of accused men. They blend photographs with design elements to picture the burgeoning gallery of perpetrators. The illustration by Oliver Munday accompanying the first of Ronan Farrow's two stories in the *New Yorker* about Harvey Weinstein, for example, depicts Weinstein's image superimposed on a blood red background, charging through white female figures (Figure 3).[11] This stylised graphic and many like it jostled side by side with the gallery of men named by those whom they had abused. In stories

Figure 3 Illustration by Oliver Munday, the *New Yorker* (23 October 2017).
Permission granted by the artist.

about specific allegations, photos dominated news reporting, as graphics attempted to respond to, organise, and make sense of the exposure of well-known, powerful men.

The eruption of graphic witness in a short time frame meant that the public sphere brimmed with previously silenced survivor speech. Inevitably, verbal and visual testimony sought compact and potent forms of reference to reveal the hidden scale of sexual violence, and also the broad range of behaviours associated with sexual harassment and assault; the lengthy time frames of grooming, stalking, shaming, failures by police, authorities of many kinds, and courts to investigate complaints or hold perpetrators accountable; and the difficulty of fully removing oneself from locations of harm, including professions, towns, and families. With so many stories being told, some asserted the need for clarity, including calling for a sliding scale of harm with transgressions and penalties clearly mapped: as if the gravest danger might arise not from the abuse, but from insufficient clarity about what kinds of bodily violations abusers could get away with; not from the failure of statutes of limitations to hold abusers accountable, but from unclear rules about the temporal boundaries victims were supposed to follow; not from the silencing and gaslighting of victims, but from questions about what kinds of allegations could even be brought forward. Sometimes in sympathy with these containment strategies and sometimes in concert with amplifying survivor speech, graphics stepped in to comment visually.

Taking up the theme of #MeToo's proliferation, Paula Scher categorised offences, assigning point values (Figure 4). Rape and paedophilia at 25 points represent 'criminal' behaviour. Pussy grabs – a reference to Donald Trump's boast about his own behaviour recorded on the Access Hollywood tape – at 20 points is categorised as 'predatory'. 'Inadvertent breast-feel, one instance only' earns 5 penalty points and qualifies as 'forgivable'. The graphic exposes some of the flawed thinking represented by the 'common sense' call for clarity. The seeing eye on the chart suggests both a new visibility on sexual abuse and a new I/eyewitness at its centre. Assigning point values to certain acts visualises the range of offences as pervasive and random. 'Mixed emotions' imagines how to let men off the hook by centring their acts and apologies rather than justice or healing for survivors.

The images and design elements I have discussed have been co-evolving in relation to contemporary protest over 2018. While many of the posters and graphics associated with the Women's March made reference to female anatomy, such as the pussy hats, much #MeToo iconography has resisted

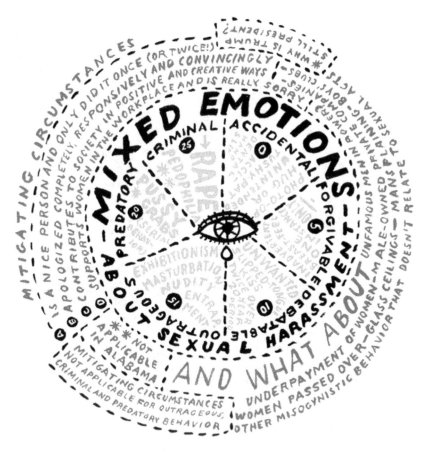

Figure 4 Paula Scher, 'Mixed Emotions' (2017). Ink and paint on paper. Originally published in 'The Reckoning: Women and Power in the Workplace' (*NY Times Magazine*, December 2017). Permission granted by the artist.

gendered anatomical reference, preferring the figuration of justice, testimony, and protest represented by speech and by hands. Graphics published around October and November 2017 often used images related to speech. The design element of a megaphone, for example, visualised how #MeToo amplified women's voices and broadcast them publicly. The iconography of speech ties #MeToo to representations of political prisoners and prisoners of conscience who are typically depicted as gagged to represent the silencing of their protest. Yet, one of the reasons I read the

#MeToo hashtag as a form of graphic witness is that it has conjured the iconic hand.[12] Initially raised to signal 'I'm here, too', the hand also makes a mark: 'I raise my hand to testify that hands grasped me against my will. I still feel those hands, I still feel that pain.' We are hailed through this testimony about manhandling to return to the violated body and its proxy and emissary, the testimonial metonym of the hand. An assemblage of graphic witness forms at the site of the hand: hand to God, hand on the Bible, hand over heart, and, as Christine Blasey Ford testified, Brett Kavanaugh's hand over her mouth to smother her screaming and terrifying her that 'he might inadvertently kill me'.[13] The hand lifted to swear in a witness joins with so many hands that rise in response to the question, 'Have you ever experienced unwanted sexual attention?'

The graphic power of the hand as symbolic of protest ties #MeToo to the haptic witness of Hands Up Don't Shoot – an embodied and performed protest following the killing of Michael Brown in Ferguson, Missouri, who witnesses said had his hands raised when he was shot by white police officer Darren Wilson – and a renewed use of the raised fist of the black power movement invoked as protest. The gesturing hand allows us to see, too, how the whole body is positioned to signify and to be read, how it is made graphic and legible in context such that when anyone takes a knee on a field of sport this season (and this gesture has travelled beyond sports), it resonates within the context of Colin Kaepernick's original NFL protest against racist police brutality.[14] The gestural and rhetorical fuse here in forms of graphic witness. Even the locution of the 'firsthand' witness, used frequently in the USA in journalism, law, and the vernacular to mean knowledge gained from the original source, underlines the linkage of being present with offering valuable testimony.[15] Hands coordinate the gesture of swearing in – one on the Bible, one lifted – and visually rhymes with the unbalanced scales that justice seeks to equalise. When we place the scale of sexual violence on the scale of justice, why does women's testimony not carry more weight?

When we understand #MeToo as the virtual follow up to the embodied mass mobilisation of the Women's March, and not, that is, primarily an eruption in response to the Harvey Weinstein case, and compelling, brave, and credible celebrity witness, it is more clearly the breaking through of the intersectional experience, analysis, and activism of feminist anger in public. Unheard anger, unacknowledged trauma, and incomplete justice: here histories begin to shimmer in the graphic space of the hashtag, as the hand that types a tweet or shares a #hashtag on a device joins the visual repertoire of other hands raised to testify.

Yet, an interdisciplinary and intersectional feminist #MeToo is necessary to prevent the current moment from descending into a confessional death spiral where we mistake the exposure of 'so much' sexual violence as 'too much' accusation. This will occur if we tolerate the non-apology re-brandings crafted for accused perpetrators by legal teams for maximum deniability that are recently being trotted out. When Weinstein initially responded publicly to allegations of rape, he tried to deflect from his accountability and, instead, blamed, variously, his accusers and the past as 'a different time'; promised to work on himself; and attempted to shift focus by promising to renew his political activism.[16] The deflection strategy is distilled by both Charlie Rose and Matt Lauer to 'I'm sorry if anyone ever felt uncomfortable, that was not my intention.'[17] Sometimes, the accused cannot even muster the feigned sincerity of the non-apology and exposes his sense that he is impervious, as with Mario Batali's sorry-not-sorry blog post that ended with a recipe for cinnamon rolls made out of pizza dough.[18] This is the banality of confession. Another round of whispering on a couch, as Foucault might say, searching out the secret, shameful side of sex, confessing, gaining absolution through spinning sex into discourse. The contemporary male quasi-confessors recycle a myth that rape is sex gone wrong. Abusers exploit this false view by apologising as if women's misunderstanding of the consensual sex the men claim they were having is what they are sorry about. Sexual assault and rape are crimes about power. Abusers use sex to enhance their own masculinity in violent ways that degrade and diminish victims. Survivors in the #MeToo movement are not confessing. They are testifying.

Confession is saturated in sin, shame, and secrecy, but it is also the discourse of victims who have been blamed so effectively that they blame themselves. Testimony produces new knowledge about trauma and justice. It asks new questions, demands new ways of understanding the life histories of those seeking to evade and survive masculine violence in institutions that normalise and enable it. Testimony aims to shift shame and the responsibility for suffering from victims to perpetrators. If we read testimony as if it were confession, we think of sex gone wrong. This is a category error, fuelled by cultural myth and the normalisation of a status quo.

Testimonial moments are vulnerable to being derailed as new subjects encounter old judgements in the arena of truth-telling. Long-standing patterns of doubt and discrediting are easily revived through infighting or backlash. We have seen these familiar obstacles to the consolidation of social authority arise in the face of many insurgent social justice movements: #BlackLivesMatter protestors are called terrorists who threaten police, the high school student survivors of the mass killing in Parkland, Florida, are called crisis actors, and survivors of sexual abuse, sexual harassment, and sexual assault are accused by commentators across the political spectrum of, variously, fomenting a sex panic, violating due process, and failing to distinguish between a pat on the butt and rape.[19]

It is hardly an accident that the persistence of #MeToo is rooted within the current political climate in the USA. We cannot underestimate the impact of the 2016 election of a man who had bragged about sexual assault, and whose stalking of Hillary Clinton in the 'Nasty Woman' debate shook many. The Women's March and the scale of global assembly the day after his inauguration were signs of how angry women are about a culture that allows sexual abuse to continue without holding perpetrators accountable. What is breaking through is not only pain. Rather, as evidenced by its history and contemporary affinities, it is the spectre of an intersectional feminist analysis of it, developed over a long time span of advocacy and activism. This is why Tarana Burke is not simply a figure to cite in order to get the #MeToo origin story right; rather, she represents marginalised, intersectional knowledge about the vulnerability of poor girls and women of colour to sexual violence and the systemic inequalities that make Indigenous women and girls and queer adolescents of colour the most vulnerable young people to sexual violence – not only in locations defined by deprivation, but also as they move from them. It is not that their identities make them intransigent victims somehow, but that their vulnerability as they move acts like a tracer that exposes the systemic networks in which male elites do harm. Currently, we are all tasked with understanding #MeToo as a form of intersectional feminist graphic witness. I wonder how much truth we will allow ourselves to bear. I hope we can bear more.

For the opportunity to present this work, I gratefully acknowledge invitations from Rice University, the Center for the Study of Women, Gender, and Sexuality, and the Gray/Wawro lecture series; Caroline Bicks, Stephen E. King Chair in Literature, and the University of Maine; Boston College Center for Work and Family; the Altman Center for the Humanities, Miami University; the Robert E. Knoll Lectureship, University of Nebraska; the Agora Society and Michaela Rhile at

Wellesley College; and Joy Castro, Theresa Kulbaga, Elizabeth Marshall, and Helena Michie.

Notes

1 'More Than 12M "MeToo" Facebook Posts, Comments, Reactions in 24 Hours', *CBS News* (17 October 2017).
2 Feminists of colour are central to the history that underlies #MeToo, and its present-day incarnation. It is important to note that #MeToo restarts a long-deferred public reckoning with workplace sexual harassment and racism that was started and swiftly shut down in the USA when Anita Hill testified that Clarence Thomas sexually harassed her. See L. Gilmore, *Tainted Witness: Why We Doubt What Women Say About Their Lives* (New York: Columbia University Press, 2017).
3 Time's Up and other organizations are moving into this space.
4 See R. Doolittle, 'Unfounded: Why Police Dismiss 1 in 5 Sexual Assault Claims as Baseless', *The Globe and Mail* (2 February 2017) and US Department of Justice, Civil Rights Division, 'Investigation of the Baltimore City Police Department' (10 August 2016).
5 K. Dotson, 'Tracking Epistemic Violence, Tracking Practices of Silencing', *Hypatia*, 26:2 (Spring 2011), 251 and 244, respectively.
6 K. Manne, 'Brett Kavanaugh and America's "Himpathy" Reckoning', *New York Times* (26 June 2018). Manne developed the concept of 'himpathy' in *Down Girl: The Logic of Misogyny* (New York and Oxford: Oxford University Press, 2017).
7 Gilmore, *Tainted Witness*, 5.
8 The *New York Times* reported on three new studies: a national online survey, a *Washington Post*/ABC News poll, and findings from the largest continuing study by the National Intimate Partner and Sexual Violence Survey by the Centers for Disease Control and Prevention. S. Chira, 'Why #MeToo Took Off: Sheer Numbers Who Can Say "Me, Too"', *New York Times* (24 February 2018).
9 Statutes of limitations allow legal responsibility for crimes to expire. This is a particular area of concern for victims of sexual violence because abuse often happens in childhood or adolescence and is traumatic. Both factors contribute to lag times in reporting.
10 J. Butler, *Bodies that Matter: On the Discursive Limits of Sex* (New York: Routledge, 1993), 13.
11 The two articles capture important episodes in the unfolding temporality of #MeToo. The initial article centred survivor stories and the second uncovered the elaborate network Weinstein established to enable his predation and threaten those he abused. See R. Farrow, 'From Aggressive Overtures to Sexual Assault: Harvey Weinstein's Victims Tell Their Stories', *New Yorker*

(23 October 2017) and 'Harvey Weinstein's Army of Spies', *New Yorker* (6 November 2017).

12 Sara Ahmed includes hands in her 'willfulness archive' as a body part long associated with metaphorical, philosophical, and phenomenological meaning, including the visual iconography I reference here. See her *Willful Subjects* (Durham, NC: Duke University Press, 2014), 13.

13 E. Brown, 'California Professor, Writer of Confidential Brett Kavanaugh Letter, Speaks Out About Her Allegation of Sexual Assault', *Washington Post* (16 August 2018).

14 M. Garber, 'They Took a Knee', *The Atlantic* (24 August 2016).

15 See H. Chute, *Disaster Drawn: Visual Witness, Comics, and Documentary Form* (Cambridge, MA: Belknap Press of Harvard University Press, 2016), who argues that from its origins, the comics form allowed for 'the work of the hand to emerge as a feature of comics of witness' and with it, the fusing of 'the haptic and the visual – a crucial connection for witness – that is recognizable in the idiom of "firsthand" information, a claim that generally indicates direct visual apprehension' (p. 71). This fusion is part of the history of graphic illustration, as well, from which the visual iconography of #MeToo emerges, in part.

16 'Harvey Weinstein Statement', *New York Times* (5 October 2017).

17 Charlie Rose tweeted his response to allegations of sexual harassment (20 November 2017). See his Twitter feed. NBC carried Matt Lauer's statement following his firing from the network: 'Transcript: "Today Anchor Matt Lauer Fired by NBC News"', *NBC News* (29 November 2017).

18 Mario Batali offered a casual apology in an online blog post on 15 December 2017 (since taken down, but easily found reproduced in full in the abundant criticism that followed it) followed by a holiday recipe for cinnamon rolls. See J. Ducharme, 'Mario Batali's Sexual Misconduct Apology Came with a Cinnamon Roll Recipe', *Time* (16 December 2017).

19 M. Gessen, 'When Does a Watershed Become a Sex Panic?' *New Yorker* (14 November 2017). On Matt Damon's comments, see B. Finger, 'Matt Damon Gets It Wrong, Yet Again', *Jezebel* (23 March 2018).

CHAPTER 3

Trapped in the Political Real: Imagining Black Motherhood Beyond Pathology and Protest

Candice Merritt

Introduction

In 'An Unnatural Woman', black woman novelist, essayist, and mother Martha Southgate recounts a most ordinary moment in her home. Standing beside the kitchen sink, she chops parsley, whips butter into pasta. Her four-year-old daughter quietly talks to herself while playing with dinosaur toys in the dining room; her seven-year-old son sits close by, writing a story, asking his mother to spell every word. Their father, Southgate's husband, has not returned home yet from the day's work. Exercising patience, Southgate shares every consonant and vowel her son needs. She continues cutting parsley and begins sensing the irony of assisting her son scribe a story while she has failed to tend to her own unfinished novel in six months. Then, within what seems like an unremarkable reflection of domestic life, narrated over six lines of text, a rupture to the idealised image of a dutiful, home-maker occurs. The knife, sharp and deliberate, continues cutting the vegeta-tion. 'I think', Southgate writes, 'briefly, of turning the knife to my wrist, a messy end.'[1] Another whispering image enters: 'Or maybe I'll walk out the door and never return, seamlessly gone, leaving behind the children, the cold pasta and chopped parsley' (p. 114). The ideation of termination – of abandon – briefly seduces. Southgate concedes: '[M]y disappearance from this scene would be easier than trying to keep going as an artist, a mother, and a wife' (p. 114). The mother, in the confines of her home, again, puts death aside; she continues cutting parsley.

I open this chapter with one black woman's daily account of maternal life in the twenty-first century as a point of departure from popular and scholarly rhetorics of black motherhood by black feminists and theorists. Reading the open expression of a black mother's intimate desire to flee her children for her artistry and life's sake, even though ephemeral, strikes me as an anomalous expression by a black mother in the contemporary political moment. In the age of the global Movement for Black Lives, commonly referred to as Black Lives Matter (BLM), the dominant narrative of black motherhood is one marked by crisis. As demands to end state-sanctioned violence against all black persons within and beyond US national borders continue, the publicised spectacles of the dead and dying (mostly black men and boys) by the hands and triggers of state agents accumulate and course through global media networks and veins of political imaginaries. Accompanying these cross-continental images of assaults and executions stand the repetition of moving images and affects of the mothers of slain children. The reproduction of the pained pleas of black women, such as Sybrina Fulton (mother of Trayvon Martin), Gwen Carr (mother of Eric Gardner), Lezley McSpadden (mother of Michael Brown), Valerie Castile (mother of Philando Castile), Geneva Reed-Veal (mother of Sandra Bland), and the many more unnamed and growing number of black women who have lost their children to state violence have coalesced into the common, yet, politically powerful trope of black maternal grief and loss.

Collectively, the visibility of anguished black mothers has played a significant role in making black death and suffering culturally legible, even as such images lack sustained efficacy in preventing the very violence they seek to protest. Coupled with the growing attention to the disproportionate rates of black infant mortality and maternal death, the oft-narrated political reality of black mothers and children in communities seems to be one singularly haunted by expected state-induced injury and/or death. The now four-decades-old black feminist adage written by Audre Lorde in 1979 seems best in describing the political conditions troubling the material and psychic life of black mothers in the new millennium: 'Raising black children – female and male – in the mouth of a racist, sexist suicidal dragon is perilous and chancy. If they cannot love and resist at the same time, they will probably not survive.'[2]

While black mothers feel haunted by raising children in a monstrous world, another social and psychic antagonism exists within black women's intimate relationships. Commenting on the racial and gendered expectations placed upon black maternal being, Southgate reflects: 'A woman loves her children. That is a given in our society, reinforced at every conceivable turn. And a black woman is the mother to the world. Look at our history – all the babies we've raised. Our own and other people's. By necessity or by choice' (p. 115). Here, Southgate speaks on the mandate for black women to be a limitless and boundless nurturer to all. As a site of excess, the 'black mother's love is supposed to be uncomplicated' and Herculean even when they may be materially overburdened and feel suffocated by the demands of others (p. 115).

Though voices of ambivalence such as Southgate's can be found in the lives of black mothers, I find them interestingly faint in contemporary black feminist rhetorics. How do the voices of black women fantasising about death and escape from the throes of being a mother and/or wife – a family woman – fail to occupy critical discursive space in black feminist theoretical landscapes in the twenty-first century, especially since feminism more broadly has sustained robust criticisms of compulsory motherhood and mothering as unmarked categories of labour? Leading motherhood studies scholar Andrea O'Reilly, however, writes that in the twenty-first century, mainstream (read white and liberal) feminists have failed to espouse a 'feminism developed from the specific needs/concerns of mothers'.[3] In contradistinction, O'Reilly considers the theoretical contributions of black feminists Patricia Hill Collins, bell hooks, and writer Toni Morrison as fruitful resources for revaluating motherhood as a site of women's empowerment. Though black feminist insights can be a corrective to mainstream feminist analyses of gender and the private sphere, I argue that black feminist discourses of motherhood also have their own limitations and critical absences.

Given the resurfaced senses of a mass movement for black liberation and the recognition of black feminism's re-emergence as 'the analytical framework for the activist response to the oppression of trans women of colour, the fight for reproductive rights, and ... the movement against police abuse and violence', this chapter historicises contemporary black feminist discourses of motherhood.[4] In doing so, I return to earlier black feminist voices of the 1970s and 1980s and trace the historic continuities and patterned analyses undergirding theorisations of black maternity as a differential and subversive formation emerging from the practices of the Transatlantic Slave Trade and US chattel slavery. While I consider the now canonical black feminist standpoint of motherhood as one born of political necessity, I point to the excisions in theory which limit contemporary black feminist treatments of motherhood, particularly the lack of engagement of mothering as a site of ambivalence and a burdensome problem of labour for black women. I argue that black feminist romances with motherhood obfuscate the normalisation of gendered labour in the lives of black women and contend that sitting with the subjugated voices of ambivalences by black mothers provides a critical opening for black feminist theorists to explore.

Roots of Black Feminist Theorising on Motherhood

Recent black feminist publications, such as the anthology *Revolutionary Mothering: Love on the Front Lines* and memoirs *We Live for the We* and *This is How We Survive*, frame the meanings of black motherhood in the wake of the 'resurgence of a civil rights movement led by Black youth and Black mamas, who are taking over . . . national conversations and proclaiming – in the words of Alicia Garza, Patrisse Cullors, and Opal Tometi – that Black Lives Matter'.[5] Popular black feminist discourse like this attempts to reimagine 'the word "mother" less as a gendered identity and more as a possible action' that can change the status quo into a more just and equitable world.[6] As such, contemporary black feminists argue that 'Mothering isn't gendered' and constitutes a skill that 'Everyone, including and especially men, must engage in.'[7]

Characterisations such as these also seek to distance black feminist perspectives on motherhood away both from historic white feminist analyses of family and women's reproduction and from mainstream publications on motherhood. Dani McClain, in *We Live for the We*, observes that the 'current wave of writing on motherhood . . . has tended to focus on white, middle-class women's experiences' and furthers that 'These writings frame motherhood as something that robs women of our professional ambitions . . . and reminds us that biology and age-old gender roles are indeed destiny.'[8] Buttressing this sense of opposition to white feminist theories are black feminist articulations of motherhood as part of a longer intellectual and political tradition of US-based black feminist thought and praxes. *Revolutionary Mothering* anthology editors Alexis Pauline Gumbs, China Martens, and Mai'a Williams express their approach to motherhood as 'intergenerational', acknowledging the works of feminists of colour of the 1970s and 1980s as 'literary and theoretical "foremothers for mothering"' (p. 5). Likewise, Dani McClain cites the early scholarship of Angela Davis, Audre Lorde, and Patricia Hill Collins as fundamental to her broadened understanding of black motherhood as politically subversive for its affirmation of collective care for all black children in a community. These now canonical works on motherhood and family by black feminists such as Davis, hooks, Hortense Spillers, Lorde, and Hill Collins should be historicised as an urgent political response to the prevalent rhetorical and material devaluation (i.e., enforced sterilisation and coercive birth control policies) of black women as aberrant racialised and gendered-sexual subjects by the gaze of government officials, scholars, and, even by some individuals in the black liberation struggles of the late twentieth century.[9] While founding works fundamentally shape contemporary feminist articulations of black mothering, the deep grooves and well-rehearsed contours of black feminist grammars that problematise white feminist understandings elide other complex processes of theorising black motherhood and its experience in the lives and psyches of black women.

The development of distinct black feminist analytical and conceptual articulations of motherhood began taking shape, like any theory, in response to the dominant political urgencies of its time. Popular scholarly and political articulations of the black woman as an emasculating matriarch circulated heavily in the 1960s.[10] By the 1970s, the spectre of familial pathology structured public discourses of black maternity. Hill Collins describes the matriarch as a 'controlling image' of black womanhood which emerged in a political moment marked by expanding US global capitalism, mass black protests against white supremacy and Western imperialism, and women's liberationist demands to end patriarchy. As an enduring trope (even at the turn of the century), the matriarch 'symbolizes the "bad" Black mother . . . who failed to fulfil their traditional "womanly" duties at home'.[11] She was too often unmarried and 'overly aggressive' – an '"unfeminine" woman' who dominated men, causing them to abandon and flee marital commitment to women and their children (p. 75). Further cementing her deviancy, this black mother was presumed to work outside the home, leaving kids neglected. The matriarch provided an ideological cover for structural racial and gender inequities by equating poverty to black culture.

The year of 1965 marked an intense consolidation of (mis)information of black women as 'bad' mothers in the rhetorical and ethnographic site named the 'black family' in the political arena. In the now famed document *The Negro Family: The Case for National Action*, commonly referred to as the Moynihan Report, US Secretary of Labor and senator Daniel Patrick Moynihan pronounced the black family as one in crisis.[12] At the time of the US federal government's War on Poverty campaign, Moynihan sought to call for federal policy to remedy the centuries of maltreatment inflicted upon African American communities. Though Moynihan named slavery, Jim Crow, and current-day discrimination as barriers to equality for black Americans, he also drew attention to what he considered a hidden problem – the historic damage of racism upon what he termed 'The Negro Family'. Using the 'white family' as both a proxy and desired horizon, Moynihan deployed the matriarchate family thesis. Writing with the powerful idiom of science and objectivity, he backed his claims through his supply of historiographic and sociological information on 'normal' practices of gender and sexual coupling, familial arrangements, and aggregate sociological data on rates of black and white female-headed households, divorce trends, rates of illegitimacy, welfare dependency, and juvenile delinquency. Moynihan drew upon the works of noted scholars on slavery, such as Nathan Glazer, and the works of respected black sociologists such as E. Franklin Frazier and Robert Staples – all noted scholars on the history of black folk culture and family.

In Moynihan's annotations, US slavery constituted the most insidious slave system to ever exist because black men could not ascend to the order of humanity nor assume the rightful role as the patriarch in the family, like white men (p. 15). Black women, a group that had little choice in engaging in labour outside the home, became understood as subsuming a masculine role in the family – a trend, according to Moynihan, continued through the eras of post-emancipation, migration, and urbanisation. Black men became known as castrated and effeminate since they could not assume the proper familial role. For Moynihan, pathological gender relations explained the lack of upward mobility and low status of black Americans. This familial abnormality, or self-perpetuating 'tangle of pathology', begat unfit black mothers and the absence of patriarchal fathers (p. 47). With the swift stroke of his pen, Moynihan shifted attention away from structural processes of inequality (racist discrimination, redlining, segregation, and more). Resulting solutions called for government efforts to elicit the development of patriarchal gender relations between black men and women through increasing rates of black male employment, military service, and marriage. Such efforts presumed to restore black male masculinity and the proper dynamic of male provider/protector and female passivity/homemaker between black men and women.

Consequently, Moynihan's study of black matriarchy became a popular way to understand black inequality not only in policy and scholarly discourses, but also among black communities. As black male castration constituted a significant sign and framework to understand racial harm, many black men and women involved in the liberation era desired the restoration of black masculinity. Male dominance and female compliance became a teleological vision of redress, particularly in black cultural nationalist segments.[13] Leading nationalists, such as Maulana Karenga and Imamu Amiri Baraka, espoused black men and women to return to presumed African cultural roots.[14] The sentiment premised compulsory heterosexuality and motherhood for black nation building. The function of the black woman in this ideological formation was to 'inspire her man, educate her children, and participate in social development'.[15] While the desired trope of the black mother-wife provided a significant symbolic and material place for women in black liberation and revolutionary movements of the era, it shared a strange affinity with Moynihanian solutions for racial progress. The seams of dominant black political mores (from radical to conservative) and normative gender and sexual ideologies of (white) civil society converged at the presumption of women's domesticity and maternity. Black women's motherhood and mothering were thus critical to black racial perpetuation, survival, and well-being.

Black feminists responded to matriarch claims by waging an intellectual and political intervention in public conversations. They deployed a critical method of counter-narrative that unearthed and stressed the forced familial severances and violent treatment of black women's reproduction by state and extra-legal apparatuses, beginning with the material conditions inscribed by their property status under the Transatlantic Slave Trade and the US chattel slavery system. The black feminist rejoinder to Moynihanian myths of the matriarchal black mother crystallised into what I consider two primary archetypes. Black feminists articulated a historically injured maternal subject, or what Spillers has referred to as 'both mother and mother-dispossessed'.[16] The dispossessed mother encompassed the historic archive of forced severances between black women and children; and continues as a sign of black maternal loss with each repetition of slain black children and their grieving mothers in the contemporary moment. The insurgent black mother formed the second archetype. Through her survival and sacrifice for kin and community against the 'odds of pulverization and murder', black feminists narrated black motherhood as a sacred social formation that perpetuated black humanity and mothering as a form of resistance against racial oppression.[17]

The dual archetypes debunked the matriarchy thesis and re-valued black motherhood. The mother-dispossessed archetype enacted a powerful narrative of injury. Through the frame of dispossession, black feminists established an evidentiary archive of sexual terrors committed against the bodies of black women under enslavement and post-emancipation political economies. Accounts of black women stripped of their infants in arms, black women nursing white children, black babies left in troughs unattended, black mothers and children standing on the auction block, and the deadly tales of lashings, rape, and slave breeding fleshed a historic fact for black feminists to deploy: that the black woman could never be a matriarch. She lacked legal claim to her body and her children, and any kinship structures, if ever formed, were subjected to the desires of property owners.[18] And while black women's reproductive dispossession produced capitalist accumulation for white men, and women, and children, mother-hood as an institution stood as an inaccessible sex-gender structure for black women to legally, symbolically, and materially inhabit.[19]

Invocations of dispossession stitched the black mother without child as a kind of master sign with critical functions in black feminist political praxis and thought. It provided a public imagining of the black mother as victim to the sociopolitical order rather than the perpetuator of its economic and moral demise. Instead, white capitalist prerogatives became the corruption responsible for producing familial separation and persistent conditions of black dehumanisation. With a victim subject at hand, black feminists could further activate their commitment to political advocacy and reparative claims in various public spheres. Not only was heavy moral sentiment carried by the dispossessed mother for political utility but it also structured what can now be recognised as the haunting landscape of black maternal loss and grief in the contemporary moment. Today, black feminists continue this tradition of counter-narrative and advocacy by emphasising black mothers' ongoing struggle to protect their children from anti-black violence and through political demands of redress.

Epistemologically the dispossessed mother in black feminist theorising carved the black woman and white woman into a binary couplet who seemingly shared little if any affects when it came to private matters of family and mothering. The black woman contrasted with her white counterpart, who benefited from 'the protections of white patriarchy'.[20] Because she worked and did not participate in a heteronormative nuclear familial structure due to racial and economic constraints, black feminists' everywoman subject structurally did not identify with the discontents of the private sphere expressed by white women. These polarised subjects thus fell into simplified camps of feelings – the white woman's ambivalence towards and/or wholesale rejection of motherhood and the black woman's desire for homemaking and children. bell hooks's summation of second wave feminists' race and class-biased terms of motherhood as a domestic trap offers an emblematic example of black feminist characterisations of this duo's affective and political orientation towards maternity. The white woman liberationist, recalled hooks, lamented: 'We are tired of the isolation of the home, tired of relating only to children and husband, tired of being emotionally and economically dependent; we want to be liberated to enter the world of work.'[21] The black woman, however, intimately knew the world of dehumanising labour and the respite of family. 'Had black women voiced their views on motherhood', surmised hooks, 'it would not have been named a serious obstacle to our freedom as women. Racism, availability of jobs, lack of skills or education ... would have been at the top of the list – but not motherhood' (p. 133). The black everywoman was imagined as harbouring an uncomplicated yearning for the home space: 'We want to have more time to share with family, we want to leave the world of alienated work' (p. 134).

In narrating the black woman as outside traditional sex-gender parameters and sentiments, black feminists framed feminist criticism of the private sphere as 'particularly problematic' and 'less applicable' to black women and families.[22] While critiques of white feminist exclusions were necessarily incisive, rendering liberal and Marxist feminist analyses, such as those by Nancy Chodorow, Simone de Beauvoir, Adrienne Rich, and Betty Friedan, as non-applicable helped curtail black feminist theoretical conceptualisations of family and mothering as sites of black women's bondage, self-denial, and alienating labour. In black feminist retrospectives, white feminists too often discarded 'the Black babies out with the bathwater of their universalism' and today are not engaged for political or theoretical utility beyond critiques of exclusion.[23]

With the domestic sphere considered a non-barrier for black women's liberation, black feminist scholarship laid the groundwork for contemporary understandings of motherhood as a subversive site. Angela Davis acknowledged patriarchy's ascription of black women to domestic duties, yet speculated that successful resistance to slavery would not have been possible had it not been forged in the domestic slave quarters and through women's leadership in this arena, away from the masters' gaze and whip.[24] Likewise, hooks emphasised how black women took the patriarchal role as mothers and caregivers and transformed the 'homeplace' into insurgent ground during the era of segregation. Black mothers here nourished black children, men, and other women, reinforcing their sense of humanity in a cold, racist world that denied them status.[25] These accounts articulate the black mother as latent in revolutionary potential – an insurgent – and the private sphere as a humanising, life-giving, and self-empowering site.

Black feminists reclaimed civil society's condemnation of black motherhood from a pathological formation to a culturally distinct and potentially transgressive reproductive practice. Articulated as either an adaptation to the conditions of slavery and/or as a lasting west African cultural custom, black feminists positioned black maternity as an organised women-centred network that exercised communal ownership to ensure the well-being of 'all the Black community's children'.[26] This shared care system challenged the premise of children as private property and the heteropatriarchal nuclear family as the ideal form of social reproduction.[27] Moreover, the labour of mothering was figured as a mutually beneficial communal provision. As black women mothered, it afforded them a socially sanctioned site of respectable self-definition and a political platform for racial uplift while black communities gained emotional and material support in return.[28]

Feeling and Thinking Ambivalently

While contemporary discourse designates past works by black feminists as critical precursors, or 'foremothers' to the 'radical' articulation of mothering, the archive of black feminist sentiments of the 1970s and 1980s was not exclusively filled with love and utopic visions of collectivity. As black feminists look to the past to fashion a sense of political promise in the present and hope for the future, I urge them to examine the 'subjugated knowledge' within their own theoretical archives of motherhood and liberatory political projects.[29] To do so requires rereading thinkers and texts now considered classic with a different disposition – one that suspends the celebratory orientation towards black women's performance of endurance and self-sacrifice for family and community. Such a positive orientation keeps sedimented understanding of black women's mothering as a necessary good for racial well-being without problematising racialised and gendered logics that conscript black femininity as an expectant anchor of naturalised caregiving. Rather than an orientation that presumes mothering as an unproblematic 'practice of creating, nurturing, and supporting life', I advocate an ambivalent position – a both/and disposition towards motherhood as an institution and experience in the lives of black women.[30] This position recognises motherhood as a structure of relation and mothering as an instrument. Each can both empower and deprive; create and destroy life; generate and expend energy; and engender affinity and enmity between social subjects. Engaging the both/and position towards black motherhood and mothering not only further opens theoretical wonder for black maternal subjectivities but also permits a complex understanding of power and subject formation within the most intimate spaces in black social life, particularly in the sites of the home, the community, and the psyche.

Importantly, I ask all black feminists, including myself, what the effects of the ambivalent black mother can unveil regarding matters of power relations between black mothers and children, men, and other women. How does the reflection of black mother Danielle Dunn, who watches 'motherhood swallow women up like fish with a minnow', illustrate the historic and political conditions which undergird a black woman's sense of feeling eaten by those most intimate in her life?[31] What can the black mother's life detail of the interstitial maps of (anti)blackness and misogyny that collide to make her an object to kin and community? What can her expressed interiority tell black feminists about the function of the structures of sex/gender, race, and capital in the quiet, private realms of living and dying in black women's lives? And how might this ambivalent sense matter (or not) to black liberation, gender, sexual, and reproductive freedom?

The anecdotes in this chapter may strike some black feminists as anomalous moments in the greater repertoire of black feminist archives of women's maternal experience. The ambivalent mother may even seem non-representative of black mothers' familial and domestic struggles of the twenty-first century. Moving with an ambivalent orientation, however, exposes how such a sense is a quiet undercurrent in black feminist thinking if one is interested in tuning into the lower frequencies. The anecdotes are haunting echoes from within black feminism itself.

Alice Walker penned an apt metaphorical axiom to assist with translating the political conditions plaguing the contemporary black mother in this chapter's opening – written in the same year Audre Lorde uttered the now famed metaphor of the racist, sexist, suicidal dragon. Walker's 1979 proposal for women to have *only* one child or else risk becoming a *sitting duck* marks motherhood and mothering as obstacles to black women's freedom in terms of time, mobility, their sense of self-fulfilment and creative expression.[32] Walker's ambivalence emphasises the potential consequences of maternal sacrifice upon her being. She writes, 'For me, there has been conflict, struggle, occasional defeat – not only in affirming the life of my own child (children) at all costs, but also in seeing . . . a fond acceptance and confirmation of myself in a world that would deny me the untrampled blossoming of my own existence' (p. 363). I hear similar contentious sentiment and conflict between mothers and familial demands echo thirty years later, as Southgate describes the pressure to be a 'good' black woman – an unfaltering caretaker.

Conclusion

How can black feminist theorists begin to move beyond the conundrum between the necessity of mothering and the costs of self-sacrifice incurred by black women's performance of care labour in families and communities?

For this question to begin to be answered in earnest, black feminist theorists must begin a sustained exploration of motherhood as an expectation imposed from within black life. It will require sitting with the less oft-told tales of black mothers, such as Martha Southgate in her kitchen considering suicide, Alice Walker who publicly wrote that having more than one child would make her a *sitting duck*, and Danielle Dunn who recalls motherhood's oceanic swallow of black women. While popular black feminist rhetorics hail mothering as critical to survival and resistance, theorists must stall considering motherhood a barrier to women's freedom as a privileged white woman problem. Mothering as costly to women's mobility, time, creativity, energy, and well-being proves to be an issue in the lives of black women too. As such, theoretical space must be opened to consider the distribution of reproductive labour within black intimate spheres as a matter of justice and equity despite motherhood's honourable status in black women's lives and feminist theorising.

Finally, a shift in optics must also occur in black feminist analytic orientations on questions of black mothering. The aesthetic and narrative repetition of historic and contemporary black maternal severances instigated by the white supremacist neoliberal nation state crowds out discourses that aim to think of messier black mother subjectivities that may express love and hate, joy and anger, warmth and coldness, and intimacy and distance. The shift to an analytic orientation committed to the interiority of maternal subjectivities may cause discomfort. It may lead to unexplored territory not only within scholarship but also within black feminist theorists' very sense of themselves.

Notes

1 M. Southgate, 'An Unnatural Woman', in C. Berry (ed.), *Rise Up Singing: Black Woman Writers on Motherhood* (New York: Broadway Books, 2004), 114. Berry's anthology features writers such as Faith Ringgold, Edwidge Danticat, Rita Dove, and Maya Angelou. Southgate's story stands out as the only contribution detailing suicidal ideation and abandon from the perspective of a mother at home. Another standout is June Jordan's 'Many Rivers to Cross' which recounts her mother as a 'good' woman who ended her life in suicide.

2 A. Lorde, *Sister Outsider* (Berkeley: Crossing Press, 1984), 74.

3 A. O'Reilly, 'Ain't I a Feminist?: Matricentric Feminism, Feminist Mamas, and Why Mothers Need a Feminist Movement/Theory of Their Own' (2014), mommuseum.org. Also see A. O'Reilly, *Toni Morrison and Motherhood: A Politics of the Heart* (Albany: State University of New York, 2004).

4 K. Taylor, *How We Get Free: Black Feminism and the Combahee River Collective* (Chicago: Haymarket Books, 2012), 13.

5 A. Gumbs, C. Martens, and M. Williams (eds.), *Revolutionary Mothering: Love on the Front Lines* (Oakland: PM Press, 2016), 3.

6 A. Gumbs, 'm/other ourselves: A Black queer feminist genealogy for radical mothering', in Gumbs, Martens, and Williams (eds.), *Revolutionary Mothering*, 23.

7 M. Williams, *This is How We Survive: Revolutionary Mothering, War, and Exile in the 21st Century* (Oakland: PM Press, 2019), 7.

8 D. McClain, *We Live for the We: The Political Power of Black Motherhood* (New York: Bold Type Books, 2019), 3.

9 D. Roberts, *Killing the Black Body: Race, Reproduction, and Liberty* (New York: Pantheon Books, 1997) provides a social history of myths surrounding black women's fertility and their role in state-sponsored birth control and sterilisation initiatives targeted at the black 'underclass' in the 1960s and 1970s and black nationalist charges of racial genocide and proposals for increased women's fertility.

10 P. Hill Collins, *Black Feminist Thought: Knowledge, Consciousness, and the Politics of Empowerment* (New York: Routledge, 2000), 74–8 and Roberts, *Killing the Black Body*, 15–17 note that studies describing black families as female-dominant and unstable were prevalent in twentieth-century sociology.

11 Hill Collins, *Black Feminist Thought*, 75.

12 D. Moynihan, *The Negro Family: The Case for National Action* (Washington, DC: United States Department of Labor, 1965).

13 See. T. Cade Bambara, *The Black Woman: An Anthology* (New York: Washington Square Press, 1970) and P. Hill Collins, *From Black Power to Hip Hop: Racism, Nationalism, and Feminism* (Philadelphia: Temple University Press, 2006) for accounts of black women's experience of misogyny within black liberation organisations.

14 Hill Collins, *From Black Power to Hip Hop*, 95–122.

15 C. Halisi and J. Mtume, *The Quotable Karenga* (Los Angeles: Us Organization, 1967), 20.

16 H. Spillers, 'Mama's Baby, Papa's Maybe: An American Grammar Book', *Diacritics*, 17:2 (Summer 1987), 80.

17 Spillers, 'Mama's Baby, Papa's Maybe', 80.

18 A. Davis, 'Reflections on the Black Woman's Role in the Community of Slaves', *The Black Scholar*, 3:4 (1971), 3; b. hooks, *Ain't I A Woman: Black Women and Feminism* (South End Press, 1981), 15; Spillers, 'Mama's Baby, Papa's Maybe', 74.

19 P. Hill Collins, 'The Meaning of Motherhood in Black Culture and Black Mother-Daughter Relationships', *Sage*, 4:2 (Fall 1987), 3; Spillers, 'Mama's Baby, Papa's Maybe', 80.

20 Hill Collins, 'The Meaning of Motherhood', 3.

21 b. hooks, *Feminist Theory: From Margin to Center* (Cambridge, MA: South End Press, 1984), 134.

22 Hill Collins, 'The Meaning of Motherhood', 3.

23 A. Gumbs, 'Forget Hallmark: Why Mother's Day Is a Queer Black Left Feminist Thing', in Gumbs, Martens and Williams (eds.), *Revolutionary Mothering*, 120.

24 Davis, 'Reflections', 4–7.

25 b. hooks, 'homeplace: (a site of resistance)', in J. Ritchie and K. Ronald (eds.), *Available Means: An Anthology of Women's Rhetoric(s)* (Pittsburgh: University of Pittsburgh Press, 2001), 382–90.

26 Hill Collins, 'The Meaning of Motherhood', 5.

27 Hill Collins, *Black Feminist Thought*, 185.

28 Hill Collins, 'The Meaning of Motherhood', 5.

29 Hill Collins, *Black Feminist Thought*, 9.

30 Gumbs, Martens, and Williams (eds.), *Revolutionary Mothering*, 9.

31 D. Dunn, 'Motherhood Will Swallow You Alive' (January 11, 2019), blackmomlife.com.

32 A. Walker, *In Search of Our Mothers' Gardens: Womanist Prose* (New York: Harcourt, 1983), 363.

CHAPTER 4

Feminism at the Borders: Migration and Representation

Emily J. Hogg

Introduction

Migration across state borders has become a defining issue of the first decades of the twenty-first century. According to Joseph Nevins, 'Increasing economic integration and liberalization' means that international boundaries are 'relatively open to flows of capital, finance, manufactured goods, and services', but the movement of people, especially people from lower-income countries, is welcomed to a far lesser extent.[1] Many migrants face death, detention, violence, and danger as they attempt to cross borders between nation states, the same borders which are 'relatively open' to financial flows.[2] I argue in this chapter that literary texts can play a crucial role in articulating a feminist approach to contemporary migration, the suffering it often currently entails, and the hope and potentiality it can embody. In her 2003 book *Feminism Without Borders*, Chandra Talpade Mohanty states that 'our most expansive and inclusive visions of feminism need to be attentive to borders while learning to transcend them'.[3] Through discussion of the representation of borders and migration in Valeria Luiselli's non-fiction book *Tell Me How It Ends: An Essay in Forty Questions* and in prose poems by Warsan Shire and Vahni Capildeo, this chapter examines literature's contribution to such visions of feminism.

Representing Migration

The feminist project of becoming 'attentive to borders while learning to transcend them' requires challenging some recurrent features of conventional representations of migration. In the 1951 Refugee Convention, a refugee is defined as a person who 'owing to well-founded fear of being persecuted for reasons of race, religion, nationality, membership of a particular social group or political opinion, is outside the country of his nationality and is unable or, owing to such fear, is unwilling to avail himself of the protection of that country'.[4] Nation states are required to grant asylum to people who are refugees, but the legal definition is limited: only a person 'persecuted' for one of the five reasons listed in the Convention is defined as a refugee. Those forced to leave their homes for other reasons – such as environmental catastrophe or extreme poverty – are not.[5]

Refugees, imagined as a relatively small group in desperate need of help, are often contrasted with another group: 'economic migrants'. In an article in *The Guardian* entitled 'Five Myths about the Refugee Crisis', journalist Daniel Trilling aims to directly challenge some of the misleading ideas about migration that circulate in popular discourse. He argues that the term 'economic migrant' has become a negative one, used 'to suggest that people are trying to play the system, that their presence is the cause of problems at the border, and that if we could only filter them out, order would be restored'.[6] In many different geopolitical contexts, there is a pervasive discourse of invasion related to migration, in which 'economic migrants' are depicted as the threatening other, putting national tradition and social cohesion at risk.[7] This refugee/economic migrant dichotomy is fraught with difficulties. According to Roger Zetter, many people who cross state borders 'are fleeing complex root causes in which persecution *and* socioeconomic exclusion are combined.'[8] Zetter also argues that – though many economies across the world are dependent on migrant labour – the laws dealing with non-refugee migration are extremely strict. As immigration laws become tighter, Zetter states that 'the label "refugee" has offered greater potential to gain access; indeed, it has been the most clearly established means of entry' (p. 183). At the same time, states are increasingly trying to limit the number of people who are recognised as refugees. This has created 'the perception that the protective label "refugee" is no longer a basic Convention right, but a highly privileged prize which few deserve and most claim illegally' (p. 184).

As an alternative to the discourse of suspicion and 'invasion' which surrounds the ambiguous categories of the 'economic migrant' and refugee, humanitarian discourse has often emphasised victimhood and suffering in an attempt to spur individual and governmental action. When three-year old Alan Kurdi, a Syrian refugee, drowned in the Mediterranean Sea on 4th September 2015, many newspapers and websites printed upsetting photographs of his body face down on the beach. His story attracted intense attention in the international media; *The Guardian* stated that 'the full horror of the human tragedy unfolding on the shores of Europe' had been 'brought home'.[9] Though not overtly discriminatory in the way that other mass-media depictions of migration are, such intense focus on individual suffering and victimhood is characteristic of a broader – and much critiqued – trend in humanitarian narratives.[10] Strong focus on one emblematic and shocking story, told in such a way as to provoke feelings of pity and sadness, can risk decontextualisation. The structural forces which produce horrifying suffering become disguised; the social and political histories which led up to a particular disaster are often occluded. As Alison Mountz and Nancy Hiemstra argue, global migration tends to be represented through notions of 'chaos and crisis', terms which 'hold in common the projection of danger, instability, panic and dramatic upheaval'.[11] The discourse of danger and panic focuses attention on moments of emergency, demanding immediate emotional responses (which then wane when the issue disappears from social media feeds and twenty-four-hour news), rather than encouraging the examination of longer histories.

Feminism and Borders

What, then, do feminist insights have to contribute to our understanding of borders today? For Mohanty, 'there is no one sense of a border' (p. 2). Borders represent 'fault lines, conflicts, differences, fears and containment', and the 'lines between and through nations, races, classes, sexualities, religions, and disabilities' (p. 2). She associates state borders, which are typically demarcated physically and require documentation to pass through, with less concrete borders, such as the divisions produced by prejudice, unexamined privilege, and misunderstanding. Mohanty's wide definition encourages us to think about the relationship between state borders and other forms of social difference and differentiation, pointing to the fundamental questions of difference and identity that underlie bordering processes. As Gabriel Popescu puts it, 'Humans erect borders as a way to mediate between the familiar of *here* and the unfamiliar of *there* ... . Border making is a power strategy that uses difference to assert control over space by inscribing difference in space.'[12] In particular, bordering often invokes longer histories of colonial domination, racialisation and othering. Mohanty's feminist approach to borders therefore reveals the connections between various forms of exclusion and domination, refusing to isolate state borders as technocratic inevitabilities, or see them as relevant only to certain, disadvantaged people.

Nonetheless, focusing on the links between these various kinds of border, the symbolic and the unignorably physical, is not without its risks. As a result of the pervasiveness of borders, and the way that the term 'border' can signify widely differing types of experience, it is easy for discussions of the topic to become primarily metaphorical or symbolic in a way that does little justice to the sheer material difficulty and signifi- cance of crossing certain kinds of border for certain kinds of people. In postcolonial literary and cultural studies, the stability and ethno- nationalism often associated with the nation state are typically criticised through contrast with the flexibility and hybridity of the migratory subject, something which fails to account for the difficulties of forced migration. Being attentive to borders must therefore mean paying close and careful attention to the way borders actually operate, and the differ- ences between various kinds of migration, rather than relying too heavily on abstract, generalisable concepts such as the hybrid. Literature can play an important role here by facilitating readers' close attention to the particular operation of borders in particular times and places through its self-conscious use of language. Not all literature employs language in this way, but one striking feature of the texts I examine here is their shared obsessive interest in words' shifting meanings, and in the ways stories are told.

'On the Same Map': The Multiplicity of Borders in *Tell Me How It Ends*

Tell Me How It Ends (2017) describes Valeria Luiselli's experiences volun- teering as a translator at the federal immigration court in New York for unaccompanied children who have crossed the border between Mexico and the USA. The children predominately come from Honduras, El Salvador, and Guatemala. Luiselli is a Mexican novelist and college teacher living in New York City, and during the period described in the book she is waiting for her green card, which will give her permanent residency in the USA. In the text, she highlights something she perceives to be missing from discourse around migration:

> The attitude in the United States toward child migrants is not always blatantly negative, but generally speaking, it is based on a kind of misunder- standing or voluntary ignorance. ... No one suggests that the causes are deeply embedded in our shared hemispheric history and are therefore not some distant problem in a foreign country that no one can locate on a map, but in fact a transnational problem that includes the United States.[13]

As this passage illustrates, Luiselli positions her writing as a counter-narrative and a corrective.

There are, she writes, 'Official accounts in the United States', which she characterises as: 'what circulates in the newspaper or on the radio, the message from Washington, and public opinion in general' (p. 83). By implication, what the reader encounters in Luiselli's book is an unofficial account, one that tries to speak back to prevailing patterns of decontextualisation and dehistoricisation, in order to insist on a 'shared hemispheric history' (p. 85). To make this concrete, Luiselli identifies a particular example. She writes that all the 'official reports' fail to note the connections between Hempstead, a city in New York state, and Tegucigalpa, a city in Honduras, because they 'almost always locate the dividing line between "civilisation" and "barbarity" just below the Río Grande' (p. 83). Accustomed to thinking of a contrast between Honduras and the USA, it becomes difficult, she argues, to understand their relationship. In fact, 'Both cities can be drawn on the same map: the map of violence related to drug trafficking', as the same gangs operate in both locations (p. 83). In the USA, the Mexican border has been rhetorically overlaid with another border – 'the dividing line between "civilisation" and "barbarity"' (p. 83). To counter this, Luiselli offers an alternative way of conceptualising space in the image of the drug-gang map that features both cities.

Importantly, she is not challenging the double border which features in the official narrative with a naïve vision of a world without borders, as if by inviting readers to simply imagine a borderless world, one can be brought into being. Maps are, obviously, not typically border-free spaces – in fact, what they often do is represent and insist upon politically determined and sometimes arbitrary borderlines. However, the borders in the official narrative are lines of demarcation and separation, lines which attempt to produce and maintain division. By contrast, Luiselli wants to draw readers' attention to points of connection. She invites us to see the Mexico–USA border not as a marker of absolute difference, but rather as a place which reveals and mediates interconnectedness. The experience of the border is not the same for citizens or residents of the USA as it is for those trying to cross the border, but nonetheless the border shapes the experiences of both. This mutual interrelation is illustrated through the way Luiselli describes her daughter's interest in the children she translates for. In particular, Luiselli writes, 'There is one story that obsesses her' (p. 55). This is the story of two other little girls, five and seven years old. The girls' mother had migrated to Long Island three years ago and then sent for them. They left Guatemala by themselves, with 'a man' (p. 56). They 'made it to the border, were kept in custody ... for an indefinite time period ... . After that they went to a shelter and a few weeks later they were put on a plane and flown to JFK' (p. 57). It seems likely that Luiselli's daughter becomes especially interested in these children because of what she and they share in terms of age and gender – that is, there is a type of identification at play here.

In the text, her daughter's intense interest in these other girls is repeatedly connected to issues of storytelling and writing and prompts Luiselli's self-conscious reflection on the form that is appropriate for recounting the extraordinary experiences of child migrants. Importantly, it also gives the book its title. Luiselli's daughter asks her: 'So, how does the story of those children end?' (p. 55). Luiselli has 'not yet been able to offer a real ending': 'I don't know how it ends yet, I usually say' (p. 55). But 'She comes back to this question often, demanding a proper conclusion with the insistence of very small children' (p. 66). Because of the complexities of the immigration court, the girls' arrival in New York is not the end of the story: 'That's just where it begins, with a court summons: a first Notice to Appear' (p. 58). At the end of the text, there is an incident which brings together these themes – the daughter's imaginative investment in the girls' migration story, the interrelationship between different types of border, and the challenge to literary style. In the book's final section 'Coda (Eight Brief Postscripta)', Luiselli describes her horror and shock at the election of Donald Trump: 'the world is so upside fucking down that Trump somehow became president of the United States' (p. 101). She feels that – as a writer of fiction – she should have known what was about to happen: 'I should have foreseen some of it: I am a novelist, which means my mind is trained to read the world as part of a narrative plot, where some events foreshadow others' (p. 101). One of the events which feels, in retrospect, like foreshadowing, involves her daughter: they are playing together with face paints when her daughter puts white paint on her face and says 'now I'm getting ready for when Trump is president. So they won't know we're Mexicans' (p. 102).

The daughter's anxieties about a Trump election victory show that, as Trilling has suggested, 'In the 21st century, a border is not just a line on a map; it is a system for filtering people that stretches from the edges of a territory into its heart, affecting those who are already in the country.'[14] The daughter's experience is not the *same* as the experience of the Guatemalan girls she is obsessed with. But this incident – the sad, jokey performance of self-erasure, her deep understanding of racialisation at such an early age – suggests the extent to which she too is shaped and affected by the policing of the border. This is an experience which connects these differently located girls. This moment feels like foreshadowing: it feels as if it should be in a novel. Nonetheless, it appears in this non-fictional text, even though being a novelist is central to Luiselli's identity. Novels, she claims, provide a 'narrative plot, where some events foreshadow others' (p. 101). To do justice to the unknown ending of stories like that of the two girls from Guatemala, and her daughter's own sense of insecurity, a novel would be insufficient.

In this way, the text's challenge to the official narrative is twofold, working at the level of form and content. It directly points out the connections between the USA and the rest of the American continent which produce migratory flows, thereby challenging the decontextualisation characteristic of the official narrative. But in its form, it also performs incompletion, and draws attention to its own distance from rigid structure (by, for example, ending with a list of eight postscripta, instead of a conclusion which draws the threads together). It is as if the story is stretching and outpacing the forms the writer has available to her. In order to centre this particular female experience, the connected experience of different kinds of border which stretches between the unaccompanied migrant girls and her own daughter, a new type of narrative has to be developed. The text's own lack of closure makes the need for new stories about migration – ones which can account for connection and the multiple types of border which currently exist – appear increasingly urgent to the reader.

Mouths: Imagery, Sexual Violence and Migration in 'Conversations About Home'

Warsan Shire's prose poem 'Conversations about Home (at the Deportation Centre)' also emphasises the relationship between state borders and wider societal patterns of oppression. It employs imagery related to mouths to evoke the vulnerability to sexual violence that is, for many women, exacerbated by migration, illuminating the gendered dimensions of travel across borders. The text has four sections, but the relationship between these sections is left open: all have a first-person speaker, who describes forced migration, but whether this is the same speaker across the sections is not clear. Mouths are mentioned repeatedly in the poem. At first home is compared to a mouth: 'home spat me out, the blackouts and the curfews like tongue against loose teeth'.[15] The home–mouth analogy then becomes more particular: 'No one leaves home unless home is the mouth of a shark' (p. 24). Then it is the speaker's mouth which moves to the foreground: 'I've been carrying the old anthem in my mouth for so long that there's no space for another song, another tongue or another language', and 'I tore up and ate my own passport in an airport hotel. I'm bloated with language I can't afford to forget' (p. 24). At first home *is* the mouth; as the poem progresses, the home country is instead *in* the speaker's mouth, symbolised by the anthem and the passport. The 'old anthem' fills up the speaker's mouth – a metaphor suggesting the difficulties of displacement (p. 24). Belonging to her own national community and inevitably shaped by it, it is difficult – even impossible – for the speaker to adjust linguistically, culturally or romantically/sexually: there is 'no space' for 'another language', 'another song', or 'another tongue' (p. 24).

This imagery continues to be twisted and transformed as the poem continues: borders become personified and they too possess mouths: 'Look at all these borders, foaming at the mouth with bodies broken and desperate', the speaker says in section 2 (p. 25). A mouth is a kind of border between the body's inside and outside: that the borders' mouths are foaming indicates an uncontrolled sickness. Then the speaker describes being far from home and watching the news depicting the terrible events which are occurring there: 'I watch the news and my mouth becomes a sink full of blood' (p. 26). The image of the mouth as a sink suggests the intensity of the speaker's corporeal, visceral response to what she sees on the news: the mouth is filled with blood, as if it is taking on the injuries of others back home. Though blood in the mouth is probably an easily imaginable experience, the comparison of the mouth with the sink makes the image surreal and indicates the speakers' sense of disorientation.

Why do mouths recur across the poem in this way? One explanation is suggested by section 3, in which the speaker describes her reasons for leaving her home. After describing the indignities and difficulties of life as an immigrant, she states: 'But Alhamdulilah all of this is better than the scent of a woman completely on fire, or a truckload of men who look like my father, pulling out my teeth and nails, or fourteen men between my legs, or a gun, or a promise, or a lie, or his name, or his manhood in my mouth' (p. 26). The speaker fears violence; this fear causes her to migrate. The violence is notably gendered. There are female victims ('the scent of a woman completely on fire') and male perpetrators: 'the truckload of men ... pulling out my teeth and nails'; the 'fourteen men between my legs' (p. 26). Early in the poem, mouths are symbolic. The danger of home is symbolised by teeth; the disaster of tightening border controls is symbolised by the foaming at the mouth. In this later part of the poem, the mouth is no longer a symbol but is, rather, the actual site of sexual violence. It is well established that sexual violence is a significant risk for women during wartime and during migration, and the repeated use of the image of the mouth in this poem, related to home, the border, and the threat of violence, works to make the link between sexual violence and migration clear.[16] Importantly, though, it does not do this through logical language or through statistics – it works in a different register. It is one thing to understand that there is a link between sexual violence and migration. But the insistent, obsessive return to the image of the mouth, its appearance in multiple, sometimes surreal locations, suggests more than the link itself. It also registers the frightening and traumatic impact of these intertwined experiences, the way they can unsettle ordinary life and make it impossible.

Refugee, Exile, Migrant, Expatriate: Vahni Capildeo's 'Five Measures of Expatriation'

So far in this chapter I have been arguing that literary writing, with its intense interest in language and in forms of storytelling, can help readers to become attentive to the connections between state borders and other forms of social differentiation and oppression, such as the experiences of racialisation and fear which link Luiselli's daughter and the girls from Guatemala she is interested in, and the specifically gendered aspects of migration, such as women's experience of sexual violence. In the final section of the chapter, I turn to the second part of Mohanty's definition of feminist thinking on borders – transcendence. I argue that, through its linguistic innovation, Vahni Capildeo's prose poem 'Five Measures of Expatriation' invites readers to contemplate the creativity, freedom, and opportunity that crossing borders can produce, without losing sight of the associated difficulties and suffering. As we have seen, the words used to describe a border-crossing person matter deeply. Luiselli argues that the USA needs to 'rethink the very language' used to describe the migrants who cross the Mexico–US border – a rethinking she considers unlikely, because of the legal significance of certain names (p. 86). A 'war refugee', she writes, 'is bad news and an uncomfortable truth for governments, because it obliges them to deal with the problem instead of simply "removing the illegal *aliens*"' (p. 87). Meanwhile, the word 'refugee' has also taken on other meanings beyond the law. The speaker in Warsan Shire's poem hears people saying '*fucking immigrants, fucking refugees*' (p. 27). 'Refugee' – legally defined as a person outside of her country of citizenship and with a well-founded fear of persecution – is here an insult.

It is against the background of the names given to border-crossers, their shifting meanings and life-changing significance, that Capildeo's prose poem 'Five Measures of Expatriation' can be read. The speaker in the poem was born in Trinidad and lives in the UK, and the poem explores a series of experiences with, and reflections on, borders. For example, it describes the party game 'where each person says the first word that comes to mind, prompted by what the person before has just said', and asks: 'If these words: expatriate, exile, migrant, refugee: turned up in the children's game, what, on the instant, would be my wordless upsurge?'[17] The section is titled 'A Record of Illegitimate Reactions', and each of the four words appears on the page accompanied by a set of associations. For example, 'Migrant geese or some such was where I first heard the word so as to note it, the word migrant actually not alone at origin, part of a phrase with white wings' (p. 102). Exile, meanwhile, 'is Joseph. Exile is Moses. Exile is a boy or a man and sand and serpents. Exile is Sri Rāma' (p. 102). The accumulation of associations includes colours ('Migrant is cerulean and khaki' (p. 102)) and recollected personal experience: '*Refugee.* Severity of the olive green cover of the J.S. Bach *Preludes and Fugues* book that was my master such long hours of my teens . . . *Refugio.* A cavern. Mary and Joseph, straw in a rough box?' (p. 101).

Listing the diverse ideas associated with each name for a border-crosser, the poem carefully attends to the shades of meaning that these words can possess. It thus distinguishes itself from a prominent trend in postcolonial literary and cultural studies, which has often symbolised migration in general through one concept: the figure of 'the unencumbered exile who rejects the need for home altogether and, through this process, finds self-actualization through authorship', as Lucinda Newns puts it.[18] The problem with the heroic exile figure, David Farrier writes, is that it 'too easily equates voluntary exiles and asylum seekers', failing to acknowledge that some movements away from home produce trauma without contributing to redemptive experiences of personal growth.[19] By contrast, 'Five Measures' is careful to distinguish various kinds of migratory experience. For example, the speaker finds 'expatriate' to be the most fitting name. This term is arrived at via the process of haphazard, responsive creation which the poem sees as characteristic of the expatriate: 'An exile, a migrant, a refugee, would have been in more of a hurry, would have been more driven out or driven towards, would have been seeking and finding not' (p. 101).

However, the poem does not only use its list of names for border-crossers to suggest that we need to be attentive to the specificity of individuals' experiences, and resist collapsing distinctions. What is so striking about the list which follows each of the words is that they float entirely free of the expected meanings: they are allusive, sometimes obscure; they follow chains of association that go off in wild directions. The poem does not only show that each name for a person who crosses a border suggests different shades of meaning, but also connects the words 'refugee', 'migrant', 'exile', and 'expatriate' to surprising, idiosyncratic, specific, and evocative ideas, phrases which recall religious practice and mythology, colour and art. In this way, it implies a rethinking of the words used to describe migration – not in the sense Luiselli means, as a way of spurring targeted political action, but rather in an imaginative sense. The poem refuses the static meanings and bureaucratic jargon of border control – the discourses that decide which label an individual will acquire, and therefore the kind of treatment they will receive. It does not regurgitate the legal or political definitions of a refugee, for example – it insists on the possibility of finding new meanings in this familiar category.

'Expatriate' is the term claimed by the speaker in Capildeo's poem. This term is chosen for circumstantial reasons, because of the bureaucratic machinery of immigration – it is not in any sense a personal experience of inner identity.

> Expatriation: my having had a *patria*, a fatherland to leave, did not occur to me until I was forced to invent one. This was the result of questions. The questions were linked to my status elsewhere. (p. 95)

The speaker is compelled to assert an identity in order to travel, but even so 'expatriate' is not simply an externally imposed label – it also opens new possibilities. The word is heavily weighted. As Mawuna Remarque Koutonin has written, 'In the lexicon of human migration there are still hierarchical words, created with the purpose of putting white people above everyone else', and expatriate or expat 'is a term reserved exclusively for western white people going to work abroad'.[20] Because it is being born in Trinidad, once colonised by Britain, that poses such problems and hold-ups for the speaker in European immigration systems, there is a certain irony in the choice of this word; it is an attempt to reclaim and reconfigure a term conventionally used to maintain racial hierarchy.

The word 'expatriate' also has gendered connotations. In feminist terms, liberation from the father is – archetypally – cast as an important movement towards individual freedom (however well-loved actual flesh-and-blood fathers might be). The poem suggests that leaving a real father can be a source of freedom: 'My father, in Trinidad, was very ill, as he had been ever since I had known him. In my early twenties, I realized that this illness was not going to change, except to get worse. In some ways this realization was freedom. I started looking to cross other waters' (p. 96). Though this 'freedom' is not uncomplicated or unambiguous, because it comes at the cost of a father's illness, the connection between the father and the father-land here is suggestive. If leaving the actual father provides some opportunity for freedom and movement and mobility as well as sadness and pain, for the feminist reader, alert to the significance of patriarchs as symbols of masculine power, there is an implication that becoming an expatriate can also become a source of new possibility in gendered terms. The poem causes the reader to linger over the meaning of the familiar word 'expatriate', and draws attention to the movement away from the symbolic figure of masculine authority, the figure of the father, embedded in the literal meaning. In this way, it suggests that the expatriate might function as a symbol of feminist possibility, even through and within the grief and pain of loss: 'Expatriate, I had acquired the confidence to hurtle into having to start over. It was a way of going on' (p. 99).

Conclusion

The texts discussed in this chapter present feminist perspectives on the injustices of contemporary bordering practices, and all three use innovative literary approaches to do so. The imagery of the mouth in 'Conversations about Home (at the Deportation Centre)' makes the connection between sexual violence and migration viscerally and uncomfortably clear, powerfully evoking the suffering experienced by many women and girls who cross borders today. An intersectional feminist politics cannot treat gender in isolation, and the texts also emphasise the racial politics and colonial histories that intersect with gender in bordering processes. *Tell Me How It Ends* self-consciously draws attention to the limitations of its own narrative form as it tries to depict the interconnected experiences of the child migrants from Guatemala and Luiselli's own daughter. Through its unsettled narrative structure, it emphasises the need for new stories to adequately reflect the 'shared hemispheric history' that links the girls (p. 85). Finally, Capildeo's poem reimagines the words 'migrant', 'refugee', 'expatriate', and 'exile', and – through playing with the word 'expatriate' – intertwines the possibilities of anti-patriarchal and migratory freedom. Through these gestures, border crossing is depicted as a source of imaginative and creative liberation, even as it is also associated with loss, pain, and grief. The feminist approach to borders that emerges when the texts are read together, therefore, is one that attends to the extreme difficulties of many migrations today, and represents the particular experiences of women as well as understanding gender in relation to racial politics and colonial histories. Against the background of intense anti-migrant sentiment, it also resolutely celebrates and defends the value, significance, and creativity of the act of crossing borders.

Research for this chapter was funded by the Danish National Research Foundation, grant number DNRF127.

Notes

1 J. Nevins, *Operation Gatekeeper and Beyond* (New York: Routledge, 2010), 10.
2 Ibid.
3 C. T. Mohanty, *Feminism Without Borders: Decolonizing Theory, Practicing Solidarity* (Durham, NC and London: Duke University Press, 2003), 2.
4 1951 Convention Relating to the Status of Refugees and its 1967 Protocol, unhcr.org.
5 J. B. Cooper, 'Environmental Refugees: Meeting the Requirements of the Refugee Definition', *New York University Environmental Law Journal*, 6:2 (1998), 480–674.
6 D. Trilling, 'Five Myths about the Refugee Crisis', *The Guardian* (5 June 2018).
7 V. Mamadouh, 'The Scaling of the "Invasion": A Geopolitics of Immigration Narratives in France and The Netherlands', *Geopolitics*, 17:2 (2012), 377–401; H. De Haas, 'The Myth of Invasion: The Inconvenient Realities of African Migration to Europe', *Third World Quarterly*, 29:7 (2008), 1305–22.
8 R. Zetter, 'More Labels, Fewer Refugees: Remaking the Refugee Label in an Era of Globalization', *Journal of Refugee Studies*, 20:2 (2007), 183.
9 H. Smith, 'Shocking Images of Drowned Syrian Boy Show Tragic Plight of Refugees', *The Guardian* (2 September 2015).
10 E. Coundouriotis, 'The Child Soldier Narrative and the Problem of Arrested Historicization', *Journal of Human Rights*, 9:2 (2010), 191–206; L. Khalili, 'Heroic and Tragic Pasts: Mnemonic Narratives in the Palestinian Refugee Camps', *Critical Sociology*, 33:4 (2007), 731–59.
11 A. Mountz and N. Hiemstra, 'Chaos and Crisis: Dissecting the Spatiotemporal Logics of Contemporary Migrations and State Practices', *Annals of the Association of American Geographers*, 104:4 (2014), 383.
12 G. Popescu, *Bordering and Ordering the Twenty-First Century* (Plymouth: Rowman & Littlefield, 2012), 15.

13 V. Luiselli, *Tell Me How It Ends: An Essay in Forty Questions* (London: 4th Estate, 2017), 85.

14 Trilling, 'Five Myths about the Refugee Crisis'.

15 W. Shire, 'Conversations about Home (at the Deportation Centre)', in *Teaching My Mother How to Give Birth* (London: Flipped Eye, 2011), 24.

16 J. Leaning, S. Barterls, and H. Mowafi, 'Sexual Violence during War and Forced Migration', in S. Forbes and M. J. Tirman, *Women, Migration and Conflict: Breaking a Deadly Cycle* (London: Springer, 2009), 173–99.

17 V. Capildeo, 'Five Measures of Expatriation', in *Measures of Expatriation* (Manchester: Carcanet, 2016), 101.

18 L. Newns, 'Homelessness and the Refugee: De-valorizing Displacement in Abdulrazak Gurnah's *By the Sea*', *Journal of Postcolonial Writing*, 51:5 (2015), 516.

19 D. Farrier, *Postcolonial Asylum: Seeking Sanctuary Before the Law* (Liverpool: Liverpool University Press, 2011), 4.

20 M. R. Koutonin, 'Why Are White People Expats When the Rest of Us Are Immigrants?', *The Guardian* (13 March 2015).

CHAPTER 5

Sex Work in a Postwork Imaginary: On Abolitionism, Careerism, and Respectability

Helen Hester and Zahra Stardust

What does it mean to envisage a future free from work, and what might that look like for sex work? This chapter examines calls to end work, contextualising contemporary understandings of sex work in light of recent developments in labour studies. It insists upon the importance of factoring sex work into 'postwork' perspectives, while critiquing the stakes involved in feminist drives to abolish sex work. Using texts from gender and sexuality studies, sex worker activism, and materialist feminism, we argue that the starting point for any postwork position on this issue must be the insistence that labour itself be perpetually interrogated, resisted, and problematised; it is work in general (and not sex work in particular) that deserves to be abolished.

Postwork: Possibilities and Limitations

Postwork theorists respond proactively to changing labour conditions in the twenty-first century, often seeking to confront the idea that advances in the automation of industrial and service work will lead to increased inequality, ever-more precarious working arrangements, and the loss of a significant number of jobs. Rather than agitating for the preservation of jobs, however – as a more conventional leftist position might – they suggest that the reduction of available work represents a moment of political opportunity. As long as automation is put at the service of people not profit, contemporary postwork theorists argue, the coming crisis can represent an unprecedented opportunity to reduce the working week, and to develop a culture beyond the glorification of the work ethic. They typically critique the idea that today's jobs are capable of delivering prosperity, purpose, and social equality, and argue instead that the left needs to resist wage labour (and the work ethic) as part of a proactive response to the current crisis. Work, these theorists argue, must be framed as a problem rather than a solution, and we must seek to be emancipated from (rather than through) our labour.[1]

Postwork ambitions are often articulated in terms of waged work, meaning that some of the work of social reproduction is excluded. Social reproduction involves various labours to reproduce people and communities on a daily or intergenerational level – activities such as cleaning, cooking, and childcare. It includes work that is often undervalued, unwaged, or even criminalised, but from which capital nevertheless benefits. The neglect of this work is a problem not merely because it unduly restricts postwork imaginaries, but also because of its gendered implications. If historically 'feminized' forms of remunerated and unremunerated labour are assumed to continue much as they always have (without concerted efforts to reduce the amount of labour they require or to substantially redistribute this labour across a wider subset of the population), then supposedly emancipatory visions of a postwork world are in fact profoundly inequitable.

In common with many other theorists of social reproduction, we include sex work under the bracket of reproductive labour, because it involves physical and affective labour intended to foster the emotional regeneration of the workforce. Postwork theorists, however, have done little to include sex work within their analyses. This is an oversight on their part, and one which inadvertently replicates the exclusion of erotic labour from wider efforts to theorise work. As Melissa Gira Grant remarks, 'even many scholars of the informal economy who've mapped the labour of trash pickers and street sellers, counterfeiters and smugglers have failed to give sex work its due – because it is criminal, because it is service work, and in many cases, because it is work gendered as female'.[2]

'Sex Work Is Work': The Rhetoric of Demand Making

Situating sex work within a broader framing of labour has been a deliberate strategy to advance social, cultural, and legal change and has aligned sex work with other intimate, caring, and domestic work.[3] Coined by sex worker activist Carol Leigh in the late 1970s, the term 'sex work' has been adopted by the United Nations, World Health Organisation, International Labour Organisation, and others.[4] The political slogan 'sex work is work' continues to appear as a powerful rallying cry in advocacy organising.[5] This position has been used to resist specific criminal laws, to push for anti-discrimination protections, to help ensure occupational health and safety standards, and to provide opportunities for collective bargaining.

Across the globe, sex workers have mobilised to insist on the recognition of their work *as work* and to demand fair working conditions. Famous examples include the unionisation of the Lusty Lady in San Francisco, which became one of the first worker-owned co-operative peepshows in the USA.[6] In Chiang Mai, Thailand, the collectively sex-worker-owned Can Do Bar splits all profits among sex workers and aims to operate with optimum workplace conditions.[7] In New South Wales, Australia, Scarlet Alliance worked in partnership with a government health department to develop workplace health and safety standards, which were adapted for use in other jurisdictions and translated into multiple languages.[8] In Calcutta, India, the Durbar Mahalia Samanwaya Committee (DMSC) represents 65,000 sex workers, involves the community in all decision-making processes, advocates for occupational and human rights and runs its own micro-credit programme for sex workers.[9] For the labourers themselves, there are real and tangible benefits to be achieved by recognising sex work as work: the removal of police as regulators, the option to access fair work mechanisms, and the removal of social and cultural barriers to accessing services (to see a doctor without undergoing mandatory medical tests, for example, or to negotiate child custody without being seen as an unfit parent).

Vectors of Dignity: Legitimacy Through Labour

Some commentators, however, have gone beyond these pragmatic gains, pointing to wider benefits in terms of the generation of cultural capital. To call something work, they argue, is to mobilise widespread social veneration for this category of activity. In these cases, the adage 'sex work is work' operates as an appeal to classify sex work as a legitimate occupation, and as *therefore* deserving of respect. Wendy Chapkis, for example, argues that sex workers need to 'insist on the dignity and respect owed to any worker'.[10] The organisation Prostitutes of New York (PONY) argues that 'efforts to deny [sex workers] of their livelihood are efforts to deny them of the dignity of earning a living', while the feminist human rights organisation CREA stresses that sex workers deserve 'dignity for their work and the same rights and recognition as other workers'.[11] In these discourses, sex work moves from being classified as a 'vector of disease', and instead, via the social recognition conventionally afforded to remunerated work, becomes positioned as a vector for dignity.

Sex workers are seen to warrant esteem here because they are as industrious and self-sufficient as waged workers from other sectors of the economy, but they repeatedly must *prove* that their work *is* work before such dignity can be bestowed. In *The Problem with Work*, Kathi Weeks discusses the 'limitations of certain efforts to claim the title of work when that also involves making use of the legitimacy conferred by its dominant ethic'.[12] In her view, activism pushing for the acceptance of sex work *as* work risks reinforcing the perceived intrinsic virtue of labour and shoring up its role as a discourse of distinction. In Weeks's words, to declare that sex work is work 'usefully demoralises the debates about the nature, value, and legitimacy of sex for wages in one way, but it often does so by problematically remoralising it in another' (p. 68). Other postwork theorists agree with this view. Peter Frase, for example, builds upon Weeks's account when he argues that '[t]he basic problem that afflicts many pro- and anti-sex work arguments is that they take for granted the desirability and legitimacy of *wage labor in general*. They are caught up in an ideology that says that work is supposed to be a source of meaning and dignity in life.'[13]

While, in Weeks's words, shifting 'the discussion from one moral terrain to another, from that of a suspect sexual practice to that of a respectable employment relation' may *seem* like a pragmatic approach, critics argue that it is fraught with rhetorical risks (p. 68). Mobilising accepted ideas about work might end up replicating some of the worst tendencies of 'respectability politics'. It is our argument, however, that sex worker rights movements do not merely 'take for granted the desirability and legitimacy of wage labour in general' but rather engage discourses of work strategically and critically.

Happy Hookers and Respectability Politics

If one were to look solely at mainstream journalistic representations, it might certainly appear that the appeal for sex workers to be recognised as workers is an assimilationist one that buys into the glorification of work. For example, when sex workers attract social acclaim or positive exposure, media narratives emphasise their high incomes, entrepreneurial attitudes, and choice of flexible working conditions. When former journalist Samantha X divorced her husband and came out as a 'high class courtesan', *Daily Mail* headlines read 'mother-of-two charges $800 an hour or $5,000 a night for her time', and news media detailed how she worked out of a high-end apartment with better hours and greater flexibility than her former office job.[14] Sex work here is selectively presented as easy, appealing, lucrative, and convenient work: this individualised and largely depoliticised narrative of sex work appeals to a cultural fantasy about autonomous working conditions but does nothing to improve the structural or systemic factors (criminalisation, policing, precarious labour, stigma, and discrimination) that govern sex work and further stratifies more marginalised forms of sex work as less acceptable.

It is the professionalisation of sex work that attracts social reward here, and a safe version of sex work that is seen to redeem the supposed transgression of sex itself. We should follow sex workers in turning a critical eye on the ways in which they are expected to perform narratives of an empowered 'happy hooker' with a job 'like any other' in order to access media representation. Juno Mac and Molly Smith are among those who have problematised the demand that, if sex workers wish to vouch for the validity of sex work as work, they must assert that they find it enjoyable: 'Anti-prostitution feminists and even policy makers often ask sex workers whether we would have sex with our clients if we weren't being paid. Work is thus constantly being reinscribed as something so personally fulfilling you would pursue it for free.'[15] As they point out, this sets an unreasonable pre-condition for all struggles for workers' rights, as the only legitimate workers would appear to be those with no need for workplace organising at all.

It is also worth noting that the sex workers who are sought out for mainstream attention are frequently white, cisgender, tertiary educated, middle class, and working as private escorts rather than street-based or brothel workers. By requiring sex workers to assert their love for the job, this 'happy hooker' narrative makes invisible the labour involved in sex work itself. As Heather Berg has argued, the expectation that sex workers describe their work as a personal identity or form of self-expression, or confess their genuine love for sex work or its altruistic reward and social benefits, in fact serves to extract more labour-power.[16] This should absolutely be of concern to postwork theorists, as it is to many sex worker rights movements.

Collective Solidarity and Dismantling Whorearchy

Sex worker advocacy is deeply concerned with what is colloquially known as the 'whorearchy' – the hierarchical systems within sex work that determine who is afforded privilege, social capital, and respectability. Belle Knox, famed as the 'Duke University Porn Star', has written about the stratification of sex work, its segregation along social and legal lines, its arrangement 'according to intimacy of contact with clients and police' and how the whorearchy is maintained through the operation of disdain among sex workers.[17] Sex worker movements are invested in fostering solidarity between sex workers, regardless of the type or legality of their work, to ensure the rights won for some do not come at the expense of others. This is epitomised by one of the key international slogans of the movement – 'No bad whores, just bad laws'.

Sex worker advocacy and outreach is focused not upon assimilating into the current work ethic, but upon protecting and supporting the most marginalised workers – those who are migrant, street-based, drug users, culturally and linguistically diverse, Aboriginal, living with HIV, trans or gender diverse, or parents. Because sex work does not always operate in the form of waged labour, the movement supports sex workers whose work is opportunistic, for trade, or for goods. C. B. Daring notes that '[i]n a Western context, sex workers' rights are connected to other prominent anarchist projects, specifically around gentrification, anti-racism, anti-police brutality, and queer rights'.[18] Sex worker organisations have built alliances with movements for unionisation, drug law reform, prison abolition, decriminalising HIV, and open borders. Scarlet Alliance, for example, has collaborated with the Cross Border Collective on a campaign in which migrant sex workers stand alongside First Nation peoples and refugees to declare that 'We don't need your pity, we need our rights.'[19] The grass-roots, bottom-up processes of sex worker organisations provide mechanisms for community consultation and accountability and seek to address systemic factors that place sex workers at risk. Objectives relate to safety not respectability, de-stigmatisation not assimilation, autonomy not legitimacy.

Abolitionist Feminism, Rescue Industries and Careerism

Sex work provides potent examples of where aspirations to abolish (certain forms of) work have missed the mark. Calls for the abolition of sex work have typically come in the guises of 'exit strategies', 'demand reduction', and anti-trafficking policies, which have variously sought to provide incentives for sex workers to leave the industry (to be redirected into other forms of 'acceptable' work – often low-status, poorly paid labour), to criminalise clients (making it difficult for sex workers to screen them for safety), and to target migrant sex workers via brothel raids, immigration checks, and deportation (instead of improving pathways for safe migration or access to industrial rights mechanisms).

In the absence of a more general critique of work, the disproportionate enthusiasm for ending sex work positions it *beyond work*. This relies on the premise that sex workers are selling more than their labour-power –

namely, their bodies or some ineffable sacred essence tied up with sex. According to this understanding, they are 'selling themselves'. In *Capital*, Marx differentiates between selling one's labour-power as a commodity versus oneself being positioned as a commodity. This, he argues, is the difference between being a capitalist worker and being a slave:

> the owner of the labour-power should sell it only for a definite period, for if he were to sell it rump and stump, once for all, he would be selling himself, converting himself from a free man into a slave, from an owner of a commodity into a commodity. He must constantly look upon his labour-power as his own property, his own commodity, and this he can only do by placing it at the disposal of the buyer temporarily, for a definite period of time.[20]

Sex workers are obliged to repeatedly assert that they are selling their services, not their bodies (common slogans such as 'Keep your laws off my body!' and 'My body, my rights' assert corporeal ownership and autonomy). They maintain that sex work, like many other kinds of labour, uses both body and mind, and involves assessing risks, negotiating prices, establishing boundaries, performing STI checks, and educating others about pleasure, anatomy, and safer sex.[21] To the extent that sex workers own their own bodies, and are therefore in a position to sell their labour-power as a commodity (as many of these workers themselves assert), we must recognise that they constitute workers under capitalism.

The overall effect of abolitionist models has been not to end sex work, nor to improve labour conditions, but rather to reduce sex workers' control over their workplaces and increase risks to their safety and well-being. There is mounting evidence about the effect of laws that criminalise the purchase (but not the sale) of sexual services. In Sweden, landlords are required to terminate tenancy of premises used for sex work, laws prohibiting anyone 'living off the earnings of prostitution' have been used to charge sex workers' children with pimping, and sex workers report being denied access to methadone treatment programmes unless they leave sex work.[22] In France, sex workers report a deterioration in their relations with the police, a deterioration of their living conditions (being pushed out of public spaces to more isolated areas), and a continued exposure to violence.[23] In Canada, sex workers face pressure from clients to rush their negotiations due to police presence, which can impede opportunities to screen clients for weapons or intoxication.[24] In Northern Ireland, sex workers report concern that criminalisation of clients will lead to increased involvement of organised crime and 'pimps'.[25] And despite the risks it brings for worker safety, research indicates that criminalisation has no effect in reducing the size of the sex industry.[26]

These approaches appear to be less about ending work and more about creating a new class of helping professionals to redirect sex workers into more 'reputable' forms of labour. Laura Agustin refers to a 'rescue industry' in which the middle classes see 'themselves as particularly suited to help, control, advise and discipline the unruly poor, including their sexual conduct', while imposing a victim identity that affords privilege and status to helpers and is 'closely linked to their *carving out a new employment sphere for themselves* through the naming of a project to rescue and control working-class women' (our emphasis).[27] Elizabeth Bernstein writes that, under the guise of 'rescue' and 'moral condemnation', helping professions have offered middle-class, white, 'young, evangelical women a means to engage directly in a sex-saturated culture without becoming "contaminated" by it'.[28] Abolitionist feminism then is not necessarily about resisting work, but rather about consolidating the sphere of 'NGOism' and strengthening the carceral state. As Jay Levy and Pye Jakobsson write, it is a form of 'patriarchal control' acting to displace women perceived to be deviant.[29] In opting to target a kind of labour that some of the most marginalised people can access (people who may not be able to obtain other kinds of work), sex work abolitionism targets the most vulnerable rather than the structures which generate and enforce vulnerability. The remedies – deportation, arrest, move-on notices, exit from the industry – strengthen a criminal justice response but do nothing to increase the safety, rights, or autonomy of sex workers, let alone to help foster a postwork future.

Anti-work Tendencies in Sex Worker Activism

In comparison, sex workers demonstrate anti-work tendencies within their resistance to the 'rescue industry'. Many of the key tenets of the sex worker movement are based not upon the celebration of work, but upon practical tactics and theoretical strategies for maximising autonomy in relation to it. The Empower Foundation's 'Last Rescue in Siam' – a short black and white film made in Thailand, inspired by the tradition of silent movies – depicts a dramatisation of sex workers running to escape from social workers, police, and 'the hero NGO'. Piling into a police van to conduct a brothel raid, these agencies ignore burglary, assault, and a motorbike accident. In the film, some sex workers avoid arrest by shooting ping-pong balls into a police officer's eyes, but another is locked away in rehab to learn to sew. In a defiant finale, this sex worker sews herself a ladder and escapes via the window, puts her heels back on and returns to work in the brothel.[30]

The global Network of Sex Work Projects (NSWP) has referred to the abolitionist and 'sex worker rehabilitation movement' as a form of 'economic disempowerment' noting that sex work appeals to some because of its higher wage and shorter hours, meaning that a lesser share of one's life is consumed by remunerated labour. In its regional report on economic and social empowerment in Cambodia, Thailand, Indonesia, Myanmar, and India, NSWP writes that:

> Anti-sex work fundamentalist feminists have quite the opposite interpretation of 'economic empowerment': they believe that sex workers are empowered when they exit sex work and are placed in programmes with alternative employment opportunities, regardless of whether the sex worker finds the work empowering or not. However, other occupations are often less appealing than sex work, as many involve long hours, violence, dangerous conditions, and sexual violations. Our research repeatedly indicates that supposed 'alternatives' pay far less and are entirely inadequate if the worker has dependents, as many do.[31]

To choose sex work, then, may be to refuse to be swallowed by the alternatives and to resist the pressure to submit to more 'respectable' forms of labour. Within this context, one can easily recognise anti-work tendencies within sex workers' rights movements – tendencies unmistakably expressed by the Asia Pacific Network of Sex Workers, whose logo features a sewing machine with a red circle and slash through it.[32] This defiant attitude is expressed even more clearly by the Prostitutes' War Group – 'an internationalist collective of anarchist revolutionary queer insurrectionist PROSTITUTES'.[33] They write that

> we believe in the formula: Least amount of labour/ for Highest rates of pay. We have no interest in careerism or 'respectable' lowly paid employment. ... We fundraise on our own terms to enable our Autonomy, the time and freedom to realise and unleash our own latent Power, and to bestow solidarity on those we respect in their offensive actions against systemic control.[34]

Mobilising discourses of distinction associated with the work ethic is clearly not the dominant concern here.

In their differing attitudes towards low-paid work, it becomes apparent that the rescue industry is far more prone to uncritically celebrate the work ethic than is sex worker activism. Whereas the struggle for sex workers' rights understands *work* as the problem with sex work, the rescue industries assume it is the *sex*. Indeed, anti-sex work discourse tends to scoop up the problems with work in general, and project them onto sex work in particular. In setting sex work apart as a unique vehicle for precarity, vulnerability, and coercion, and in holding it up as *the* privileged example of Big Bad Work without addressing the complex and systemic web of labour relations under capitalism, it lets wider cultures of labour off the hook. This, we argue, is part of a wider trend towards sex work exceptionalism – a trend that needs to be examined in order to better understand the possibilities of abolishing all work.

A Lever Not an End Point

As the sex worker, labour-rights activist, and anti-work thinker Morgane Merteuil reminds us, there is a fundamental difference between the situations of housewives and sex workers: 'unlike domestic labour, sex work is criminalized and stigmatized'.[35] Nevertheless, we feel there is an instructive comparison to be drawn between the approaches of contemporary sex worker movements and that of the 1970s International Wages for Housework Campaign, which demanded recognition and remuneration for the labour of cooking, cleaning, and caring. As Weeks points out, when campaigners 'maintained that the family is a site of social production and . . . demanded that women receive wages for the work they do there, the point was not to extol the virtues of domestic work'.[36] In activist materials from the height of the campaign, authors stress that the wage is not an endpoint but a lever – a means for facilitating the eventual refusal of work. Indeed, Silvia Federici famously renames the campaign 'Wages Against Housework' and points out that to 'say we want wages for housework is the first step towards refusing to do it, because the demand for a wage makes our work visible, which is the most indispensable condition to begin to struggle against it, both in its immediate aspect as housework and its more insidious character as femininity'.[37]

Aligning housework with activities that are socially visible *as* labour – via the mechanism of the wage (or rather, the demand for the wage) – is a means of problematising and *denaturalising* gendered reproductive labour. Something similar can be said of the claim that sex work is work. Despite sometimes being viewed as a transhistorical inevitability – the 'oldest profession' – financial exchange, combined with a context of criminality, helps to set sex work apart from the naturalising cultural mythologies surrounding other 'labours of love'. As Eva Pendleton writes, the mere act of charging money 'reverses the terms under which men feel entitled to unlimited access to women's bodies.'[38] Leopoldina Fortunati asserts that reproduction work – housework and prostitution – has a dual character. The former presents itself to capital as a natural force of social labour, hence as non-work, and posits itself to the [masculinized waged] worker as a personal service .... The latter is for capital an unnatural force of social labour, and for the worker is a personal service paid for by money.[39]

That being said, sex work does currently operate at the level of identity to some extent. Within cultures in which this labour is heavily stigmatised, sex work becomes culturally sticky; it ceases to be seen as something one does and is instead imagined as something one is. To call these services 'work' can be seen as part of an effort to separate the labour from the labourer and to restore sex work to its status as a process rather than an identity: sex workers are offering a service for money, not selling themselves 'rump and stump', as Marx would put it.[40] It is the start of a process of disidentification – a means of saying *we are not that work*. The claim that 'sex work is work' does not need to be freed from the short-sighted valorisation of the category of labour, then, because *it is already* performing the dual movement of naming activities as work, the better to reject work itself.

Conclusion

While we agree that tying ideas about human worth to the notion of remunerated labour is fundamentally unhelpful, the political risks and practical benefits associated with this approach should be viewed in context. The trend to situate sex work as work should be understood as a political strategy rather than as an unequivocal statement about the inherent essence of work itself. While the term 'work' can be rhetorically exploited, the radical anti-work tendencies already embedded in sex work advocacy suggest that sex workers have a more sophisticated and critical attitude to work than sex work abolitionists, whose approach is less about postwork politics and more about creating a rescue industry, protecting elite careers, and reinforcing a carceral state. Governments and NGOs can hardly be heard clamouring for the abolition of house-work, or for the physically and emotionally demanding toil of care work to be made illegal for carers' own protection. But like the Wages Against Housework campaign, the goal of sex worker advocacy is not to reify work, but rather to make visible under-recognised labour as part of a longer-term project to forcefully resist it. To claim that 'sex work is work' is the necessary starting point for any emancipatory position on contemporary erotic labour, rather than a betrayal of postwork principles.

Notes

1 See, for example, A. Bastani, *Fully Automated Luxury Communism: A Manifesto* (London: Verso, 2019) and N. Srnicek and A. Williams, *Inventing the Future: Postcapitalism and a World Without Work* (London: Verso, 2015). Other recent and forthcoming texts exemplifying a postwork tendency include D. Frayne, *The Refusal of Work: The Theory and Practice of Resistance to Work* (London: ZED Books, 2015); D. Graeber, *Bullshit Jobs: A Theory* (London: Simon & Schuster, 2018); and H. Hester and N. Srnicek, *After Work: The Fight for Free Time* (London: Verso, 2021).

2 M. Gira Grant, *Playing the Whore: The Work of Sex Work* (London: Verso, 2014), 49.

3 C. Wolkowitz et al., (eds.), *Body/Sex/Work: Intimate, Embodied and Sexualised Labour* (Basingstoke: Palgrave Macmillan, 2013).

4 C. Leigh, *Unrepentant Whore: The Collected Writings of Scarlet Harlot* (San Francisco: Last Gasp, 2002); Amnesty International, 'Policy on State Obligations to Respect, Protect and Fulfil the Human Rights of Sex Workers' (2016), amnesty.org; Joint United Nations Programme on HIV/AIDS (UNAIDS), United Nations Population Fund (UNFPA), United Nations Development Programme (UNDP), *Sex Work and the Law in Asia and the Pacific* (2012), 10.

5 Global Network of Sex Work Projects, 'Consensus Statement: On Sex Work, Human Rights and the Law' (2013), nswp.org.

6 See *Live Nude Girls Unite!*, dirs. V. Funari and J. Query (Brooklyn: First Run/Icarus Films/Query Productions, 2000).

7 See the working conditions listed on the Empower Foundation's website for Can Do Bar: www.empowerfoundation.org/barcando_en.html.

8 Scarlet Alliance, *Principles for Model Sex Work Legislation* (Redfern: Sydney, 2014), 46, scarletalliance.org.au/library/principles_2014.

9 Durbar Mahlia Samanwaya Committee, durbar.org.

10 W. Chapkis, 'Sex Workers: Interview with Wendy Chapkis', in S. Seidman, N. Fischer, and C. Meeks (eds.), *Introducing the New Sexuality Studies: Original Essays and Interviews* (London and New York: Routledge, 2007), 244.

11 Prostitutes of New York, 'Statement on the Dignity of Sex Workers' (2005), nswp.org; CREA, 'Sex Work Is Work' (2017), creaworld.org.

12 K. Weeks, *The Problem with Work: Feminism, Marxism, Antiwork Politics, and Postwork Imaginaries* (Durham and London: Duke University Press, 2011), 67.

13 P. Frase, 'The Problem with (Sex) Work' (27 March 2012), peterfrase.com.

14 E. Crane and L. Cheer, '$800-a-Night Escort Samantha X Defends her Lifestyle Claiming it Makes No Difference to Her Two Children', *Daily Mail* (1 September 2014); IVillage Team, 'So, is "High Class Call Girl" Really the Perfect Job for a Busy Mum?' *Mamamia* (1 September 2014).

15 J. Mac and M. Smith, *Revolting Prostitutes: The Fight for Sex Workers' Rights* (London: Verso, 2018), 42.

16 H. Berg, 'Sex, Work, Queerly: Identity, Authenticity and Laboured Performance', in M. Liang, K. Pilcher, and N. Smith, (eds.), *Queer Sex Work* (London and New York: Routledge, 2015), 24.

17 B. Knox, 'Tearing Down the Whorearchy from the Inside', *Jezebel* (7 February 2014).

18 C. B. Daring, 'Queering Our Analysis of Sex Work: Laying Capitalism Bare', in C. B. Daring, J. Rogue et al. (eds.), *Queering Anarchism: Addressing and Undressing Power and Desire* (Chico, CA: AK Press, 2012), 193.

19 Scarlet Alliance, *Sex Work Legislation*, 99. See also E. Jeffreys and J. Fawkes, 'Staging Decriminalisation: Sex Worker Performance and HIV', in A. Campbell and D. Gint (eds.), *Viral Dramaturgies* (Basingstoke: Palgrave Macmillan, 2018), 69–90.

20 K. Marx, *Capital: A Critique of Political Economy*, Vol. 1, trans. S. Moore and E. Aveling, ed. F. Engels (Moscow: Progress Publishers, 1887), 119.

21 Scarlet Alliance, *Sex Work Legislation*.

22 S. Dodillet and P. Ostergren, 'The Swedish Sex Purchase Act: Claimed Success and Documented Effects', conference paper presented at the International Workshop 'Decriminalizing Prostitution and Beyond: Practical Experiences and Challenges', The Hague, 3–4 March 2011, 3, petraostergren.com; and the interview with P. Jacobsson, 'A Swedish Sex Worker on the Criminalisation of Clients' (30 August 2011), youtube.com.

23 H. L. Bail and C. Giametta 'What Do Sex Workers Think About the French Prostitution Act: A Study on the Impact of the Law from 13th April 2016 Against the "Prostitution System" in France', *Synthesis* (April 2018), n.p.

24 A. Landsberg et al., 'Criminalizing Sex Work Clients and Rushed Negotiations Among Sex Workers Who Use Drugs in a Canadian Setting', *Journal of Urban Health*, 94:4 (2017), 563; A. Krüsi et al., 'Criminalisation of Clients: Reproducing Vulnerabilities for Violence and Poor Health Among Street-based Sex Workers in Canada: A Qualitative Study', *BMJ Open*, 4:6 (2014), 4.

25 S. Huschke et al., 'Research into Prostitution in Northern Ireland', Belfast Department of Justice (2014), 16.

26 Bail and Giametta, 'What Do Sex Workers Think', 4.

27 L. Agustin, *Sex at the Margins: Migration, Labour Markets and the Rescue Industry* (London and New York: Zed Books, 2007), 7–8.

28 E. Bernstein, 'Militarized Humanitarianism Meets Carceral Feminism: The Politics of Sex, Rights, and Freedom in Contemporary Anti-trafficking Campaigns', *Signs: Journal of Women in Culture and Society*, 36:1 (2010), 45; E. Bernstein, 'The Sexual Politics of the New Abolitionism', *Differences* 18:3 (2007), 128–51.

29 J. Levy and Jakobsson, 'Abolitionist Feminism as Patriarchal Control: Swedish Understandings of Prostitution and Trafficking', *Dialectical Anthropology*, 37:2 (June 2013), 333–40.

30 *Last Rescue in Siam*, dir. Empower Foundation (Chang Mai: Bad Girls Film, 2012), youtube.com.

31 Network of Sex Work Projects, 'Sex Workers Demonstrate Economic and Social Empowerment', Regional Report: Asia and the Pacific (2014), nswp.org.

32 See the Asia Pacific Network of Sex Workers website: www.apnsw.info.

33 Prostitutes War Group, 'Pro-Festo of the Prostitutes War Group' (2017), pr ostituteswargroup.wordpress.com.

34 Ibid. The PWG refuse the term 'sex worker' for being reformist. We would argue that some of the group's anti-work spirit is in evidence even within less strident forms of activism (even if packaged in less dynamic and confrontational ways).

35 M. Merteuil, 'Sex Work Against Work', *Viewpoint Magazine* (31 October 2015).

36 Weeks, *The Problem with Work*, 123.

37 S. Federici, *Revolution at Point Zero: Housework, Reproduction, and Feminist Struggle* (Oakland: PM Press, 2012), 18–19. We also find this viewpoint in the work of Mariarosa Dalla Costa, Selma James, The Power of Women Collective, Wendy Edmond, Suzie Fleming, and others.

38 E. Pendleton, 'Love For Sale: Queering Heterosexuality', in J. Nagle (ed.), *Whores and Other Feminists* (London and New York: Routledge 1997), 73.

39 L. Fortunati, *The Arcane of Reproduction: Housework, Prostitution, Labour and Capital* (New York: Autonomedia, 1995), 22.

40 Marx, *Capital*, 186–7.

CHAPTER 6

The New Plutocratic (Post)Feminism

Diane Negra and Hannah Hamad

Navigating a series of instructive and symptomatic examples across the spectrum of contemporary celebrity culture, including entertainment media-cum-advocacy figures such as Emma Watson, and culminating in an analysis of high-profile (pseudo) political icon Ivanka Trump, this chapter briefly explores some vexed issues in contemporary discourses of femininity. We contend that gender discourse in the current cultural climate is frequently, and crucially, characterised as being marked by a mix of residual postfeminist formations and proliferating new feminisms; and that both, though the latter in particular, are often associated with high-end celebrity exemplification and embodiment. Celebrity is therefore an important lens through which this prevalent discursive mix comes into view, and through which to understand the rise to discursive prominence of points of overlap in this mix. Celebrity also provides a useful frame for understanding the emergence from this discursive mix of figureheads of what we are here calling the new plutocratic feminism, and of which Ivanka Trump is the celebrity embodiment par excellence.

We argue that a complicating factor in the changing hierarchy of discourses that mark the co-existence of postfeminist ideologies with these new feminisms, and one that impedes a straightforward understanding of these as discursively discrete and distinct from one another, is the emergence of what bell hooks has influentially called 'faux feminism', espoused and embodied by high-profile plutocrat celebrities like Trump.[1] The new plutocratic feminism is thus associated with highly culturally visible figures such as former Facebook COO Sheryl Sandberg and the brand of corporate workplace-oriented 'lean in' feminism that she espouses in her now infamous book of the same name.[2] It is also associated, in a slightly more qualified way, with entertainment industry icons such as Beyoncé, who, alongside her zealous commitment to the promotion of black subjectivities in predominantly white spaces, grounds her celebrity in an incoherent ideology produced by the confluence of her insistent and public avowal of feminism, her iconicity as a floating signifier of individualistically postfeminist discourses of empowerment and choice, and her material status as a functionary of global capitalism.[3] However, epitomic of the new plutocratic feminism is the aforementioned dynasty heiress and entrepreneur Ivanka Trump.

Broadly speaking, we see evidence of a newly stressed postfeminism whose operating manual fits poorly with a social landscape of heightened awareness of dramatic inequality. In this chapter we argue that the new (faux) feminisms of privilege disassociate themselves from notions of social justice except in the most cursory rhetorical fashion, cleaving instead to neoliberal individualism and global capitalism. This intensely market-based form of feminism joins together female affective composure as a hallmark with safe performances of empowerment and, in the case of Trump in particular, displays of family capital; in so doing, it bids to soothe cultural tensions with regards to race, class, technology, and social power. We thus offer this investigation into the nature and functions of this new style of feminism and assess its value to current hegemonies of class and capital.

Residual Postfeminisms and New Feminist Formations

Scholars have begun to explore, interrogate, and theorise the tensions, contradictions, and complexities that characterise the fraught relationship between the persistence of postfeminist ideologies and the new proliferation of purportedly feminist discourses that have exploded in media culture over the course of the 2010s. Most notably, Rosalind Gill has, with a deliberate degree of scepticism, offered up the term 'post-postfeminism' as a potential means to understand this, demonstrating the need to 'think together feminism with anti-feminism, postfeminism and revitalized misogyny'.[4] She posits that the postfeminist sensibility that she has long argued has characterised contemporary media and culture remains persistent and tenacious, the new 'rise of popular feminism' notwithstanding (p. 610). She stresses therefore that it is now incumbent upon feminist media scholars to 'unpick some of the complexities of a cultural moment seemingly characterised by a multiplicity of (new and old) feminisms which co-exist with revitalized forms of popular misogyny' and to join her in debunking the idea that in this context 'the concept of postfeminism has nothing to offer in reading the current moment' (p. 612). On the contrary, Gill makes clear the extent to which some of what is self-presenting in mediated spheres as feminism 'is in fact distinctly postfeminist in nature' (p. 612).

Gill and a number of other scholars have correspondingly noted and begun to interrogate the public resurgence of feminism and its renewed visibility in media and culture in the 2010s. Nicola Rivers, for example, notes that 'feminism has been undergoing something of a revival in the last few years', pointing to evidentiary phenomena such as Laura Bates's 'Everyday Sexism' campaign, attempts by UK politicians such as Ed Miliband and Nick Clegg to harness the cultural currency of feminism by aligning themselves with it, and the now widely discussed phenomenon of celebrities' self-identification and self-disclosure as feminists.[5] As Gill observes, 'While a few years ago it sometimes felt difficult to make *any* feminist arguments *stick* in the media, today it seems as if *everything* is a feminist issue. Feminism has a new luminosity in popular culture.'[6] A touchstone instance of this luminosity occurred at the 2014 MTV Video Music Awards at which aforementioned pop icon Beyoncé famously self-proclaimed her feminism by standing in silhouette before an outsized and illuminated projection of the word itself. As Jessalynn Keller and Maureen Ryan note, '[p]erhaps unimaginable a decade earlier', at the height of millennial postfeminism, 'Beyoncé's performance was only one example of the ways in which feminism has become increasingly visible within popular media cultures.'[7] This flashpoint example is likewise symptomatic of the fact that access to (high-profile, commercialised) feminist rhetorical space seems to require a pre-sold status and elevated levels of celebrity capital. The de-stigmatisation of feminism has therefore come at the cost of its articulation through figures of privilege. All the same, the field of feminist commentary in popular media and culture has correspondingly broadened in recent years, with the latter day resurgence of high-profile ostensibly feminist bestsellers – what Anthea Taylor calls 'feminist blockbusters' – having a comedic bent (as in books by Caitlin Moran, Tina Fey, Mindy Kaling, Amy Schumer and Amy Poehler) or a business self-help bent (with empowerment oriented titles such as *Lean In, You Are a Badass, #girlboss, Girl Code: Unlocking the Secrets to Success, Sanity and Happiness for the Female Entrepreneur*).[8] For some, the campaign against sexual assault operating under #MeToo constitutes proof of feminism's new power in the public domain. Nevertheless, a surge in popular misogyny exemplified by the rise of 'pick-up artists' and the seduction industry, the heightened profile of 'incels' (involuntary celibate men who call for the distribution of women as sexual chattel to men who fail in the dating market), and the success of men's rights guru Jordan Peterson are undeniable elements of the current gender landscape.[9]

The New Plutocratic Feminism and Contemporary Celebrity

Highlighting some of what is ideologically at stake in uncritically celebrating the new feminist formations, especially with regard to the co-optation of feminism and feminist discourse by global capitalism, Nancy Fraser observes that '[i]ncreasingly, it is liberal feminist thinking that supplies the charisma, the aura of emancipation, on which neoliberalism draws to legitimate its vast upward redistribution of wealth', and it is this aspect of the phenomenon that anchors our investigation into a (faux) feminist formation, embodied by a number of high-profile female celebrities of extreme wealth and privilege, that we argue manifests in its exemplary forms as a new feminist plutocracy.[10] Further, and as indicated above, in line with the broader celebritisation of all spheres of public life, and alongside the reorientation of media cultures around and towards the cultural logics of celebrity that has taken place in recent decades, particularly since the normalisation in the Global North of digital media and online cultures of connectivity, celebrity has emerged as a key prism through which the new plutocratic feminism must be seen and understood. As Nicola Rivers correspondingly writes,

> the fourth wave championing of feminism in popular culture through … megastars such as Beyoncé, Taylor Swift, and Miley Cyrus … navigates a complicated path between postfeminism(s), relying on promoting the achievements (and frequently the lifestyle) of successful women, whilst also demanding that all women be elevated to – or more worryingly, emulate – this individualised, neoliberal, and capitalist vision of "success".[11]

We argue that Emma Watson and Ivanka Trump differently embody this capitalist vision and signify this version of female success. Both thus represent residual postfeminism at an intersection with new feminisms, and while both are differently epitomic of a shift in public feminism, 'as it is increasingly invoked by celebrities for whom it often functions as a credential of entrepreneurial self-branding', the latter has parlayed her celebrity into an unelected government role and a discourse of femininity.[12]

The figure of the new plutocratic feminist has not simply appeared from a vacuum at this particular historical conjuncture – rather, she has emerged at this specific time, with her constituent and formative elements and characteristics having germinated during millennial postfeminism via the pointed and ideologically charged neoliberalisation of feminist discourse that took place during that period, arguably peaking in the mid-2000s prior to the onset of the global financial crisis from 2007 onwards.[13] Writing in the mid-2000s, Tasker and Negra seemed to anticipate the subsequent rise to discursive prominence of the new but related gender discourse of plutocratic feminism that we now argue has emerged since, in shining a light on what they identified then to be '[p]ostfeminist culture's centralization of an affluent elite'.[14]

Further, no discussion of the fraught discursive relationship between the persistence of the postfeminist sensibility and the emergence of the new feminisms in the 2010s can proceed without attention to the work of Catherine Rottenberg and her conceptualisation of what she terms 'neoliberal feminism', wherein ideologically loaded discourses of choice, equality, and freedom are invoked in order to negotiate a highly individualistic notion of feminism, and to posit that women are responsible for their own successes and failures irrespective of the social fact of entrenched inequalities and structures, or inequities of access to opportunities and the possession of power.[15] The cultural logic of neoliberal feminism therefore dictates that consideration of historical barriers to women's full participation and progression in workplace (particularly corporate) cultures be elided, and attention paid instead to what is offered up in place of these things: a lack of ambition in individual women. The attention that this logic declines to pay to factors such as the intersection of class and race, as well as gender, makes clear both the discursive overlap with the logic of postfeminism and why most of neoliberal feminism's most prominent figureheads are white women of inherited class privilege.

As Keller and Ryan write in their explanation of the importance of Rottenberg's work to understanding potential ideological pitfalls that are thus bound up with new feminist discourses, it 'highlights the ambivalences of some of these emergent feminisms, calling attention to the ways in which emergent feminisms can remain affectively "stuck" (Ahmed 2004) to seemingly appealing postfeminist sensibilities'.[16] An important take-away from this, therefore, especially thinking ahead to the negotiation of feminist discourse in the celebrity embodiments and exemplifications discussed hereafter, is that 'emergent feminisms may not always offer us progressive politics or activist agendas' (p. 11). Rather, as Rivers argues, 'fourth-wave feminism is fractured and complex, frequently reinforcing the advancement of the individual and centering the seductive notions of "choice," "empowerment," and "agency"'.[17]

The 'Feminism' of Emma Watson and Residual Postfeminist Body Politics

Highlighting one instructive instance of some of the ideological incoherence which marks specific formations of the new feminisms, particularly those that exist in something of a mutually constitutive relationship with postfeminist discourse, Rivers points to the fourth-wave feminist activist group Femen as symptomatic of this. 'Their insistence', she writes, 'on the disruptive power of baring their breasts in protest is seemingly reliant on accepting a postfeminist sense of "playfulness," or at least a postfeminist irony whereby any notion of a feminism that critiques the sexualisation of women's bodies is firmly consigned to the past' (p. 24). This example thus shines a light on the ambivalences that inhere in some of the new feminist formations and is particularly pertinent to a media flashpoint that occurred arising from the similarly ideologically malleable (faux) feminism of film actor and celebrity humanitarian Emma Watson, who became a key celebrity figurehead for contemporary feminism after she was appointed UN Women Goodwill Ambassador in 2014.[18]

When the March 2017 edition of US popular culture and current affairs magazine *Vanity Fair* was published, a controversy arose from the inclusion in the issue of images from a photo shoot that featured Watson (who was promoting the imminent release of her then current star vehicle, Disney's *Beauty and the Beast* (2017)) as that month's cover star. One image subsequently proved to be particularly inflammatory. In the picture, Watson is framed in mid-shot, facing the camera, her hair in a tousled up-do, her lips parted, and her arms crossed in front of her torso. She is wearing a white lace skirt, and a small sheer ruff on her neck, and draped on her shoulders sits a very loosely crocheted see-through bolero with oversized white stitching. She is thus posed (nearly) topless, save only for a pair of thickly stitched fabric loops. By this point in her career, Watson's public profile had long since transcended the bounds of the persona created by the roles that collectively comprised her film career. Beyond this she had become the de facto media face of a particular formation of privileged white 'commodity feminism' after being appointed to her aforementioned UN ambassadorship in July 2014 as part of its campaign for global gender equality.[19] She was also named the 'fresh face of feminism' for 2014 as part of a feminist-themed issue of *Elle* magazine that featured Watson on its cover, and named the 'top' so-called 'feminist celebrity' of 2014 by the *Ms.* foundation collaborating with *Cosmopolitan* magazine.[20]

The media, spanning the spectrum of tabloid news and platforms for celebrity gossip to more niche outlets for feminist commentary and debate, were thus primed to respond to the charged and ideologically malleable scenario of a publicly outspoken feminist celebrity posing almost semi-nude in a mainstream publication, ostensibly as part of a publicity drive for her forthcoming film release. At one end of the spectrum, notoriously recidivist UK tabloid newspaper *The Sun* gave over almost a full page to reproducing the image under the headline 'Beauty and the breasts', knowingly and significantly placing it on its infamous 'Page 3', on which it had famously printed oversized images of topless glamour models on a daily basis from 1970 to 2015, and which had been a lightning rod for contemporary feminist activism in the UK following the formation of the 'No More Page 3' campaign in 2012.[21]

The inevitability of ensuing feminist debate over this in the public sphere was plain, but it was sparked when British columnist and broadcaster Julia Hartley-Brewer took to social media in protest, lambasting Watson for what she interpreted as her hypocrisy in using her public profile to champion feminist causes such as the gender pay gap on the one hand, and using (or allowing) sexualised imagery of her body to sell the Hollywood film in which she was starring on the other. Watson herself was quick to fall back on the typically cis, white, Western, and privilege-blind rhetoric of 'choice' so symptomatic of millennial postfeminist discourse, and so widely critiqued by feminist scholars, in asserting that 'feminism is all about giving women a choice'.[22] She was also candid in revealing her naivety-cum-ignorance about the historically entrenched and ongoing fraught relationship between feminism, postfeminism, and body politics, asserting weakly, 'I really don't know what my tits have to do with it.'[23]

In the media storm that followed, a number of well-rehearsed feminist and postfeminist debates were staged and restaged about, for example, the cultural policing of women's bodies, women's agency, and control over the circulation of meanings attached to sexually charged images of the female body, as well as the limitations, political vacuity, and ideologically misguided or disingenuous nature of some new formations of feminism, as they are articulated in the mainstream media and celebrity culture, embodied by figureheads such as Watson. Taylor observes of Watson that 'it has been her seeming lack of awareness about her own privilege that appears most irksome to feminists', going on to note that 'the exclusions of Watson's brand of feminism are indeed troublesome in terms of race, class, gender, and sexuality, so perhaps we should not be surprised . . . that its elisions have prompted intense debate about the ongoing exclusions of dominant ways of figuring feminism'.[24]

Watson represents just one of the higher profile examples of how 'feminism has become a marked feature of contemporary celebrity discourse' and this flashpoint moment in her celebrity is highly symptomatic of the confused ideologies that emerge from the intersection of residual postfeminism and new formations of feminism.[25] The next case study raises the stakes of this ideological incoherence and of the ambivalences inherent to the new faux feminisms.

Ivanka Trump – Plutocratic Feminism *Par Excellence*

This section explores the nature and functions of the new plutocratic feminism through an investigation of Ivanka Trump, assessing its value to current conceptualisations of gendered aspiration and attainment, with particular regard to the regressive adulation of the wealthy.[26] This mode of (post)feminist discourse is strongly allied to what Nathan Heller has called the 'Organization Celebrity', a type defined by proficient multitasking that he points out 'tends to be emphasized in its female form'.[27] For Heller, 'female celebrity ... is moving toward a work and achievement culture, and such re-narrativization requires active reinforcement in the public eye'.[28] Celebrities of this kind document a vacillation between a (post) feminism that accedes to and takes full part in neoliberal capitalism and one which is devoted to fantasy corrections of it. Ivanka Trump personifies the Organization Celebrity and her claims to feminism resonate within the new gendered affective landscape of neoliberal capitalism. The exploitative production conditions associated with her branded goods, moreover, offer a stark illustration of the way in which 'the postfeminist rhetoric of triumphalism not only makes race disappear ... but it also uses the global capitalist hierarchy of the Global North and Global South to make multinationals' exploitation of female workers disappear'.[29]

As her father's political status accrued in 2016 and into 2017, Ivanka Trump's adept performance of moral thoughtfulness indirectly gratified a fantasy that the presidency would compel civility and decency from Donald Trump. The highly touted bond between the two served initially as a key part of his political mythology, helping to repair the president's amply documented misogyny, his track record of divorce, and the public limitations of his current wife. In Donald Trump's symbolic re-activation of the American Dream, he fills the role of crude cretin capable of producing progeny who are polished elites with (potential) altruistic intent. This is one reason why Ivanka Trump is so key to his mythology, since his other children conspicuously fail to fill that role.

The irrational hopefulness that was attached to Trump in the lead-up to her father's presidency and in its first six months is hard to source. Trump's pre-casting for an idealised role may be attributed in part to twenty years of princess-oriented popular culture which normalised elite intergenerationalism and dynastic privilege. Media coverage of Chelsea Clinton, the Bush twins, and the Obama daughters stoked interest in the figure of the first daughter, as did films such as *Chasing Liberty* (2004) and *First Daughter* (2004). Nevertheless, the intense media interest in Ivanka Trump has no real precedent in the annals of presidential daughterhood. A preoccupation of the high-end press and female commentators, Trump was frequently imagined as a mitigator of her father's worst inclinations, a counterbalancing moral check on his heedless disregard for constituencies other than the privileged. Further, Trump was positioned as a female ideological alternative to Hilary Clinton; in a *New York Times* article that sought to explain Donald Trump's success with women voters, nearly every woman profiled expressed antipathy towards the Democratic nominee, several noting their preference for Ivanka Trump over Clinton in explaining their decision-making, taking for granted the nepotistic involvement in any Trump administration of a person whose name was not listed on any ballot.[30]

The affective contrast between Ivanka Trump and the Democratic candidate was all in the former's favour. Where Clinton was categorised using the old misogynist descriptor 'shrill', Trump is serene, where Clinton was cast as too old to be president, Trump is young, having attained influence and profile beyond her years in a nepotistic context. Where Clinton is associated with a difficult marriage, Trump is warmly lit in campaign ads glorifying her family life. Serenity, transcendence, and composure are Trump's performative keynotes; these are experienced as a relief from the duress and anxiety of precarity and she is exonerated from appearing simply a rich dilettante because she combines the appearance of these qualities with entrepreneurial 'hustle'.

In Ivanka Trump's persona, dynastic privilege is rewritten as exemplary achieved confidence. 'Confidence chic', as identified by Laura Favaro, is part of a cultural turn whereby 'negative affect is rapidly silenced and with that goes the transformative force of collective anger at structural realms of injury and injustice'.[31] Yet Trump's display of 'confidence chic' is hazardous, narrowly avoiding problematic excess, as when she took her father's place at the G20 Summit in Hamburg in July 2017, drawing widespread condemnation. Trump is an iconic figure for an era in which 'the promotion of self-confidence has surfaced as the site for expanded, heightened, and more insidious modes of regulation often spearheaded by those very institutions invested in women's insecurities' (p. 283).

Trump's anodyne positioning as wife and daughter is bound up with insistent cultural messaging that the (marketised) family is the only safe space for American women. She strikingly illustrates Rottenberg's claim that, '[n]o longer deeply interested in the struggle for equal rights or for an end to gender discrimination, neoliberal feminism focuses principally on the notion of work-family balance'.[32] In an era in which marriage and motherhood operate as markers of personal success and (increasingly) socioeconomic security, Trump's status marriage to Jared Kushner can usefully be understood as a form of assortative mating and elite social behaviour that has long existed but that has become more conspicuous in the era of renewed wealth triumphalism. Noting that 'the wife has morphed into postfeminist media culture's most favoured icon', Suzanne Leonard observes that 'marriage occupies new ground as a cultural status symbol'.[33] As she puts it, 'wifedom is newly professionalized as an occupation in its own right and the regulatory and affective investments that characterize contemporary labor relations also ground American wifedom' (p. 12).

Trump's position as her father's alibi signals ideological reversion to a nineteenth-century conception of gendered capitalism in which women's public activities were frequently tied to their attributed role as agents of moral uplift whose influence kept men functional and incentivised within the prevailing economic order. Her bid for public recognition as a feminist, concretised and commercialised in her book *Women Who Work: Rewriting the Rules for Success*, marked a break with the earlier discourses of aggressive capitalism showcased in her previous publication *The Trump Card: Playing to Win in Work and Life*.[34] The shift in focus from the family name in the first book to 'women' in the second illustrates Trump's shifting target of identification and affiliation. Moreover, the 'women who work' tag, as the *New York Times* has reported, originated in a 2013 strategy session held by Trump, her husband, and several of her employees designed to generate a quasi-feminist motto that could follow the surging popularity of Sandberg's 'lean in' slogan.[35]

The audacity of Ivanka Trump's claims to feminism require careful contextualisation. They must be situated, for instance, against the rise of corporate or what has been called 'gestural feminism', well exemplified by the 2017 placement of a bronze statue of a young girl, hands on hips, seemingly situated in an act of moral confrontation with the charging bull on Wall Street.[36] 'Fearless Girl' was commissioned and funded by financial services company State Street and the timing of its desire for public association with feminism looks suspicious, given the company's then recent agreement to pay $64 million to resolve fraud charges and the fact that despite the statue's stated purpose as celebrating 'the power of women in leadership', State Street itself has a dismal record of placing women in executive posts. We may note that 'Fearless Girl' is positioned to undertake the same symbolic role often attributed to Ivanka Trump – namely to act as a moral check on unfettered capitalism.

With fantasies and enmities swirling around Ivanka Trump so intensely, the question of why she rivets so many people's attention deserves complicating. At a prosaic level it is worth reiterating the sheer conspicuousness of her gender difference in a political administration that regularly and unapologetically releases photos of clusters of white men ostensibly doing the nation's business as if it were the nineteenth century. Kellyanne Conway drew high levels of opprobrium for a photo in the Oval Office in which just such a group gathered in the mid and background while she was pictured in the foreground, barefoot and with her legs drawn up under her on a sofa, a pose that many deemed disrespectful and symptomatic of the casualisation and crudity of the office under Trump. Like Conway, Trump is continually placed as the female figure of exception and she stands out for that very simple reason.

However, public absorption and fascination with Ivanka Trump is importantly tied to the pressing question of what women's relationship to crony capitalism is. In an era in which capitalism is increasingly in disrepute, should women be moral counterweights and figures of opposition to it or full and enthusiastic participants, 'leaning in' to get their piece of the pie? Ivanka Trump, it seems, is trying to be both. She personifies on the one hand women's traditional moral obligation to stand apart from markets – to segregate themselves from the most aggressive forms of capitalism. On the other hand, simultaneously and with great meticulousness about how she is presented, she epitomises dynastic privilege, capitalist zeal and, ultimately, the new plutocratic (post)feminism.

As Rivers writes in her explanation of the ideological vagaries of some of the new feminisms: 'the fourth wave is clearly not characterized solely by a newly galvanized "left-wing" intent on dismantling neoconservatism and neoliberalism'.[37] If anything, in light of the emergence of the new plutocratic (post)feminism, this reads like an understatement. Rather, '[t]hose seeking to celebrate the emergence of this "new" wave of feminism, particularly in seeing it as signalling the death knell of postfeminism or in ushering in

uncomplicatedly pro-feminist times, should perhaps proceed with caution'
(p. 25). Our observation here that some forms of public feminism are
divested of social justice concerns and made to harmonise with technocratic
and neoliberal discourses is presented in support of such a cautionary
approach.

Notes

1 A. McRobbie, *The Aftermath of Feminism: Gender, Culture and Social Change*
(London: Sage, 2009); b. hooks, 'Dig Deep: Beyond *Lean In*', *The Feminist
Wire* (28 October 2013); A. Taylor, *Celebrity and the Feminist Blockbuster*
(London: Springer/Palgrave Macmillan, 2016), 5.

2 S. Sandberg, *Lean In: Women, Work and the Will to Lead* (New York: Alfred
A. Knopf, 2013); see also hooks, 'Dig Deep' and G. Marchetti, 'Lean in or Bend
Over? Postfeminism, Neoliberalism, and Hong Kong's *Wonder Women*', in
J. Keller and M. Ryan (eds.), *Emergent Feminisms: Complicating a Postfeminist
Media Culture* (New York and London: Routledge, 2010), 193–210.

3 D. Chatman, '"Pregnancy, Then It's Back to Business"', *Feminist Media
Studies*, 15:4 (2015), 926–41; N. Weidhase, '"Beyoncé Feminism" and the
Contestation of the Black Body', *Celebrity Studies*, 6:1 (2015), 128–31; J. Keller
and M. Ryan, 'Introduction: Mapping Emergent Feminisms' and
C. Thompson, 'The *New* Afro in a Postfeminist Media Culture: Rachel
Dolezal, Beyoncé's "Formation," and the Politics of Choice', both in Keller
and Ryan (eds.), *Emergent Feminisms*, 1–21 and 161–75 respectively.

4 R. Gill, 'Post-Postfeminism?: New Feminist Visibilities in Postfeminist Times',
Feminist Media Studies, 16:4 (2016), 625.

5 N. Rivers, *Postfeminism(s) and the Arrival of the Fourth Wave* (Basingstoke and
New York: Palgrave Macmillan, 2017), 7; S. Cobb, 'Is This What a Feminist
Looks Like? Male Celebrity Feminists and the Postfeminist Politics of
"Equality"', *Celebrity Studies*, 6:1 (2015), 136–69; H. Hamad and A. Taylor,
'Introduction: Feminism and Contemporary Celebrity Culture', *Celebrity
Studies*, 6:1 (2015), 124–7; B. Renninger, '"Are you a *Feminist?*": Celebrity,
Publicity, and the Making of a PR-Friendly Feminism', in Keller and Ryan
(eds.), *Emergent Feminisms*, 42–56.

6 Gill, 'Post-Postfeminism?', 614.

7 Keller and Ryan, 'Introduction', 1.

8 Taylor, *Celebrity and the Feminist Blockbuster*, 4; Sandberg, *Lean In*; J. Sincero,
*You Are a Badass: How to Stop Doubting Your Greatness and Start Living an
Awesome Life* (London: Hachette, 2016); S. Amorusi, *#girlboss* (London:
Penguin, 2014); C. Alwill Leyba, *Girl Code: Unlocking the Secrets to Success,
Sanity and Happiness for the Female Entrepreneur* (London: Penguin, 2017);
C. Moran, *How to Be a Woman* (London: Ebury Press, 2011); T. Fey, *Bossypants*
(New York: Reagan Arthur Books/Little, Brown and Company, 2011);
M. Kaling, *Why Not Me?* (New York: Random House, 2015); A. Schumer,

The Girl With the Lower Back Tattoo (New York: Gallery Books, 2016); A. Poehler, *Yes Please* (New York: Harper Collins, 2014).

9 For a full delineation of the seduction industry, see R. O'Neill, *Seduction: Men, Masculinity and Mediated Intimacy* (London: Polity, 2018).

10 G. Gutting and H. Fraser, 'A Feminism Where "Lean In" Means Leaning on Others', *The New York Times* (15 October 2015).

11 Rivers, *Postfeminism(s)*, p. 25.

12 D. Negra, 'Claiming Feminism: Commentary, Autobiography and Advice Literature for Women in the Recession', *Journal of Gender Studies*, 23:3 (2014), 275.

13 D. Negra and Y. Tasker, 'Introduction: Gender and Recessionary Culture', in D. Negra and Y. Tasker (eds.), *Gendering the Recession: Media and Culture in an Age of Austerity* (Durham and London: Duke University Press, 2014), 1–30.

14 Y. Tasker and D. Negra, 'Introduction: Feminist Politics and Postfeminist Culture', in Y. Tasker and D. Negra (eds.), *Interrogating Postfeminism: Gender and the Politics of Popular Culture* (Durham and London: Duke University Press, 2007), 2.

15 C. Rottenberg, 'The Rise of Neoliberal Feminism', *Cultural Studies*, 28:3 (2014), 418–37.

16 J. Keller and M. Ryan, 'Introduction', in Keller and Ryan (eds.), *Emergent Feminisms*, 11.

17 Rivers, *Postfeminism(s)*, p. 24.

18 Hamad and Taylor, 'Introduction', 124–7; Taylor, *Celebrity and the Feminist Blockbuster*, 277.

19 J. Keller and J. Ringrose, '"But then Feminism Goes Out the Window!": Exploring Teenage Girls' Response to Celebrity Feminism', *Celebrity Studies*, 6:1 (2015), 132–5.

20 Taylor, *Celebrity and the Feminist Blockbuster*, 276.

21 N. Fahey, 'Beauty and the Breasts', *The Sun* (1 March 2017), 3; A. Bingham, 'Pin-Up Culture and Page 3 in the Popular Press', in M. Andrews and S. McNamara (eds.), *Women and the Media: Feminism and Femininity in Britain, 1900 to the Present* (New York and London: Routledge, 2014), 184–98; L. Holmes, *How to Start a Revolution* (New York and London: Random House, 2015).

22 N. Zieminski, 'Actress Emma Watson Says Revealing Photo Does Not Undermine Feminism', *Reuters* (5 March 2017). For a critique of choice, see E. Probyn, 'New Traditionalism and Post-Feminism: TV Does the Home', *Screen*, 31:2 (1990), 147–59 and S. Projansky, *Watching Rape: Film and Television in Postfeminist Culture* (New York: New York University Press, 2001).

23 Zieminski, 'Actress Emma Watson'. On the relationship between feminism, postfeminism and body politics, see C. Lumby, *Bad Girls: The Media, Sex and Feminism in the 90s* (Sydney: Allen and Unwin, 1997); R. Gill, 'From Sexual Objectification to Sexual Subjectification: The Resexualisation of Women's Bodies in the Media', *Feminist Media Studies*, 3:1 (2003), 100–5; F. Attwood, 'Pornography and Objectification', *Feminist Media Studies*, 4:1 (2007), 7–19.

24 Taylor, *Celebrity and the Feminist Blockbuster*, 277 and 278 respectively.

25 Negra, 'Claiming Feminism', 285.

26 The focus here is on the USA and UK but Trump is also a figure of inspiration in China where her associations to nepotism and corruption do not signify pejoratively, with the former typically read as dynastic connection and the latter as common business practice: J. C. Hernandez, 'The "Goddess" Yi Wan Ka: Ivanka Trump is a Hit in China', *New York Times* (5 April 2017); J. Fan, 'China and the Legend of Ivanka', *New Yorker* (11 April 2017).

27 N. Heller, 'The Multitasking Celebrity Takes Center Stage', *New Yorker* (23 June 2016).

28 Ibid.

29 T. A. Kennedy, *Historicizing Post-Discourses: Postfeminism and Postracialism in United States Culture* (Albany: SUNY Press, 2017), 159.

30 S. Chira, '"You Focus on the Good": Women Who Voted for Trump in Their Own Words', *New York Times* (14 January 2017).

31 L. Favaro, '"Just Be Confident Girls!": Confidence Chic as Neoliberal Governmentality', in A. S. Elias, R. Gill and C. Scharff (eds.), *Aesthetic Labour: Rethinking Beauty Politics in Neoliberalism* (Basingstoke and New York: Palgrave Macmillan, 2017), 296.

32 C. Rottenberg, 'The Neoliberal Feminist Subject', *Los Angeles Review of Books* (7 January 2018).

33 S. Leonard, *Wife Inc.: The Business of Marriage in the Twenty-First Century* (New York: NYU Press, 2018), 4 and 13 respectively.

34 I. Trump, *Women Who Work: Rewriting the Rules for Success* (New York: Portfolio/Penguin, 2017); I. Trump, *The Trump Card: Playing to Win in Work and Life*, (New York: Touchstone/Simon & Schuster, 2009).

35 J. Kantor, R. Abrams, and M. Haberman, 'Ivanka Trump's West Wing Agenda', *New York Times* (2 May 2017).

36 G. Bellafante, 'The False Feminism of "Fearless Girl"', *New York Times* (16 March 2017).

37 Rivers, *Postfeminism(s)*, p. 24.

11
Fields

CHAPTER 7

Feminism and Literary Disability Studies

Susannah B. Mintz

The millions-strong, worldwide Women's March that followed the US presidential inauguration on 21 January 2017 called for unity under the 'bold message' that 'women's rights are human rights'.[1] As Amanda Hess reminded us in the *New York Times Magazine*, however, 'the women's movement has not always been a site for unity', beset throughout its history by conflicts primarily of race and class, and many feminist commentators in the wake of the election worried about 'how far the tent can stretch', in Susan Chira's words, 'without leaving some outside'.[2] How many know, to press the point, that a virtual march was also taking place, the Disability March, organised in protest against such alarming campaign promises as the demolition of Medicare, directly affecting people with disabilities? The Women's March, demanding mobility, stamina, and tolerance for crowds, with its able-bodied, feel-good protectiveness – what is sometimes called *inspiration porn* – made obvious a critique that disabled feminists have been levelling for decades: mainstream feminism simply 'assumes', to quote Alison Kafer, 'that a feminist future is, by definition, one without disability and disabled bodies'.[3] If, as Hess suggests, twenty-first-century feminism is a pop-cultural affair – with Lady Gaga and Miley Cyrus its avatars – disability will endure as the suppressed metaphor for the vulnerability that empowerment teaches us to deny. Despite its rhetoric and its intentions, activism is often ableist.

Feminist disability scholars have long argued that a disability perspective can redirect feminist inquiry in provocative and consequential ways. Susan Wendell succinctly articulated the problem in *The Rejected Body* (1997), writing that feminism has 'worked to undo men's control of women's bodies, without undermining the myth that women can control our own bodies'.[4] Quoting Adrienne Rich's dictum in the influential *Of Woman Born* (1976) that women 'require ... *control* of our bodies' (p. 21; italics in original), Wendell cautions her readers that until feminists 'criticize our own body ideals and confront the weak, suffering, and uncontrollable body in our theorising and practice, women with disability and illness are likely to feel that we are embarrassments to feminism' (p. 93). In *Feminist Queer Crip* (2013), Kafer takes on another foundational feminist text, Marge Piercy's novel *Women on the Edge of Time* (also from 1976). Still popular after forty years, Piercy's novel is 'a powerful, productive text for feminist theorists concerned with the role of technology in the lives of women and committed to envisioning an egalitarian, just world'.[5] And yet the utopian future it depicts does not just ignore disability; in Kafer's words, disabled people 'have intentionally and explicitly been written out of it. . . . [I]t is their very absence', in fact, 'that signals the utopian nature of this future' (p. 73). Following Wendell, Kafer argues that to 'eliminate disability' from our notions of what constitutes worthwhile living is to 'eliminate the possibility of discovering alternative ways of being in the world, to foreclose the possibility of recognizing and valuing our interdependence' (p. 83).

Kafer's reading of Piercy aligns with an important trend in current disability literary scholarship in which critics study not just *what* we read (a matter of representation) but also *how* we read and how narrative is formulated (a matter of knowing). In this chapter, I will suggest that the project of cripping feminism is a fundamentally epistemological enterprise that requires redrawing the contours of the realities we take for granted, and that much literature by women outside of mainstream realist fiction and autobiography directly challenges a still-prevalent – and still-hidden – feminist presumption that 'everyone craves an able-bodied/able-minded future' (p. 84). It is to the very possibility of alternatives that authors Ana Castillo, Alison Bechdel, and Octavia Butler direct their speculations – a word I use deliberately to capture what Sami Schalk has discussed as literature that 'brings *aspects* of reality into newly constructed worlds' and that is 'not restrained by patriarchal realities' (italics in original).[6] In what follows, I will explore what happens to habits of knowing and being in books less invested in correcting stereotypical representations than in thinking *through* disability as a way of engaging with questions of how we make meaning. The Disability March sought to establish an alternative collective defined by non-normative modes of sensing, moving, thinking, communicating. So too do the authors discussed in the following speak/write/draw to the imperatives of a feminist *cripistemology*, in Robert McRuer and Merri Lisa Johnson's important terminology, which contests a pathologising, corrective, also sentimental construal of disability and brings multiply situated embodied subjects together in 'new ways of being-in-common'.[7]

* * * *

I have written elsewhere about the dynamics of pain in Ana Castillo's *Peel My Love Like an Onion* (1999), a novel often categorised as magical realism.[8] Here, I want to concentrate on what the protagonist, the beautiful flamenco dancer Carmen la Coja, refers to as 'crippled-girl style' (p. 16) as it relates to how the narrative moves and shapes our engagement with its reality. Carmen is disabled from childhood polio and experiences increasingly severe post-polio syndrome as she ages. We are instructed to read that physical condition as entangled with the socioeconomics of white America, where lack of access to decent employment as well as affordable medical care creates a no-win loop: inadequate insurance means untreated pain and muscular degeneration, which prevents Carmen from working in jobs that would guarantee benefits; without money to pay for care, her symptoms worsen, which means it gets harder and harder to hold on to jobs. There is nothing playful or postmodern about these material conditions, which are starkly realistic; disability intersects with gender, class, and ethnicity in ways that have profound consequences for Carmen's physical and psychological well-being.

And yet 'reality' is a contested concept throughout *Peel My Love*, which knowingly frustrates a reader's desire for linear progression, generic stability, characterological continuity, and bodies that correspond with accepted identity categories.[9] For one thing, Carmen 'the Lame' renegotiates the spacetime of flamenco according to the needs and preferences of her body, with its chronic pain and 'long bent stick of a leg', its 'foot curved like a beggar's hand' (p. 85). She forces her partners and musicians to slow to her pace and eventually 'dances' with just arms and hands, sitting on stage to manage her pain. This crip flamenco rhythm is then writ large across the novel, which similarly disrupts itself through the overlap of various realms, perspectives, and bodies. It can be challenging to pinpoint where we are in Carmen's timeline; flashbacks and fragments of vignette, alternation between present and past tense, suspend us in temporal opacity. The absence of quotation marks makes it hard to attribute speech without Carmen's guidance. Is this, in fact, a novel? Its title is the first line of a poem that appears before the table of contents; its 'Installments', titled by their first sentence, mimic the cantos of epic verse. This is romance, a magical story of love, but also a scathing critique of racism, ableism, sexism, and homophobia as these are scaffolded by global capitalism.

Peel My Love writes difference and variation into its imagined world. The onion metaphor implies a truth one might steadily pursue, yet the instruction to *peel my love* only repeats, never reveals. One epigraph to the novel, 'God is dead, Marx is dead, Freud is dead, and I'm not feeling so well myself, is identified as having been overheard by Carmen, but Simone de Beauvoir is also quoted in a juxtaposition that scrambles our conviction about who the 'real' feminist is – especially since de Beauvoir is famous for saying that women are not born but rather gendered by culture, through the very master narratives that Carmen hears the dismantling of: religion, patriarchy, psychoanalysis, the promise of revolution, even the very notion of a stable self from which to pronounce one's subjective experience.[10] That makes sense, given the text's preoccupation with authenticity and its potent critique of the damage done to bodies of colour. But making ourselves up – what a culture tells itself about who its people are – is not wholly rejected either, as numerous references to indigenous storytelling make clear. The Carmen Santos who works in a pizza parlour at the airport also invents herself as – and is crafted into – the enchanted dancer of asymmetrical form, whose 'one-legged flamenco style' (p. 68) is 'famous all over town' (p. 69). What matters is that neither of these is primary. Carmen embodies the principle of intersectionality, where gender, class, race, disability, sexuality, and religion are thoroughly imbricated in who she 'is' – which in turn is always at once corporeal and discursive, a product of narrative both self-generated and other-imposed, a body shaped by pleasure and grace, impairment, and pain.

Nearly *every* body in *Peel My Love* is in some sort of flux (including an arthritic dog). Some are costumed, flamboyant, performed; others are injured or violated – many are both. Carmen walks with crutches and a brace, and her parents are medicated and ill. Her friends include Vicki, who also had polio as a child and keeps her lesbianism hidden at the bank where she works; and Vicki's brother Virgil, a star soccer player, who disappears into the 'underground' of AIDS (p. 189). Carmen has sexual encounters with both in what she describes as a hermaphroditic triangulation that cripqueers the confluence of sexed and gendered identities and channels erotic energy along alternate lines of desire. She has two other long-term lovers over the course of the story, Agustín (who has an injured hand) and Manolo, both of whom identify as gypsy, and both of whom Carmen 'unmasks' – the former as a college graduate who remakes himself as a troubadour, the latter a Spanish-Mexican 'all-American boy' (p. 84) who turns out to be a 'gambling, gold-tooth thug' (p. 207). In these various instances of ambiguity, the novel stages an inevitable slippage between longing to be 'calorro through and through' (p. 84) and the fact that 'being one hundred percent anything' (p. 33) is always already a fiction. Interrogating essentialism, as the novel certainly does, requires not only a critique of social prejudice but also a frank appraisal of how strongly we may feel impelled to conform, how much we may wish, as Carmen does, for a form of belonging secured by the body.

This array of liminal, transgressive corporeality is a tactical exaggeration that gives the lie to the body as a reliable, or *inevitable*, source of knowledge about identity. This is why Carmen's friend Chichi, a transsexual prostitute, is found dead in her apartment building – because the betrayal of expectations can enrage – but also why Carmen's disabled female body, marked by race and class and imperilled by ableist ideals of independence and mobility, is never 'corrected'. To the contrary, its condition worsens as Carmen gets older, such that she can no longer perform the flamenco that created her as *la Coja*. But the point at which she must stop dancing marks the start of a new (wildly successful) singing career, so that plot keeps regenerating according to the condition and contour of Carmen's physicality. Disability is the medium through which Carmen learns language, dance, love, work, the limitations of American healthcare and the lessons of ableist infrastructure, feminist community, and the body's extraordinary range of sensation – but her body does not represent the sum total of Carmen la Coja. The novel's happy ending is not *fairy tale* transformation, precisely. Ugly duckling and beautiful swan have always been one and the same, and Carmen repudiates 'faraway Grimm fairy-tale countries' (p. 212) for their myths of wholeness and in a highly ironic slam against the dominance of European literary cosmology.

What does *Peel My Love like an Onion* teach us, then, about what we know and how we know it – be it story, embodied self, or ideological law? Two things are true of this text. One is its unmistakable concern for the lived experience of embodiment within fluctuating vectors of self-actualisation and cultural discrimination; bodies become themselves in context, from the 'School for the Handicapped' where Carmen learns she is 'defective' but also forms fast friendships, to the liberatory world of flamenco where a gimp dancer can court and flout both male and non-disabled gazes. Another is that nothing is *straightforwardly* linear – *straight* and *forward* both steeped in norms about women's bodies and the lives they should direct themselves towards. 'Oh shut up!' Carmen cries to one of her lovers, who speaks to her as if reciting lines from a second-rate romcom. 'You are in the twenty-first century' (p. 143). Her own story, though, fiercely committed to the hard truths of impoverishment and oppression, spins its own old tale of magical fantasy with an unlikely protagonist and to unfamiliar effect. From an amalgam of rhetorical styles and tones, time frames and perspectives, intimacies and collectives, comes Carmen – a Bizet anti-heroine, a marginalised Chicagoan, a 'defective daughter' (p. 108), also a woman 'who belonged to nobody and everybody at some time or another and in the end only to herself' (p. 151). Possession and solitude, if also 'how women love and are loved' (p. 118), become the key terms in a quasi-utopian feminist future that does not erase but rather depends on Carmen's 'individualized dancing style' (p. 146). Impairment is much more than a metaphor here. It is what allows a woman to dance 'her own dance every day in her own world' (p. 119).

* * * *

Alison Bechdel's *Fun Home* (2006) and *Are You My Mother?* (2012) are by definition hybrid works that test the possibilities of visual and narrative form in the context of self-definition.[11] Both exploit the refractory quality of memoir – wherein a writer creates a speaking self who narrates the remembered self of the past – as Bechdel draws herself becoming herself, largely through reading. As critics have noted, *Fun Home* tells a coming-of-age story through literature; in Ariela Freedman's words, '[t]he most tantalizing possibility that books offer is the possibility of self-invention'.[12] The origin story of *Fun Home* is modernist and paternal, dominated by references to F. Scott Fitzgerald, James Joyce, Henry James, and Proust, but I would argue that Bechdel's incorporation of those male literary forebears has less to do with 'making a space for herself on the shelf of modernist literature', as Freedman suggests (p. 126), than with the tension between artifice and authenticity to which *Fun Home* obsessively returns.

Bechdel stages an explicit 'epistemological crisis' (p. 141) at the heart of her text. The autobiographical conundrum of her father's death – what were its circumstances? – resists explanation: did Bruce Bechdel commit suicide, or was he accidentally hit by a truck while crossing a road? Further ambiguities unfold behind this one, as Alison's disclosure of her sexual identity prompts her mother, Helen, to announce her father's 'affairs. With other men' (p. 58), thereby 'demot[ing]' Alison 'from protagonist in [her] own drama to comic relief in [her] parents' tragedy' (p. 58). Bechdel thus presents the impulse towards agency and self-actualisation as compromised by secrecy, a 'blurry' line 'between reality and fiction' (p. 59), and a complex 'inversion' (p. 98) between father and daughter that is itself thoroughly entangled with performance and textuality. What was 'real' for Bruce ('having sex with men for years' (p. 59)) was still notional for Alison ('hadn't even had sex with anyone yet' (p. 59)); where the father loaned books to boys he may have also been sleeping with, Alison finds her sexual self in books about queerness long before she is in bed with other women. 'My parents are most real to me in fictional terms', Bechdel writes

(p. 67), explaining her many literary allusions but also capturing the slippage between one form and another – her own visual-textual interplay in which genres, images, temporalities, perspectives constantly collide.

The hoped-for 'emancipat[ory]' moment (p. 59), then – in which Alison would write herself out of a 'suffocating' identification with her father marked by books like Joyce's *Portrait of the Artist* (p. 201) and into her own autobiography – results instead in 'abrupt and wholesale revision of [her] history' (p. 79). It seems fitting that in the panel above which Bechdel writes that she declared her lesbianism to her parents 'via letter' (p. 77), Alison is shown thumbing through *Roget's Thesaurus* – as if to insist on the ambiguity of signs and the foregone given of epistemological confusion (or perhaps, simply, multiplicity) where saying who we are is concerned. The queer archive, in the pages of *Fun Home*, leads not to certainty of self but to a fraught epistolary exchange and the stark overlay of Helen's typed response and a text box in which Bechdel announces, simply, that she 'was devastated' by her mother's disapproval (p. 77). Importantly, in fact, and in the non-linear manner of the book, 'gaps, erasures, and other lacunae' predominate over 'truth', which can only '[worm] its way . . . toward daylight' (p. 172), such that definitives – like the 'moral validity' of orgasm (p. 171) – are surrounded by 'vagaries', 'qualifiers, encryption', 'unknown quantities', and symbols 'so nondescript [they] could mean practically anything' (p. 169).

What crips all of this is the explicit interweaving of obsessive-compulsive disorder through a tale that, in unclosetting the father and interrogating his death, has already queered normative configurations of family, gender identity, life arc, and patriarchal authority. It is disability, paradoxically, that prevails over semiotic incoherence – or to put this differently, it is OCD that makes all that linguistic free play a matter of creative productivity. *Fun Home* is preoccupied with performance, and the speculation that 'affectation can be so thoroughgoing, so authentic in its details, that it stops being pretense . . . and becomes, for all practical purposes, real' (p. 60) is fraught with anxiety about what to trust. Bechdel's compulsive habits seem to emerge from, and then to exacerbate, an intense suspicion that nothing can be known with any surety, so that everything comes under erasure: not only writing, as an increasingly large series of carets subsumes Alison's journal entries into obscurity, but even Alison's sense of embodied presence, as shown in drawings of her trying to 'navigat[e]' spaces, dress herself, or maintain comforting physical intimacy with her stuffed animals (pp. 136–7). In a provocative conflation of the real and the metaphorical, Bechdel suggests that her childhood rituals were a kind of autistic stimming – what she calls 'a self-soothing autistic loop' (p. 139) – behaviour that quelled the 'dark fear of annihilation' brought on by the chaos of her parents' fighting (p. 139) and life in a family twice drawn as isolated figures in separate parts of the house (pp. 134 and 139).

But though a *crisis* of knowing – the terrifying sense that nothing is 'absolutely, objectively true' (p. 141) and that words and meaning do not reliably coincide – might be survived, 'disorder' itself endures. At the centre of the chapter detailing OCD are two maps, one from *The Wind in the Willows*, the other showing the Bechdels' neighbourhood. This chapter also initiates a 'deracination' whereby the author differentiates herself from the father, who is 'planted deep' (p. 145) in Pennsylvania. These maps, which readers will understand as representational but which reassure ten-year-old Alison as a 'mystical bridging of the symbolic and the real' (p. 147), lead directly to a new form of *self*-representation borne of obsessiveness: co-authorship between Alison and her mother in the pages of her journal – a journal whose 'first three words' are in the '*father's* hand-writing' (p. 140; my italics). Linear progression is hinted at, as Alison's life story is first written *for* her by the father and then taken down in dictation *from* her by the mother, as lonely disparateness seems replaced by caretaking interdependence, as the 'obsessive-compulsive year' (p. 147) leads to 'recovery' (p. 149).[13] But like maps that are, but also always *not*, precisely where we are, nothing is exactly resolved here, since Alison is 'as obsessive in giving up the behaviors as [she] had been in pursuing them' (p. 149), and ironically so, because an excess of orderliness, revelling in edges and lines, the exactitude of method, become the comic artist's *métier*, the very text we are reading.[14]

On the chapter's final page, mother and daughter are drawn in different states of physical closeness as Helen records Alison's diary entries, in one panel turned towards each other, in the next the mother turned subtly away, Alison cradling a teddy bear as if mother to her own baby self. Below these, father and daughter are drawn from behind in shadow, beholding a sunset, the girl's body leaning towards the man, who stands in 'wordless' contemplation (p. 150). Where is disability in these dynamic bodily arrangements? One implication, again, is that mother and daughter crip the process of composition in mutually undertaking the writing of storied self (mother and daughter 'compose' one another, as *Are You My Mother?* explicitly states (p. 14)); another is that disability makes Bechdel a certain kind of creator, which necessitates her individuation from that mother. The father, conversely, is associated here with silence, a shutting-down of verbal play; neither father nor child can speak. At the same time, what the pair seem to be regarding, 'the infinite gradations of color in a fine sunset' (p. 150) – which the reader cannot *see* in *Fun Home*'s grayish-green palette but might certainly imagine – does invoke visual beauty in a way that connects father and daughter as artists, as much as they are also readers. The fact that the loss of this 'morally suspect' (p. 16) man – the 'old artificer' (p. 14), a creator of 'sham[s]' and simulacra (p. 17) – is described as the phantom-limb pain of an amputee makes physical disability another driving force of the memoir: not a problem to be fixed, but a fact of life that 'resonate[s]' (p. 23) throughout Bechdel's work. Like the '"crippled child" game' described in *Mother?* (pp. 19 and 287), which begins in 'flat feet' and 'corrective shoes' (p. 19) and ends as 'the moment my mother taught me to write' (p. 286), OCD and phantom limb are complex layerings of Bechdel's attempts to locate what's 'real' by means of artistic playfulness, in the crucible of love and loss.

Disability in Bechdel's work is thus best understood as a mode: of connection between people, of making art, of contesting regulatory norms of being and behaviour, of identifying rather than differentiating or discriminating. The turn of phrase that makes 'a mildly autistic colony' of an 'artists' colony' suggests the mash-up of forms that cuts across borders and gutters in the fun house of this text (p. 139). As Cynthia Barounis also argues, *Fun Home* 'performs the very compulsions that it thematizes' in its 'endlessly recursive' and 'disorder[ed]' narrative structure.[15] This is a text defined by radical unknowing, where neither books nor bodies can fully divulge *singular* truths.[16] They can, though, bring forth a thing or two about disabled truth. Freedman suggests we read graphic narratives as 'the queer bastard child of high modernism', to which Bechdel insists we add crip forms of engaging the world (p. 138).

* * * *

Michael Bérubé argues in *The Secret Life of Stories* that disability is a structuring mechanism in narrative as often as it is a character trait attached to specific individuals. Many of the texts Bérubé examines do not, in fact, contain disabled characters, and that is his point: 'disability in the relation between text and reader *need not involve any character with disabilities at all*. It can involve *ideas about* disability, and ideas about the stigma associated with disability' (italics in original).[17] When disability does appear representationally in a text, moreover, we should be wary of reading practices that assume too neat a dichotomy between 'good' – that is, 'realistic' – portrayals and 'bad' – that is, metaphorical, instrumental, pedagogical ones, since, in Bérubé's words, the 'real' is 'just as weird as everything else' (p. 55) and reading disability '*as reading* . . . changes the way we read' (p. 52). Disability can do many things in a text (not just shore up the edges of able-bodied normativity), one of which is to establish the rules of our engagement with narrative.

Octavia E. Butler's dystopian novel *The Parable of the Talents* (1998), second in what was to be a trilogy featuring black, disabled heroine Lauren Oya Olamina, is set in a not-too-distant future USA.[18] With uncanny prescience about our current political moment, the novel's 'Christian America' is dominated by religious fanaticism and extreme economic disparity.[19] Whole towns – not just sports arenas – are corporatised, the poor are routinely arrested into indentured slavery, public education has failed, and a zealot intent on 'silenc[ing] all women' (p. 101) and waging war against friendly Canada has just been elected president (his message is 'make American great again' (p. 20)). Conditions for the poor, especially in health care and basic subsistence, border on the nineteenth century. 'CA' crusaders are raiding both established neighbourhoods, like the black, middle-class, walled-in community of Lauren's youth, and enclaves of displaced peoples, such as the one Lauren and her husband, Bankole, later establish, called Acorn, in northern California. Detractors are burned as 'witches' (p. 50). Women's tongues are 'cut out' (p. 50).

Talents juxtaposes this oppressive theocracy against the belief system its heroine has created, called Earthseed, whose fundamental precepts are that God is change and that human beings need purpose and community to create sustainable, co-operative, equitable lives. The 'destiny' of Earthseed is not reward in any heaven but to take to the literal skies to settle other worlds. Lauren is denounced as a cult leader, and she must gather followers stealthily; her invitation to potential members is to choose: to 'go on building and destroying' or to 'make something more of ourselves. To grow up ... to become some combination of whatever we want to become and whatever our new environments challenge us to become' (p. 358). The friction is between systems of thought: when does a legitimate desire to solve social problems become tyrannical, repressive? When is a religion a cult? How much flexibility can be allowed in any ideology before it devolves into chaos? Which beliefs are 'real', which 'science fiction' (p. 157)? These questions emerge through structural conversation (form following content) as Lauren's journals are interwoven with writing by Bankole, Lauren's brother Marc, and the adult writing of Lauren's daughter Asha (abducted from Acorn in infancy by vigilante Crusaders) – all of whom have different takes on Earthseed, Lauren herself, and the general state of things. Knowing 'what happened' in this story, what is 'true', is complicated from the start by competing perspectives.

Into this mix comes hyperempathy, a condition in which 'sharers' 'feel the pain and pleasure that ... others experienc[e]' (p. 12). The novels explain hyperempathy as resulting from a mother's addiction to 'Paracetco', a prescription 'smart drug' intended to counteract Alzheimer's disease. Curing the one creates the other, in a move that Schalk links to Butler's critique of sci-fi faith in a technologically advanced – and disability-free – future. As Schalk points out, by setting the action in a recognisable yet defamiliarised world, and by creating a disorder that does not exist, Butler demands that we read hyperempathy in context. We cannot impose contemporary assumptions about disability upon it: to have the syndrome is a culturally specific experience, meaningful according to the novel's circumstances rather than ours. In this sense, the hyperempathy of *Talents* teaches us to interpret. To avoid assuming we know what it means to have it, we must pay close attention to how the condition is situated in the plot, even as it is itself a mechanism of intimate connection between people who might otherwise occupy wildly divergent social positions. In the novel's era, hyperempaths experience far more pain than pleasure not because disability is inherently negative, but because *everyone*, given the ravages of the social environment, is in greater proximity to violence and suffering. That said, 'malnutrition, climate change, poverty, and ignorance' (p. 95) do not wreak havoc equally across socioeconomic, racial, or gendered lines, and Lauren's hyperempathy is thus an especially 'rough disability' – in Butler's own words – for a black woman who dares to defy the status quo of her time.[20]

As a boundary-crossing syndrome, hyperempathy suggests both the expansive possibilities of disabled knowing and the dangers of disrespecting unique subjectivity. It is epistemological by definition, communicating aspects of emotion and corporeal experience, pleasure, and pain that are often difficult for one person to articulate to another. What is distressing in dangerous circumstances would carry a different potential elsewhere; that Lauren and other sharers must guard themselves against the 'filthy, twisting agony' (p. 255) produced in them when they witness violence insists on its own opposite: the possibility of knowing another's joy, *and* of becoming sensitised to others' experiences in ways that might augment compassion and understanding. Butler says in *Talents* that some of the 'old diseases are back', thanks to the inadequacies and inequities of resources (p. 95), but the syndrome she invents is significantly one of *empathy*, differentiated from commiseration by degrees of knowing. The future, in other words, is far from having solved our every problem, but the new syndrome that emerges by a literal mistake also metaphorises a manner of intersubjective knowing with important social and political implications. Hyperempathy is not a gift, not 'magic' (p. 12) – Lauren is no supercrip, endowed with compensatory powers to counteract the disablement of pain – but rather a possibility. Or, it simply *is*, a phenomenology of selfhood that some manage more comfortably than others, like any other feature or trait. It is, on the one hand, a consequence of a medicalised world in which pills promise to cure our mortality, but on the other a mechanism of relationality. Whether the content of knowledge is harmful or blissful derives from context, not from the 'problem' of individualised disability.

Lauren and her conviction about Earthseed are also described, both positively and negatively, as 'obsessive' (p. 42). Asha writes, not quite complimentarily, that her mother had 'obsessive purpose' (309). Marc says that he knew his sister was 'obsessed' (p. 42). What 'engages us' most powerfully, according to Lauren, is a '[p]ositive obsession' (p. 45). Purpose is in fact the fundamental message of Earthseed: humanity must 'grow up' by having some 'difficult, long-term purpose to strive toward ... something that [people] could make real with their own hands' (p. 179). It is left to readers to determine whether Lauren's 'religion' is rightfully denigrated as estranging and weird or admired as a commitment to human potential, and so, in turn, whether 'obsessiveness' is an impairment of excess and rigidity or a creative, generative quality of mind. I would argue that where hyperempathy is a condition *of* some people's future, Lauren's obsessiveness *is* humanity's future, presented as what might bring about an end to 'chaotic, apocalyptic periods of murderous craziness' (p. 179) and conduct us, not towards perfection, but fulfilment.

In a dream recounted early in the novel, Lauren's hyperempathy has disappeared, and she cannot share the pain of her brothers. 'Pleasure is rare, pain is plentiful', Lauren says, '[s]o why do I miss it now? ... I'm afraid. A part of me is gone' (p. 12). Much later, Lauren tells a fellow sharer, 'We're all wounded. We're healing as best we can. And, no, we're not normal. Normal people wouldn't have survived what we've survived. If we were normal we'd be dead' (p. 346). Sharing may not be 'an ability or a power' (p. 33), but it constitutes identity and is a means of interdependence that fosters what Lauren elsewhere describes as the fundamentally rhizomatic nature of 'how the world works, how all sorts of things interact and influence one another' (p. 148). Sharing is part of the texture of connectedness that *Talents* promotes as lifesaving, in traditional family relationships as well as alternative kinship structures that emerge from the fracturing effects of war and oppression – and that also, in forming the basis of new communities, represent the possibility of humanity's ongoingness. It is significant that, acknowledging both the hardship and advantage of being hyperempaths, Lauren's friend Len quotes the *'sweet and powerful / Positive obsession [that] / Blunts pain'* (p. 346; italics in original). Disabilities, in these moments, are coded as the realisation of a promise: to be what we are challenged to become.

The future of *Parable of the Talents* is, in part, humanity's past, as electronic torture collars replace chains and time seems to loop backwards to 'two and a half centuries' of chattel slavery (p. 270). That implied collapse of time frames participates in the novel's refusal of state-sanctioned, patriarchal histories and the presumption of a unified, better future in which race, class inequity, and disability are simply excised – or rewritten as 'extraterrestrial' – in the name of progress. For Butler, like Castillo and Bechdel, the future can only be imagined as an amalgam of 'differing bodyminds', in Rosemarie Garland-Thomson's words, 'moving through environments together, navigating barriers, and finding pathways, both materially and metaphorically'.[21] Mythmaking, protest and resistant truth-telling, manoeuvring towards the unknown, atypical family bonds, artistic and political potential, cripqueer desires, survival *as* rather than in spite of non-normative corporeality – these are the hallmarks of gimp-dancing, gutter-jumping, time-travelling, boundary-crossing feminist disability literatures. There is no 'getting better' in these books. The crip flamenco star Carmen la Coja simply 'take[s] [her] time (p. 68). The obsessive cartoonist Alison Bechdel writes herself in 'reverse narration' (p. 232). The hyperempath Lauren understands that 'there's no manual for this sort of thing. . . . I suppose that I'll be learning what to do and how to do it', she says, 'until the day I die' (p. 371).

Notes

1 See womensmarch.com and disabilitymarch.com respectively.
2 A. Hess, 'How a Fractious Women's Movement Came to Lead the Left', *New York Times Magazine* (7 February 2017) and S. Chira, 'Feminism Lost. Now What?', *New York Times* (30 December 2016), 4.
3 A. Kafer, *Feminist Queer Crip* (Bloomington: Indiana University Press, 2013), 70.
4 S. Wendell, *The Rejected Body* (New York: Routledge, 1996), 93.
5 Kafer, *Feminist Queer Crip*, 72.
6 S. Schalk, *Bodyminds Reimagined: (Dis)ability, Race, and Gender in Black Women's Speculative Fiction* (Durham, NC: Duke University Press, 2008), 21–2.
7 R. McRuer and M. L. Johnson, 'Cripistemologies: Introduction', *Journal of Literary & Cultural Disability Studies*, 8:2 (2014), 138.
8 For a fuller discussion of *Peel My Love Like an Onion* (New York: Anchor Books, 1999), see my chapter 'The Path of Pain: On Narration and Plot', in *Hurt and Pain: Literature and the Suffering Body* (London: Bloomsbury, 2013).

9 For more on the tension between the 'real' and the postmodern in discussions of disability, see chapter 2, 'Dismodernism Reconsidered', in L. J. Davis, *The End of Normal: Identity in a Biocultural Era* (Ann Arbor: University of Michigan Press, 2013), 15–30. See also Ellen Samuels's discussion of Judith Butler and applications to disability studies in 'Judith Butler's Body Theory and the Question of Disability', in K. Q. Hall (ed.), *Feminist Disability Studies* (Bloomington: Indiana University Press, 2011), 48–66.

10 Cf.S de Beauvoir, *The Second Sex* (New York: Bantam Books, 1970).

11 A. Bechdel, *Fun Home: A Family Tragicomic* (Boston and New York: Mariner Books, 2007) and *Are You My Mother? A Comic Drama* (Boston and New York: Mariner Books, 2013).

12 A. Freedman, 'Drawing on Modernism in Alison Bechdel's *Fun Home*', *Journal of Modern Literature*, 32:4 (2009), 130.

13 Interdependence itself, of course, essentially crips that linear progression, since 'growing up' seems to demand *independence*, while *inter*-dependence is frequently invoked in disability provocations of neoliberal autonomy.

14 As Tammy Clewell writes of *Are You My Mother?*, Bechdel's resistance to 'curing' her psychological wounds and symptoms 'enable[es] the artist to embrace the messy neuroses of her everyday life not as symptoms of a psychic disturbance to be resolved but as a core component of her identity, particularly her identity as a graphic memoirist. What her resistance to a classic psychoanalytic cure makes possible, then, is the very creation of the work we encounter'. See T. Clewell, 'Beyond Psychoanalysis: Resistance and Reparative Reading in Alison Bechdel's *Are You My Mother?*', *PMLA* 132:1 (2017) 53.

15 It is well known that Bechdel's compositional process is painstaking – obsessive, by her own account – entailing digital photographs of herself in poses she subsequently draws and what Cynthia Barounis describes as 'an elaborate system of erasure and revision' in ' Alison Bechdel and Crip-Feminist Autobiography', *Journal of Modern Literature*, 39:4 (2016), 146. Clewell also comments on Bechdel's 'fastidious[s], even obsessive[e]' self-archiving in 'Beyond Psychoanalysis', 54.

16 'Any cripistemology worth its name', declares Jack Halberstam, 'should identify modes of not knowing, unknowing, and failing to know', quoted in R. McRuer and M. Johnson, 'Proliferating Cripistemologies: A Virtual Roundtable', *Journal of Literary and Cultural Disability Studies*, 8:2 (2014), 152.

17 M. Bérubé, *The Secret Life of Stories* (New York: New York University Press, 2016), 19.

18 O. Butler, *Parable of the Talents* (New York and Boston: Grand Central Publishing, 1998).

19 This is also reminiscent of M. Atwood, *The Handmaid's Tale* (New York: Houghton Mifflin Harcourt, 1986).

20 Quoted in Schalk, *Bodyminds Reimagined*, 98.

21 R. Garland-Thomson quoted in McRuer and Johnson, 'Proliferating Cripistemologies', 154.

CHAPTER 8

Feminism's Critique of the Anthropocene
Samantha Walton

The Anthropocene is the anticipated new designation for our current geological epoch in which human activity has decisively altered earth ecosystems, global natural processes, and the geological record. This chapter investigates the relationship between feminist thinking and the Anthropocene, establishing the gendered dimensions of environmental crisis, and examining intersections between ecological and feminist scholarship. By taking the Anthropocene as a central and guiding provocation, existing and emergent potentials within ecological thinking can be brought together with diverse (and often contradictory) traditions and tendencies in modern academic feminism. What Anthropocene feminism might achieve is an emboldened reorientation of ecological concerns within gender justice struggles.

Ecofeminist scholars have long critiqued feminised constructions of 'Nature', and the masculinism of capitalism, technology, science, and the environmental movement itself. This cultural work can be seen as part of a long history of women-led environmentalism, which has frequently intersected with wider gender-rights campaigns, including reproductive rights and health, autonomy and equality in work and the home, representation and participation in the public sphere, and feminist and queer critiques of militarisation and colonialism. As this chapter hopes to show, a feminist critique of the Anthropocene can – and must – be both human and eco-centred. While a false division between the human and 'nature' has created the conditions for the Anthropocene, responding in any meaningful way to the crisis of the present demands a recognition that ecology has shaped and will determine the success of all rights and justice struggles, gender-based and otherwise.

In significant ways, this deviates from a tendency in early ecocriticism to sideline civil rights and social justice critiques in favour of a more 'eco-centric' approach to environmental problems. In the introduction to the *Green Studies Reader*, Laurence Coupe ranks green literary activism as 'the most radical of all critical activities', which 'must surely rank as even more important' than readings focused on class, race, and gender, as 'with no planet, there is no future, and so no other battles to be fought'.[1] In a similar vein, Western-led environmental and conservation movements have often been rightly criticised for pursuing neocolonial, classist agendas in their approach to land and species protection in postcolonial countries. In response, this chapter considers how the 'Anthropocene' may be used to investigate and further intersectional ecological activisms which seek to improve the material conditions of women's lives, recognising that there can be no gender justice without social and environmental justice.

The Anthropocene

In cultural scholarship, the Anthropocene offers a potent tool to think with, and a conceptual means of readdressing the relationship between humanity and nature. It is also a scientific reality, demanding a response for ecological survival and environmental, social and multispecies justice. Paul Crutzen and Eugene Stoermer proposed the neologism in 2000, although terms such as 'Anthroposphere' and 'Homogenocene' have been used since the 1980s.[2] In 2009, the Anthropocene Working Group of the Subcommission on Quaternary Stratigraphy (AWG) was established to debate the scientific acceptance of the term. In 2016, they proposed that the 'Anthropocene' is a 'geologically real' epoch, rather than a longer era or period. This brings an end to the Holocene, which began around 11,700 years ago at the end of the last glacial period.

Justification for the change of epoch comes from diverse geoscientific fields. In geomorphology, the Anthropocene marks the period in which 'mining, construction, and deforestation [have] come to surpass the effects of nonhuman forces', leaving marks as vast and discernible as those produced by geological processes of erosion and eruption.[3] This places particular emphasis on changes to the earth's crust and upper mantle, although the AWG also addresses anthropogenic changes to the biosphere, atmosphere, and hydrosphere.[4] The AWG cites 'large-scale perturbations in cycles of carbon, nitrogen, phosphorus and other elements, the inception of significant change to global climate and sea level', as well as plutonium fallout from atomic bombs, and residues of plastic, aluminium, and concrete in the earth's strata.[5] Human societies have also radically altered earth biota. Shifts between geological epochs, era, and periods often mark extinction events – for example, the end of the Ordovocian period coincided with the first mass extinction (443 million years ago), while the close of the Paleozoic (251 million years ago) marks the onset of the 'Great Dying', when around 86 per cent of species were wiped out in under two million years.[6] The Intergovernmental Panel on Climate Change suggests that the earth is now experiencing a major extinction event in which around 30 per cent of species on earth are at risk, a consequence of anthropogenic issues including urban expansion, changing temperatures, habitat collapse, and ocean acidification.[7] The 'Anthropocene' therefore observes the catastrophic damage done to life on earth by human societies, as well as irreversible geological changes.

The need for a change of epoch is no longer in doubt, but when did the Anthropocene start? Archaeological traces of humanity can be found prior to the Holocene, but suggested start dates for the 'age of man' mark the first human use of fire, the augmentation of agricultural economies, the industrial revolution, the proliferation of nuclear weaponry, or the global use of chemical pesticides. The AWG proposes that the Anthropocene proper begins in 1950, although its roots lie in the 'extensive and roughly synchronous worldwide changes to the earth system in terms of greenhouse gas levels, ocean acidification, deforestation, and biodiversity deterioration', which began around 1750 with the Industrial Revolution.[8]

What's in a Name?

Arguments for the Anthropocene, particularly from the sciences, start from the premise that something has materially changed in the geological record, which demands taxonomisation and study. This largely avoids political questions around naming: a new epoch has begun, it demands a title, and the Anthropocene seems to fit the bill. However, as earth sciences professor Jill Schneiderman points out, naming conventions, much like scientific practice, have never been objective, ahistorical, or apolitical. In feminist-standpoint theory, Sandra Harding questions the neutrality of masculinist traditions of scientific knowledge and the patriarchal assumptions that underpin it, while Donna Haraway demonstrates the situated quality of knowledge, challenging the assumption that the objective observer offers a value-neutral perspective.[9] Scientists do not have a rational, detached, 'conquering gaze from nowhere': they are affected by and affective of the phenomena they observe. The naming of the Anthropocene therefore calls for cultural, as well as scientific, deliberation. Indeed, it is arguably within culture and the humanities that the Anthropocene has spurred the most vigorous discussion, making calls for an 'Anthropocene' marker as much an activist and philosophical as a scientific enterprise. The change of *cene* is not merely the bland statement of geological fact: it is a political provocation which determines culpability and demands a meaningful reaction in terms of behavioural change on macro and micro levels.

As a critical intervention in the ecological crisis, placing *Anthropos* at the heart of the new designation registers the damage on an epic and epochal scale, recognising the absolute entwining of human and natural history – a movement which began with Darwinian science, and has been a rallying cry within the ecohumanities since their rise in the late twentieth century. However, 'human' history, like the *Anthropos*, is not for, or about, everyone. The 'Anthro' of the Anthropocene addresses a universalised masculine position, located somewhere in the Global North in conditions of middle-class affluence and capitalist consumption. The 'Anthropocene' constructs a sense of 'man as such, the human as such', which 'emerges from an inscriptive technological trajectory that does not include all humans, and certainly not all life'.[10] This evades the ways in which wealth, like climate change, is unevenly and unequally distributed across the industrialised and postcolonial world, as well as erasing differentials including race, gender, and culture. Resistance to the false universals of the 'Anthropocene' presents meaningful and valuable alternatives of which science should take note.

Alternative titles abound. The Plantationocene and Capitalocene aim to better target blame on colonialism and capitalism, which turned ecology and the human into resources and commodities on a global scale, homogenising earth biota in unprecedented ways and precipitating a fluctuation in levels of CO_2, among their numerous other effects.[11] These titles also draw attention to the origins of the Anthropocene in the late seventeenth to mid-nineteenth century, with the Imperial expansion of European states into the New World, the laying of vast plantations across the Americas and the Indian subcontinent, and the mass transportation and enslavement of African peoples to work them. Fuelled by ideologies of 'beneficent' cultivation and racial superiority, colonial agriculture and biology augmented the military, financial, and cultural hegemony of European nations, laying the foundations of modern capitalism and creating immediate, deep-rooted and enduring human catastrophes, social injustices, and ecological crises across the world.[12] While the 'Plantationocene' and 'Capitalocene' attest to these points of origin, the Anthropocene, with its almost heroic and ahistorical construction of the species 'Man', instead lays blame equally across all economic and agricultural systems and cultures, erasing the specificity of these historical relations and their consequences.

Alternative names such as the Corporatcene and Androcene also lay blame, specifically on the toxic combination of globalised corporate hegemony and possessive individualist masculinities. Centring gender difference within the new geological marker is as accurate as centring capitalism and colonialism: as Claire Colebrook puts it, 'if there had not been sexual difference in its narrowest sense (man and woman), there could not have been the nuclear family, division of labor, and then industrialism'.[13] However, the relationship between cultural and scientific constructions of sex and gender in the Anthropocene calls for some careful reflection. While organic life produces forms of sexual difference beyond the binary of 'male' and 'female', Colebrook argues that the production of binary gender difference in heterosocial cultures relies 'on the same processes of "civilisation" that generated the Anthropocene' (p. 8). These differences, of course, predate capitalism. In their work on gender abolition, Joshua Clover and Juliana Spahr describe gender as a differential – rather than a monolithic difference – which capitalism seizes upon and transforms, before it becomes 'itself the producer of the gender difference' for its own ends.[14] Informed by the Wages for Housework movement and Italian Marxist feminisms of the 1970s, they propose that the 'subjugation of women to the role of housewife who cares and feeds and otherwise maintains labor power, and provides this service without any direct wage ... is a necessary condition for capital's capacity to extract surplus value toward the accumulation on a world scale' (p. 153). A Marxist ecological feminism demands, they argue, a gender abolitionist position, as only by 'annihilating the value-productive differential' of gender can ecofeminists achieve 'the making-inoperable of capital with the annihilation of an unpaid and gendered domestic sphere' (p. 155).

While critical alternatives to the Anthropocene draw attention to the relations and forces which have produced it, other critics have attempted to disrupt those relations by proposing alternative terms which might move us beyond the conditions and constraints of the Anthropocene. Physicist and ecofeminist Vandana Shiva proposes the 'Ecocene' as a way of avoiding the false universals of the Anthropocene, and also promoting a kind of cosmic humanism which will 'embrace our identity as one humanity' in the task of addressing the damage. 'The Ecocene', she states,

> is informed by the increasing awareness among humans of the ecological processes of the earth that shape and sustain life. We are part of the earth community. We are earth citizens. The earth has rights, and we have a duty to care for the earth, all her beings, and our fellow humans. The Ecocene asks us to correct and transcend the mistakes, false assumptions, and limitations that have brought us to the precipice of ecological collapse.[15]

While many theorists resist gendering 'Mother Earth', Shiva looks to the Sanskrit gendering of '*Prakriti*', a 'She' who 'is the creative force of the universe'.[16] This is an uncomfortable premise for ecofeminists from European philosophical traditions. Colonial and misogynist discourses were, as Val Plumwood influentially determined, founded on a notion of passive nature and the inferiorisation of 'nature and women – of nature-as-body, of nature-as-passion or emotion, of nature as the pre-symbolic, of nature-as-primitive, of nature-as-animal and of nature as the feminine'.[17] As such, the Mother earth gendering favoured by Shiva is not easy to translate into modernist academic thought – feminist or otherwise. Certainly, ecofeminists have long struggled to recast 'nature' as other than 'woman', while the flourishing of ecoqueer thought and creative practice has deconstructed 'natural' gender and sexual identities, experimenting with multifarious 'eco-genders, eco-sexualities and the eco-erotic.'[18] It remains to be seen whether these trajectories in queer ecological thought might co-exist with an ecofeminism which genders nature in ways beyond the Western binary. Certainly, Shiva's approach recognises that '[m]ost nonindustrial cultures have viewed the earth as living, as Mother Earth', and concurrently have developed practices for living with the earth which have been considerably less exploitative, and radically different from Romantic, industrial, and scientific constructions of feminised N/nature.[19] A decolonised Ecocene located around an expansive notion of *Prakriti* may offer possibilities for co-existence and mutual action which the patriarchal, Eurocentric, and anthropocentric Anthropocene does not.

Donna Haraway's Chthulucene also centres feminism in its critique of the Anthropocene. The name does not come from H. P. Lovecraft's 'misogynist racial-nightmare monster Cthulhu', but from 'the diverse earth-wide tentacular powers and forces and collected things' including Gaia, Spider Woman, Pachamama, Oya, Medusa, and Gorgo.[20] These figures – feminised and feminine – are evoked as forces and energies to think with, embodying values which have become essential in contemporary environmental philosophy. These include an insistence on humanity's enmeshment and entanglement in ecology; an expression of kinship with more-than-human life; and a respect for the otherness of nature and its desire and capacity to flourish beyond human needs and understanding. These principles are favoured over rights discourse and liberal individualism because, thanks to their failure to create equitable and mutually sustainable worlds, they have 'finally become unavailable to think with' (p. 5). Instead, Haraway explores the potential of multispecies empathy and companionship to provide means not just to survive, but also to culture new ways of living together and shaping change in a damaged world. Interweaving storytelling with multispecies and multicultural histories, and activist provocations, Haraway eschews conventions of academic discourse, allowing uncertainty, creativity and emotion, as well as reason, to fruitfully co-exist and inform one another. Rather than evoking futurism – that is, speculating beyond our immediate ecological realities – her 'speculative feminist fabulations' point to new and emergent possibilities for human nature co-existence and co-becoming in a damaged world (p. 81).

Compared to the Anthropocene, 'Chthulhucene' represents a less fatalistic approach to the present. While the Anthropocene implies an apocalyptic, almost glorious vision of the end of nature and the coming of a new 'age of man', the Chthulucene demonstrates a commitment to address the crises 'somehow in the presence of those who will bear the consequences' of it (p. 12). However, the Anthropocene remains the high-profile technical term with which environmentalists and feminists must grapple. The task now is to respond meaningfully to the ecological crises that it names, and to address its injustices and erasures in material actions which express the critiques of Capitalocence and Plantationocene, and embody the best qualities of Ecocene and Chthulucene.

Feminist Concerns in the Anthropocene

Within ecologically oriented cultural criticism, the rise of diverse identity-based subfields has produced distinctive moments of encounter and tension; for example, the gender essentialism of older iterations of eco-feminism has been unbound by the queering of the categories 'nature', 'gender', and the human; the whiteness of early ecocritical canons has been exploded by postcolonial ecocriticism and a new focus on nature–culture relations in Black studies and subaltern studies; reactions against cultural appropriation have altered the discipline's relationship with indigenous ontologies and epistemologies, led by First Nations and indigenous scholars, writers and activists. Although by no means a decolonised discipline, ecocriticism, like feminism, is now more meaningfully geared to addressing intersecting forms of oppression and speaking to diverse rights struggles, while exposing the Eurocentric and patriarchal origins and norms of 'rights' discourse itself.

Increasingly, ecocriticism and green activism have addressed the ways in which environmentalist movements have been inhibited by the very inequalities and injustices which were once dismissed as sideshow issues. In the UK, environmental groups such as Black2Nature are addressing the lack of Black, Asian, and minority ethnic (BAME) representation on the boards of major conservation charities, while the Fair Trade movement seeks to develop a supply chain which is environmentally and economically just, tackling issues such as debt slavery, dangerous working conditions, and chemical run-off, which overwhelmingly affect poor female garment workers in the Global South. In such practical initiatives and protests, the gendered inequalities of environmental crisis and economic exploitation are all too evident. However, thinkers have often got themselves into a conceptual bind: we cannot save the planet until we destroy patriarchy, *but* destroying patriarchy in itself will not save the planet. Anthropocene feminism risks becoming an unproductive zero sum game if one struggle is seen as inherently limiting to the validity and efficacy of the other. Instead, Anthropocene feminisms are better framed both symbiotically and dialectically, with both feminism and environmentalism looking to extend and advance the other, while seeking for points of intersection and solidarity.

Ecocriticism has demonstrated its meaning and value through its willingness to correct its canonical erasures – that is, to re-centre social inequalities within its response to the devastation of nature. In turn, the various trends of contemporary feminism must grapple with the ecological dimensions of their own theorising and practice. That might mean searching for interrelations between environmentalism and, for example, the MeToo movement, campaigns for reproductive rights, Black Lives Matter, or trans rights. Environmental justice and the Black Lives Matter movement notably intersect in the ongoing scandal of water pollution in Flint, Michigan, where predominantly African American communities are oppressed by a toxic combination of governmental indifference to black suffering, and an environmentally insensitive approach to water management. Stacy Alaimo notes how in North America, 'exposure to toxins correlates most directly with race, and then with class, as toxic waste sites, factories, and other sources are most often located near the neighbourhoods of African Americans or other people of colour'.[21] This is, of course, a global crisis: in the e-waste recycling fields of China, the Athabasca watershed of Canada, the Niger Delta, or the Bhopal region in Madhya Pradesh, poor and/or indigenous communities are exposed to contamination, often leading to catastrophic birth defects. Feminism aligns absolutely with fights for the environment and against racism, classism or castism in many of these communities. In Bhopal, women's groups have led marches to state agencies, carrying urine in transparent containers and insisting that it be tested for toxins; in Northern Alberta,

Lubicon Cree activist Melina Laboucan-Massimo draws attention both to the specific spike in violence against indigenous women in resource-extraction communities and to the systemic relationship between misogyny and ecological destruction. She writes:

> The systems of patriarchy, capitalism, colonization, and imperialism are based on a system of power and dominance. When you have these types of systems governing the way a society lives, that's how people are being treated on the ground. That's how the Earth is being treated. Indigenous people have always known that. Our relationship with Mother Earth is an attempt to be reciprocal.[22]

Some iterations of feminism, however, have been poorly aligned with ecological questions. Most notably, liberal and capitalist feminisms' 'lean in' ethos has done nothing to critique the demands for growth which despoil ecosystems, dispossess poor women, and produce gross wealth disparities in colonised and industrialised nations. Indeed, the demands of social justice and environmentalism have produced many points of tension for Western feminism. Anyone seeking to live in feminist, environmental, and anti-capitalist ways in the Global North will find themselves making emotive and politically fraught decisions in the course of everyday life in order to make some kind of difference to these catastrophes: establishing kinship relationships in traditional familial versus co-operative arrangements; using hormonal contraceptions and/or SSRIs which negatively impact aquatic life; choosing reusable menstrual products over disposable tampons, or swapping synthetic fabrics for organic cotton.[23] Making the personal the environmentally political challenges the ethos of choice and consumerist autonomy which defines modern Western feminism, and also produces more complex cuts when poverty or disability make some ecological choices economically or physically inaccessible. Environmental campaigns can polarise groups in ways that reveal the intersecting demands and oppressions at stake: such cases reveal the ways in which ecologically minded and single-issue movements often fail to take diverse needs into account, becoming a blunt tool which can add to the load of already vulnerable people, and divide rather than unite a movement.

One particularly heated debate concerns the relationship between population growth and ecological harm. In 2017, a wide-ranging study analysed the environmental impact of a range of individual lifestyle choices in developed countries, concluding that the four actions most effective in limiting personal greenhouse gas emissions are, in order of impact: 'having one fewer child, living car-free, avoiding airplane travel, and eating a plant-based diet'.[24] Most striking, however, is the gap noted between the first and second action. Living without a car for a year saves 2.4 tonnes of CO_2, while having one fewer child saves 58.6 tonnes per year.

Discussions about limiting birth rates in the name of environmental or resource protection, however, are thorny territory, to say the least. In the spirit of 'staying with the trouble', Haraway is one of the few contemporary writers making difficult interventions in this area, under her slogan 'Make kin, not babies!'[25] Policies to control population, she notes, 'demonstrably often have the interests of biopolitical states more in view than the well-being of women' (p. 6). Autonomy over reproduction – both having and not having children – has by necessity been a core demand of feminist organising, trumping 'the demands of patriarchy or any other system' (p. 6). In consequence, ecofeminists have been unwilling to address the climate consequences of childbirth, for the fear of sliding 'once again into the muck of racism, classism, nationalism, modernism, and imperialism' (p. 6). In the contexts of the Anthropocene, however, the problem takes on new dimensions. In 1950, the global population was reckoned to be around 2.5 billion people; in 2018, it was 7.4 billion; demographers predict that it will reach eleven billion by 2100. A priority for feminists globally must be to increase education for women, strengthen the rights that women hold within and outside of marriage, provide protection from abusive partners and improve access to contraception and safe elective abortion. Confrontation with the Anthropocene, however, also involves thinking in disruptive scales, over long temporal expanses, and in ways that are radically different from our current modes. For Haraway, this means culturing models of kinship beyond the nuclear family and its models of social reproduction, ancestry, and genealogy. She proposes a 'smychthonic' mode of kin-making: building relations of care and kind-ness between 'diverse human beings and other critters'; making, without domesticating, kin, with multispecies flourishing rather than individual or genealogical survival in mind (p. 103).

Struggling through the individual and collective ethics of these debates can be daunting, not least because the personal autonomy of women may seem to be being sacrificed in the name of the planet. At heart, the problem with debates about consumption and procreation is their excessive focus on the individual as bearing responsibility for climate change. During a devastating global heatwave in summer 2018, journalists at the *New York Times* and stalwart advocate for climate justice Naomi Klein debated whether a weakness of 'human nature' was to blame for the failure to address climate crisis in the 1980s, or a 'screamingly homogenous group of U.S. power players', in thrall to the interests of capital and the fossil fuels industry.[26] This debate exposed the vast scales of carbon emissions from industry and the sheer catastrophe of our predicted 2–4 degree world temperature rise. For anyone seeking to bring about a climate revolution, it made it dishearteningly obvious that without unprecedented multilateral and international agreement, a moratorium on fossil fuels and a complete change in industrial practice, climate change will not even be mitigated, let alone 'averted'. The green consumerism we have been sold offers a false autonomy, which supposes that it is the inherent selfishness or self-serving ignorance of individuals and consumers that is to blame.

However, rather than adopting an end-of-times hedonism or nihilism, it is more vital than ever to resist the self-interested, voracious construction of the individual that capitalism has used as a justification and smokescreen for its own destructiveness. Simplistic Marx-ish claims that there is 'no ethical consumerism under capitalism' may usefully gesture to the systemic nature of climate injustice, but can also beleaguer attempts to launch grassroots anti-capitalist movements, to make real reductions to human and ecological harm, and to support the emergence of alternative economies. Anthropologist Anna Tsing has explored idiosyncratic processes of accumulation, value creation, and exchange operating on the margins of global capitalism. She writes: 'Only when we begin to notice the elaborate and heterogeneous making of capitalist worlds might we usefully discuss vulnerabilities, points of purchase, and alternatives.'[27] Supporting feminist-led, low-carbon co-operatives and avoiding corporations with poor records in staff welfare and ecological harm might be only part of a broader environmental justice movement. However, the fact that corporations and governments have relied on consumer apathy and ignorance for so long demonstrates the need to participate in the process of making other ways of living in the world possible, to find 'points of purchase' for alternative modes of organisation and collective flourishing.

Other Ways of Being

Ecofeminism has long debated the relationships between ethics and efficacy, ontology and activism, in self-other, human nature, and gender relations. In the context of the Anthropocene, these debates become both more complex, and starker. According to Carol Adams and Lori Gruen, ecofeminism:

helps us to imagine healthier relationships; stresses the need to attend to context over universal judgments; and argues for the importance of care as well as justice, emotion as well as rationality, in working to undo the logic of domination and its material and practical implications.[28]

In diverse ecofeminist approaches, core principles of relationality, situatedness and care for the other rest upon ontologies of interconnectedness and co-becoming. Rejecting Cartesian divides between humanity and nature, post-anthropocentric ecofeminism has pursued accounts of 'being' based on non-Western ontologies, indigenous knowledges, and alternative accounts found in experimental physics and the life sciences.

Robin Wall-Kimmerer, an indigenous botanist and Professor of Environmental Science, has described how the language of the Potawatomi Nation radically transformed her understanding of natural forces of growth. Using language and grammar which recognises the agency and personhood of ecological processes, animals and other living entities, Wall-Kimmerer describes a form of knowledge that is relational, situated, and concerned with care and nurturing rather than supposedly 'objective' observation and control.[29]

New ecofeminist approaches have many points of similarity with Wall-Kimmerer's indigenous botany, though derived from distinct intellectual traditions. Some new feminist materialists reappraise outsider and innovative sciences and counter-traditions of Western thought – for example, Jane Bennett looks to theoretical physics and neovitalism; Haraway has been influenced by the process philosophy of Alfred Whitehead; Stacy Alaimo draws from Gilles Deleuze and Félix Guattari's theory of the assemblage. Although they build on intellectual traditions shaped by men, these loosely grouped 'life-centred' theorists push further than their predecessors in crafting ontologies that address the conditions of the Anthropocene. Haraway's 'compostist' science feminism, and what Rosi Braidotti calls 'zoe-centered' new materialism, describe the intra-active qualities of matter and disturb the complacency with which 'we' interact with the so-called world around us.[30] Processes of growth, decay, flow, and exchange attest to the vitality of the material world, and suggest that life should not be reduced to mechanical explanations or formulas. 'Zoe', for Braidotti, 'stands for the mindless vitality of Life carrying on independently and regardless of rational control', while Bennett advocates on behalf of vibrant matter because her 'hunch is that the image of dead or thoroughly instrumentalised matter feeds human hubris and our earth-destroying fantasies of conquest and consumption'.[31] Ontology, in these accounts, is productive of novel ethical relations which may underpin feminist and ecologist responses to environmental crisis.

A pertinent critique, which can be applied to the ontology-building work of new material feminism, comes from the work of Joanna Zylinksa. In *Minimal Ethics for the Anthropocene*, she criticises the masculinist 'intellectual trend towards ontology building' – the 'desire to build "worlds" and pass them off as reality'.[32] As Zylinksa does, one may fairly question whether it is useful to speculate about the agency of plants, waterways, and metals (as Bennett does) when so many women and oppressed groups are denied basic rights and access to power. New materialisms, such as Bennett's, work best when they take into account the dangers of promoting a fully 'horizontal' democracy (levelling any difference between our commitment to human and non-human needs), and explore theories 'designed to open democracy to the voices of excluded humans', as a way of promoting a more socially and environmentally just demos (p. 104).

Zylinksa's 'minimal ethics', in contrast, edges away from such theorising. It is 'less about building a better world as an external unity and more about making better cuts into that which are naming the world' (p. 88). In order 'to avoid becoming yet another masculinist enterprise which knows in advance and once and for all what it is striving for', a minimal ethics must 'embrace the very openness and vagueness of its premises', recognise 'the indecency, the gaudiness, the masquerade of any attempt to make philosophy, and then try to make it better – which perhaps means smaller, less posturing, less erect' (p. 88). This statement proves that it is impossible to get through a chapter on feminist responses to the Anthropocene without at least one joke about the law of the phallus. In general, however, feminist eco-theory works best when it is not concerned with abstract world-building, but is actively entangled in the trouble – making a cut into a world it is simultaneously trying to understand afresh.

In her theory of transcorporeality, Stacy Alaimo develops a philosophy of being which is uniquely implicated in the physical world. Transcorporeality describes the movement of materials between bodies, gesturing towards humanity's physical co-becoming and continuity with other lives, processes, and material manifestations. As Alaimo states: 'transcorporeality suggests that humans are not only interconnected with each other but with the material flows of substances and places'.[33] Divisions such as 'human' and 'nature' are ecologically meaningless, as the coalescence of matter which makes up seemingly discrete biotic and abiotic entities is always temporary, marked by material exchanges which disturb self–other and inside–outside dichotomies.

Transcorporeality has been helpful in describing and advancing a politics of co-existence, as flows of toxicity and pollution across watery and fleshy bodies of all kinds demand reconceptualisations of agency, materiality, and slow violence, as well as a renewed politics capable of addressing issues played out across deep temporal and planetary scales, across different cultures, nations, language traditions, land-masses, and water systems. Emerging from and informed by health and social justice movements, transcorporeality is inherently concerned with how intersecting forms of oppression are produced by, and productive of, environmental damage. While Zylinska rightly critiques the posturing and hubristic claims of philosophical world-building, Alaimo's theory proves its worth when it articulates injustices which may otherwise seem too dispersed to track: chemical poisoning, toxicity, industrial run-off, occupational sickness, cancers, and carcinogens. The flows, decompositions, and recompositions described in transcorporeality also provide ways of reflecting on the more-than-human damage of the Anthropocene. Alaimo has criticised clichéd visual representations of our new epoch – characterised by aerial shots of urban and industrial developments – because they suggest that the immensity of the Anthropocene 'is safely viewed from a rather transcendent, incorporeal perspective, not from a creaturely immersion in the world'.[34] Aerial technoscapes erase ecological networks and relations, obscuring the flight paths of migratory birds and the flows of water and wind. Alaimo rejects this iconography, instead locating the Anthropocene in markers such as the dissolving bodies of deep-sea shells, and in human bodies subject to toxicity and sickness. The emphasis is on precision, immersion, and an incisive (though often speculative and tentative) engagement in a living ecosphere.

An Anthropocene Feminism

While early ecofeminism was concerned with deconstructing the toxic relationship between femininity, nature, and the body, contemporary feminist responses to the Anthropocene are tasked with bringing thought back to the body, to gender-based inequalities, and to the ecosphere. The Anthropocene reveals, definitively, that it is no longer possible to tell the story of human history without natural history: the long Enlightenment project of mastering the 'forces of nature' has failed, with devastating consequences for all, and for indigenous and poor communities most catastrophically. Women and oppressed communities will be affected by climate injustice in the most pointed and unevenly distributed ways, as drought, resource scarcity, flooding, and pollution continue to affect reproductive health, access to medicines, climate refugees, gender-based violence, forced marriage, and wage inequalities. There is no way for feminism *not* to address the environmental crisis, or for environmentalism to intervene in our current crisis without the insights, energies, and dexterity of intersectional feminism at its core.

Notes

1 L. Coupe, 'General Introduction', in Coupe (ed.), *The Green Studies Reader* (London and New York: Routledge, 2000), 5.

2 J. Schneiderman, 'The Anthropocene Controversy', in R. Grusin (ed.), *Anthropocene Feminism* (Minneapolis and London: University of Minnesota Press, 2016), 170.

3 R. Grusin, 'Introduction: Anthropocene Feminism: An Experiment in Collaborative Theorizing', in Grusin (ed.), *Anthropocene Feminisms*, viii.

4 Schneiderman, 'Anthropocene Controversy', 171.

5 'Media Note: Anthropocene Working Group (AWG)', *University of Leicester* (August 2016).

6 Schneiderman, 'Anthropocene Controversy', 180.

7 From the IPCC report: J. J. McCarthy et al., *Climate Change 2001: Impacts, Adaptation, Vulnerability* (Cambridge: Cambridge University Press, 2001), 238–9.

8 Schneiderman, 'Anthropocene Controversy', 190.

9 See S. Harding (ed.), *The Feminist Standpoint Theory Reader* (London and New York: Routledge, 2004).

10 C. Colebrook, 'We Have Always Been Post-Anthropocene', in Grusin (ed.), *Anthropocene Feminism*, 8.

11 The Plantationocene was collectively generated by academics at the University of Aarhus in October 2014. See D. Haraway, A. Tsing, N. Ishikawa, G. Scott, K. Olwig, and N. Bubandt, 'Anthropologists are Talking – About the Anthropocene', *Ethnos* 81:3 (2015), 1–30. Capitalocene was suggested by Andreas Malm in 2009, see D. Haraway, *Staying with the Trouble* (Durham and London: Duke University Press, 2016), 206, fn. 6.

12 See R. Grove, *Green Imperialism: Colonial Expansion, Tropical Island Edens and the Origins of Environmentalism, 1600–1860* (Cambridge: Cambridge University Press, 1996); R. Guha, *Environmentalism: A Global History* (London: Penguin, 2014).

13 Colebrook, 'We Have Always Been Post-Anthropocene', 8.

14 J. Clover and J. Spahr, 'Gender Abolition and Ecotone War', in R. Grusin (ed.), *Anthropocene Feminism*, 154.

15 V. Shiva, 'The New Nature', *Boston Review* (11 January 2016).

16 Ibid

17 V. Plumwood, *Feminism and the Mastery of Nature* (London: Routledge, 1993), 21.

18 G. Gaard, 'Toward New EcoMasculinities, EcoGenders and EcoSexualities', in C. Adams and L. Gruen (eds.), *Ecofeminism* (London: Bloomsbury, 2015), 230.

19 Shiva, 'The New Nature'.

20 Haraway, *Staying with the Trouble*, 101.

21 S. Alaimo, *Bodily Natures: Science, Environment and the Material Self* (Bloomington and Indianapolis: Indiana University Press, 2010), 117.

22 S. Bernard, 'Making the Connections on Tar-sands Pollution, Racism, and Sexism', *Grist* (27 August 2015).

23 L. Nikoleris, 'Oestrogen in Birth Control Pills has a Negative Impact on Fish', *Lund University* (3 March 2016); C. Hsu, 'Antidepressants Found in Fish Brains in Great Lakes Region', *University of Buffalo News Centre* (31 August 2017).

24 S. Wynes and K. Nicholas, 'The Climate Mitigation Gap', *Environmental Research Letters*, 12.7 (July 2017), n.p.

25 Haraway, *Staying with the Trouble*, 5–6.

26 N. Klein, 'Capitalism Killed Our Climate Momentum, Not "Human Nature"', *The Intercept* (3 August 2018).

27 A. Tsing, 'Salvage Accumulation', *Cultural Anthropology* (30 March 2015), n.p.

28 C. Adams and L. Gruen, 'Introduction', in Adams and Gruen (eds.), *Ecofeminisms*, 1.

29 See R. Wall-Kimmerer, *Braiding Sweetgrass: Indigenous Wisdom, Scientific Knowledge, and the Teachings of Plants* (Minneapolis: Milkweed Editions, 2013).

30 Haraway, *Staying with the Trouble*, 150; see also R. Braidotti, *Transpositions* (Cambridge: Polity Press, 2006).

31 Braidotti, *Transpositions*, 37; J. Bennett, *Vibrant Matter: A Political Ecology of Things* (Durham and London: Duke University Press, 2010), ix.

32 J. Zylinksa, *Minimal Ethics for the Anthropocene* (Ann Arbor: Open Humanities Press, 2014), 79 and 86.

33 S. Alaimo, 'The Naked World: The Transcorporeal Ethics of the Protesting Body', *Women and Performance: A Journal of Feminist Theory*, 20 (2010), 23–4.

34 S. Alaimo, 'Your Shell on Acid: Material Immersion, Anthropocene Dissolves' in R. Grusin (ed.), *Anthropocene Feminism*, 92.

CHAPTER 9

Queer Feminism

Sam McBean

I am a Visiting Scholar in the Women's, Gender, and Sexuality Studies Department at Stony Brook University in New York, on my first sabbatical from my job in the UK. Women's studies was my first disciplinary home, but in the UK I work in an English Department – being here, I have a feeling of being back 'home' and also anxieties about whether I now belong in quite the same way. I worry that I am not up to speed with all the conversations happening around me. I am trying to keep up, which is also a feeling of being behind. I think often of Robyn Wiegman's formulation of the 'difficulty of being in time with feminism', which she uses to describe the ways in which a 'political and intellectual project that is itself historically transforming and transformative' is by its very nature tempo-rally multiple.[1] Knowing that there is no way to be in time with feminism (that there is not even one feminism) does not ameliorate my anxieties, but Wiegman gives me vocabulary for this as well – I am feeling the unsettling agony of the gap between 'the postulation and one's learning' (p. 161). I am learning. I attend a brilliant talk by Jennifer Nash, a talk partly about intersectionality, or what she terms the 'intersectionality wars'.[2] I am enlivened by her critique of the 'use value' that has become attached to the term 'intersectionality' in the academy and I am in awe of her careful tracing of a genealogy of the work this term does within the field of women's studies in particular. I love these kinds of projects, these kinds of arguments – arguments that trace the formation of fields, highlight critical attachment, and, integrally, unravel the desires and trials of the field of women's studies.

Yet, as I listen to Nash I have to quiet the niggling sensation that the 'field' of women's studies that is being addressed in this talk is one that I have difficulty translating into the UK context. The current institutio-nalisation of women's studies, gender studies, and sexuality studies (not to mention critical race studies or postcolonial studies) in the UK exists much more commonly as 'centres', 'research groups', or 'research

clusters' housed within or across other departments, rather than autonomous departments or centres that employ full-time academic members
of staff.[3] These spaces, which often rely on an enormous amount of
voluntary labour to sustain, do not make the discipline any more insecure
than Women's Studies Departments in the USA – departments close,
people leave – but it does make them less of an institutional 'home'.
While it is possible to do postgraduate degrees in women's studies or
gender studies in the UK, there are no BAs in Women's Studies or
Gender Studies. While listening to Nash, I remember Sara Ahmed's
reflection on a moment where she too felt estranged, in the UK, from
a story about women's studies anchored in the US context. Rather than
turn from a scene of misrecognition though, Ahmed cleaves to it, insisting that 'we do not need to recognise each other's versions to know they
bear some relation'.[4] I am feeling the isolation of not being able to relate
to Nash's story about women's and gender studies, which compounds my
anxieties about being behind conversations in the field happening in the
USA, when suddenly, Nash swerves. In an offhanded comment, she
remarks that we, scholars who travel under the sign of women's studies,
'have spent too much time on the feminist/queer divide'. I scribble this
down verbatim. In this claim that we need to stop spending time
addressing this 'divide', I wonder about what I will write for this edited
collection, this chapter. My anxieties about displacement, translation,
and feeling behind US scholarship (and feminism in particular) seemed
to have reached a crescendo. Is to be interested in the relationship
between feminism and queer to dally behind ground already settled? Is
it to indulge needlessly in debates and conversations that are not only
over, but also possibly distracting? Are we 'over it', exhausted and bored?
Am I? Are you?

The relationship, or, rather, antagonism as the relation, between
feminism and queer is an old story, a narrative bound up with
a version of the beginnings of queer theory. Wiegman suggests that the
'inaugural act of queer theory, the analytic precondition for its elaboration of a range of anti-identitarian critical and political commitments'
was the splitting off of sexuality as an object of study distinct from
gender and the insistence on the need for a new theoretical paradigm to
attend to this object.[5] In this story, the separation of sexuality from
gender enables queer theory to emerge as the disciplinary home for
sexuality, and solidifies gender as feminism's rightful object. This origin
story is usually traced back to Gayle Rubin's 1984 essay, 'Thinking Sex:
Notes for a Radical Theory of the Politics of Sexuality' and Eve Kosofsky

Sedgwick's 1990 book, *Epistemology of the Closet*. While neither text contains the word 'queer', they are both retrospectively claimed as beginnings for queer theory via a shared insistence that feminism might be insufficient to attend to sexuality as object. In Rubin's essay, in a section titled 'The Limits of Feminism', she admits that '[f]eminism has always been vitally interested in sex' because 'much of the oppression of women is borne by, mediated through, and constituted within, sexuality'.[6] Yet, writing in the wake of the pornography debates, Rubin argues that a feminist analytic struggles to imagine sexuality outside of its expression within a patriarchal framework (where either women will be liberated by sexuality and desire, or are enslaved by it) (p. 28). Rubin considers the way that the framework for thinking about sexuality from within feminism is limited to theorising women's gender-based oppression. She concludes that '[f]eminism is the theory of gender oppression' and to assume that this also makes feminism the theory of sex is to 'fail to distinguish between gender, on the one hand, and erotic desire, on the other' (p. 32).

Sedgwick builds on Rubin's suggestion that perhaps gender and sexuality are different (if related) objects of study in *Epistemology of the Closet*. Her second axiom in her list of starting points for an anti-homophobic theory is: '*The study of sexuality is not coextensive with the study of gender; correspondingly, antihomophobic inquiry is not coextensive with feminist inquiry. But we can't know in advance how they will be different.*'[7] For Sedgwick, while gender and sexuality are bound together, they are 'nonetheless not the same question' (p. 30). In much the same way that Rubin argues that feminism cannot think sexuality outside of women's status under patriarchy, Sedgwick suggests that it might be that 'a damaging bias toward heterosocial or heterosexist assumptions inheres unavoidably in the very concept of gender' (p. 31). In an attempt to detach sexuality from gender, Sedgwick insists that the gender of the object-choice seems relatively unimportant for some aspects of desire and sexual practice, such as 'desires attaching to mouth, anus, breasts, feet, etc.', and also suggests that some forms of desire do not distinguish object-choice based on gender '(e.g., human/animal, adult/child, singular/plural, autoerotic/alloerotic)' (p. 35). Sedgwick thus tells a story of desire and sexuality that may not involve gender at all, seemingly solidifying the unsuitability of feminism as the privileged site from which to theorise this version of sexuality. In both Rubin and Sedgwick, the split between feminism and a radical theory of sexuality happens concurrently with the splitting off of sexuality from gender. The opening utterance of the 1993 *The Lesbian and Gay Studies*

Reader seems to condense the arguments of both Rubin and Sedgwick: '[l]esbian/gay studies does for *sex* and *sexuality* approximately what women's studies does for gender'.[8]

However, this is a contentious split. Judith Butler, in 'Against Proper Objects', offers a sustained critique of the claim that lesbian/gay studies 'owns' sexuality and that women's studies 'owns' gender. Butler argues that in assigning gender as feminism's 'proper object', the editors of *The Lesbian and Gay Studies Reader* obscure feminism's complex history of theorising sexuality and foreground gender and sexuality in both feminism and lesbian/gay studies at the expense of their attention to other markers of difference, including race and class.[9] Moreover, a too tidy division between gender and sexuality makes it near impossible to explore the ways in which the regulation of sexuality is intimately linked to gender – for Butler, it is the imperative of heterosexuality which produces binary gender.[10] Butler thus critiques the version of feminism that is offered as the discipline from which a more radical theory of sexuality needs to split. In other words, she responds from the position of a feminist theory that does not recognise the version of itself that is narrated by the burgeoning field of queer theory. The special issue in which 'Against Proper Objects' is first printed becomes a book in 1997, *Feminism Meets Queer Theory*, and gains a new introduction in which one of the editors, Elizabeth Weed, explains that the aim of the special issue was '*to look squarely at the way the intersection of feminism and queer theory has been rendered by queer theory*'.[11] Within this introduction, Weed makes clear that the special issue was necessary because queer theory was making feminism 'unrecognizable – not to say illegible – to many feminist theorists' (p. viii). As Butler suggests, the restriction of feminism to gender appears as 'a prescribed restriction of feminist practice to terms illegible to feminist criticism'.[12]

In the laments over what happens when feminism meets queer theory, it is apparent that this meeting 'does' something to feminism. As well as restrict feminism's object to gender (at the expense of the multiple ways feminist theory has not only attended to sexuality but also gender's intersection with a wealth of other markers of social difference), Butler points out that gender itself is rendered in a curious way. She notes that the editors of *The Lesbian and Gay Studies Reader* offer a parenthetical definition of gender as 'whether male or female'.[13] In opposition to gender's supposed fixity (male or female), sexuality (as is evident in Sedgwick's formulation of desire's multiplicities), becomes much more mobile. This characterisation of sexuality then becomes a property of queer theory, producing queer as anti-foundational or radically mobile precisely because of its connection to sexuality, rather than the seemingly much more rigid object of gender, stuck to male and female, which feminism supposedly owns as object. In Biddy Martin's words, queer claims to anti-foundationalism require feminism as the repository of 'fixity, constraint, or subjection'.[14] It is not so much that feminism and queer theory encounter each other in the 1990s, but that queer theory emerges out of a cleaving from feminism, which is also a cleaving of sexuality from gender. This is a cleaving that both produces gender as feminism's proper object of study and imagines gender (and thus feminism) as much more rigid a category than the unhinged, free-floating sexuality that queer theory will claim as its object (and whose supposed unfixed energy will become a property of queer theory itself).[15]

In the 1997 book version, 'Against Proper Objects' gains a preface, a preface in which Butler laments that explorations of encounters between feminist and queer theory can quickly be 'misconstrued as a war'.[16] In opposition to this, Butler argues against proper objects, for the necessity of disagreement, the productiveness of debate, and the importance of immanent critique. Butler is tired of the queer/feminist divide in 1997. She argues that '[a]lthough we may posit the heuristic possibility of a world in which acts and identities would be fully separable, it still remains for us to describe what it might mean to live that very separation' (p. 3). This call for difference and immanent critique attempts to rewrite the feminist/queer divide away from division. Rather than settle the relationship between feminism and queer theory, she holds the door open, wanting to keep the possibilities of their relationship alive – highlighting that the stakes of the relationship between acts and identities, gender and sexuality, is far from settled, far from clear.[17] In this interest in immanence, she curiously returns us to Sedgwick. It is Sedgwick, after all, who frames her splitting of gender and sexuality through the caveat that *we can't know in advance* what differences might emerge between the study of gender and the study of sexuality.

* * * *

My book *Feminism's Queer Temporalities* has been out for over a year. After initially worrying over whether it was ever going to be reviewed, I manage to forget about it. One day, I stumble across a review published months ago and I cannot believe I missed it. It is a lovely review and I am flattered that it seems to capture something of the spirit of my work – notably the love and care I feel for my disciplinary home, for the field, objects, and thinkers that taught (and continue to teach) me how to think. The book in part challenges the idea that feminism's time is somehow linear, progressive, and generational and that queer time is precisely its opposite, by suggesting, via a reading of feminist cultural objects, that feminism's time might be queer. In this, the book aims to counter a narrative of feminism's relationship to queer that, as Annamarie Jagose puts it, resists 'the temporal disciplining of feminist from queer thought that stages them as the before and after of some narrative of critical advancement'.[18] Yet, in response to this aim, the reviewer, Melissa Gregg, confesses something: 'I never seriously thought of queer theory as a linear successor to feminism.'[19] Gregg notes her particular relationship to the fields of feminism and queer theory via her disciplinary home – the place she studied as a graduate student and where she was a former faculty member – suggesting that 'queer politics is essential to the way feminist theory is taught and practiced' (p. e2). In other words, from Gregg's perspective, the divide has been settled, the relationship one of harmony, disciplinary compatibility. Gregg's point returns when I am at Nash's talk, when she advises that we need to collectively move on from the queer/feminist divide. I hear again that I am out of time. We have spent too much time on the relationship between feminism and queer theory; it is time to move on, we have all moved on, why are you still stuck? Victoria Hesford's endorsement, printed on the inside of my book reads: 'This is a book that lays to rest once and for all the misconception that feminist and queer theory are generational antagonists locked in a drama of disidentification and forgetting.'[20] My book has finally ended this pointless drama. Has it? Am I over it? Are we done?

Not long after finding the review, I receive an email from Jennifer Cooke in which she explains that she is developing a volume of essays for Cambridge University Press. She writes, 'having enjoyed *Feminism's Queer Temporalities*, I would like to invite you to contribute a chapter on queer feminism'.[21] My book's supposed laying to rest of the divide between feminist and queer theory has produced an invitation to revisit 'queer feminism'.[22] What does it mean to be still writing about something that is over? Settled? Laid to rest? I think I am supposed to be past the 'divide' and just tell you a story of what 'queer feminism' is. Yet, I feel wholly ill-equipped. I am reminded of Elizabeth Freeman's suggestion that she might be 'still after' queer theory. She rehearses the different meanings of 'still after': being 'embarrassingly here' even after something has been declared over; being frozen, 'paralyzed, with nothing to say'; and, with the inflection on the 'after', being attached, in pursuit still of the desired object.[23] I am not sure I know how to tell you what 'queer feminism' is without a focus on the importance of the 'queer/feminist divide', without an interest in repetition, without the embarrassing admission that I might have nothing new to say, and without admitting that I am still after what queer feminism is, in any case.

Claire Colebrook describes the time of feminism via the 'stratigraphic', a geological term and process of time scaling that looks at the various layers or 'strata' of the earth. When applied to feminism, it becomes a way to both acknowledge historicity and describe the complexities of the ways we encounter the past. Colebrook makes the seemingly obvious yet prescient claim that feminism's archive can never be approached from the ground up. She suggests that 'to read Beauvoir today is not only to read her *after* Irigaray; it is also to read Irigaray, Butler, Grosz or Spivak with a complex sense of a long-negotiated terrain; any feminist claim in our present is in harmony and dissonance with a choir of past voices'.[24] I should admit something here. My introduction to the debates about the relationship between feminism and queer came not from initial encounters with Rubin and Sedgwick, or even Butler, but via an encounter with Jagose's 2009 article, 'Feminism's Queer Theory'. The significance of this is that I encountered the relationship between queer and feminism not via queer divergence, but via feminist convergence. Jagose's title, 'feminism's queer theory', signals a shift away from the 1997 collection, *Feminism Meets Queer Theory*. In Jagose, feminism is not having a shock encounter with the representation of itself that it finds in queer theory. Instead, 'feminism's queer theory' insists that queer theory belongs to feminism, or at the very least, stakes a claim on that hypothesis. The influence of Jagose's formulation is evident in my own book's title, *Feminism's Queer Temporalities* (rather than 'feminist and queer temporalities', for instance) and in the insistence I share with her that queerness might belong to feminism. Yet, much like queer theory's emergence comes out of (and thus possibly needs) the divergent energy of a split from feminism, Jagose's later convergence requires this earlier divergence – holding on is holding on only if something is trying to get away. Jagose's claims about the relationship between feminism and queer are built on top of a choir of other voices – she asks us to consider origin stories, ordering, belonging, historical time. Indeed, she suggests that 'thinking feminist and queer theory together can productively occasion a turn away from linear historical time with its implicit prioritization of the present and its reliance on heteronormative tropes of lineage, succession and generation' (p. 160).

It is a focus on time that Wiegman sticks with in *Object Lessons*, where she invokes the 'discordant temporalities of feminism and queer theory' (p. 116). For Wiegman, it matters first of all that despite the frequency of the pairing 'feminism and queer theory', they are not equivalent terms. Equivalents might be 'feminist theory and queer theory' or 'feminist activism and queer activism'. The pairing of feminism and queer theory binds a social movement (feminism) with an academic mode of critique (queer theory). Wiegman does not aim for more precision with our terms, exactly, but rather suggests that the repetition of the pairing 'feminism and queer theory' necessitates that we be more (not less) attuned to what difference this makes. As Wiegman explains it, feminism 'acquired its political resonance' as 'a *preinstitutional* discourse', by which she means that feminism as a movement pre-existed its institutional inauguration (p. 117, emphasis in original). Feminism's inauguration as academic practice is one effect of the movement's insistence that the study of women is a political practice. If feminism is a political movement that then inaugurates an academic discourse, queer theory references not a 'preinstitutional' existence, but rather a critique of a prior institutionalisation of sexuality, Gay and Lesbian Studies. As Wiegman explains it, 'queer theory departs from the identity project that most centrally bore it, Gay and Lesbian Studies, to question the construction of homosexual identity as the primary means for advancing a critical understanding of sexuality' (p. 117). In parsing out the different institutional temporalities indexed by 'feminism' and 'queer theory', Wiegman suggests that in the debates over the relationship between the two we have not been careful enough to interrogate the ways that the politics of institutionalisation are often collapsed into political contestations – the differences between feminism and queer theory might be more divergent than our desires for convergence let us see. Perhaps the relationship between feminism and queer theory has little to do with proper objects, and much more to do with the timing of institutionalisation (and the effects that this has on how a field develops). Another way to put this is that in Wiegman's story about the relationship between feminism and queer theory, she turns away from the objects of sexuality and gender (and the desires attached to what they are, who owns them, and what a better description/analysis of them might achieve), and turns feminism and queer theory themselves into the proper objects so that we might consider our attachments to them, our investments in what they might do, and their travels within institutional and activist contexts.

* * * *

I am still in New York, in a flat in Brooklyn that I am subletting. I am sat at the big, round kitchen table, curled up, reading Ti-Grace Atkinson's collection of essays, *Amazon Odyssey*. On 21 February 1970, Atkinson gave a talk titled 'Lesbianism and Feminism' at Juniata College, Huntingdon, Pennsylvania. It starts with this line: 'It has seemed clear to me, for about two years, that there is some important connection between lesbianism and feminism.'[25] She explains that her attention was brought to the possible connection between the two by the repetition of the charge that the women's movement was 'just a bunch of lesbians' and she sets out in the speech to 'figure out the meaning of this connection' (p. 83). Atkinson poses the following questions early on, questions that summarise the problem, as she sees it: 'Is lesbianism political? If so, what is its analysis and program? Does feminism, intrinsically, have a position on sex? Is sex inherently political?' (p. 84). By December of the same year, she concludes that lesbianism is the 'commitment, by choice, full-time, of one woman to others of her class' and it is this commitment that 'constitutes the political significance of lesbianism' (p. 132). Less than a year after Atkinson was pondering the relationship between lesbianism and feminism, she had decided that 'if the government *succeeds* in isolating lesbianism to *any* degree from feminism, feminism is lost' (p. 134, emphasis in original). The relationship between lesbianism and feminism was far from secured in the 1970s.[26] Atkinson's talks are situated within broader conversations about lesbians within the women's movement and the relationship between the politics of lesbianism and the politics of women's liberation. Yet, as I read her essays from my sublet kitchen, thinking about the queer/feminist divide, I am struck by the notion that Atkinson was grappling with the relationship between sexuality and gender and the political programme that might be built around these two seemingly related but also different objects. It seemed that the very objects (gender and sexuality) that would later be so central to the queer/feminist divide, were pivotal to Atkinson's grappling with the relationship of lesbians to the women's movement. What happens to the figure of the lesbian in 'queer feminism'? Does a history of lesbian feminist thought sit in excess of the narrative that is told about queer theory coming after feminism? Is the lesbian, as Clare Hemmings puts it, 'outside of the competition between queer and feminist perspectives'?[27] What are her stakes in the divide? In my fears about being still after queer feminism, my anxieties about belatedness have seemingly left me arriving impossibly early – thinking with 1970s lesbian feminism.

In 2014, Robyn Wiegman publishes 'The Times We're In' and claims the category 'queer feminist criticism'. An endnote after the first appearance of this term explains that in earlier, lecture versions of the article, she was 'repeatedly asked about the seeming "strangeness" of the category [she] invent[s]'.[28] The responses coalesce around her bringing together what some audience members wanted to insist upon as two discrete categories of criticism: queer and feminist. In this first endnote, Wiegman argues that despite a history of 'antagonism and dissensus as the political and analytic relation between queer critique and feminist criticism', there are those scholars refusing this legacy and revisiting the imbrication of the two terms (p. 20). Wiegman anchors queer feminist criticism in Sedgwick, but not the Sedgwick of *Epistemology of the Closet*, who is the more traditional origin point for queer theory. Instead, Wiegman attaches thinkers such as Ann Cvetkovich, Elizabeth Freeman, and Heather Love to the Sedgwick that gives us 'reparative' reading.[29] Reparative reading is offered, by Sedgwick, as a methodological approach that would counter what she argues has become the dominant mode of reading – a paranoid mode that is always on the lookout for hidden meaning, is motivated by suspicion, and grants critical sovereignty to the reader in their ability to master the object. In contrast, reparative reading, among other things, rejects this symptomatic reading strategy and 'the critical act is reconfigured to value, sustain, and privilege the object's worldly inhabitations and needs' (p. 7). Wiegman argues that queer feminist critics, following Sedgwick, 'all put faith in their objects of study as affectively rich environments for cultivating a response to the conditions of the political present' (p. 16). Jagose had, in 2009, suggested that perhaps the most interesting thing about holding together feminist and queer was the temporal possibilities of this pairing, and Wiegman, in 2012's *Object Lessons*, elaborates on the ways to think the temporal politics of the pairing (via institutional timing). This more recent insistence by Wiegman is that what queer feminist criticism might be is a methodological approach to the present, one imbricated in complex ways with affect theory, evidencing a commitment to 'defining and analyzing the affective in temporal terms and vice versa' (p. 6). In Wiegman's version of queer feminist criticism, a new origin story is told, anchored to Sedgwick, but not the divergent Sedgwick of *Epistemology of the Closet*, the reparative Sedgwick most often anchored to *Touching Feeling*. Wiegman, in other words, re-articulates the relationship between feminism and queer away from divergence (in Sedgwick), and instead, drawing on Sedgwick's later affect theory, argues that she provides an origin for queer feminist criticism that is reparative. Moreover, Wiegman's new origin story for queer feminism relies on the production of a new object; queer feminism's object is neither gender nor sexuality per se, but rather the dual analytics of affect and time.

It would be too easy to end here, with the suggestion that Wiegman offers a new genealogy for thinking together queer and feminist that somehow 'solves' the problem or ameliorates the discordances between the two terms. A new origin story equals a new object equals a new 'queer feminist criticism'. But the story does not end here, the story ends with a return (again) to what exactly happens to feminism when it is paired with queer. Wiegman's piece, published in a special section of *Feminist Theory*, is followed by numerous responses. Hemmings, in her piece, remains stuck on the formulation 'queer feminist'. She asks, 'Is queer the descriptor here, that qualifies "feminist"? . . . Can "feminist" only remain relevant – critically or politically – when dragged out of anachronism through "queer" re-description?'[30] For Hemmings, 'queer theorists and not feminist theorists appear to be having all the fun' (p. 29). In a later piece by Hemmings from 2016, she elaborates on her response to Wiegman by exploring the ways that to be aligned with queer theory (over feminism) seems to mark 'the people doing so as fully contemporary . . . as part of the present and future rather than of a necessarily co-opted feminist past'.[31] In other words, Hemmings worries precisely over the politics of the present that would see queer theory as the more contemporary project – queer feminist criticism becomes, in Wiegman, not only a methodology for grappling with the present, but also the timeliest of methodologies. To reclaim some theoretical edge for feminism, Hemmings suggests returning to unstick gender from the seemingly binary and heteronormative connotations that it accrues in Rubin and Sedgwick. Hemmings, in other words, goes back to the origin of the queer/feminist divide to offer a re-narration of gender as object, describing the ways we might approach gender not as rigid or bound to heterosexuality but as 'an unfinished, conflicted site of engagement' (p. 94). Hemmings pulls back ever so slightly on Wiegman's desires to claim the present for queer feminist criticism, and cleaves to gender as object, offering a more reparative reading, refusing to let go of the unfinished business of gender (a move that Wiegman might, as it turns out, claim as 'queer feminist criticism').

The queer/feminist divide is a site of repetitious return. As a divide or divergence, it might tell us a story of queer theory's origins. As a suturing or convergence, it might tell us something of feminist theory's reparative work. The queer/feminist divide becomes its own kind of curious object – not a disagreement, settled terrain, or something from the past, but an object in its own right that we might track, a pairing that does a lot of work. It might be a site to keep thinking through what kind of objects gender and sexuality are (and what their relationship might be), it might enable us to think through institutional time and the desires we attach to both objects and disciplinary homes, or it might be a methodology for thinking with time's affective structures in the present. Disciplinary homes are unsettling. To work under a sign (such as queer feminism) might also involve being open to the discordances of that sign. Perhaps 'queer feminism' forces us to keep being unsettled; perhaps it even provides a methodology for precisely this – to keep unsettling narratives of gender and sexuality, of identity politics, of institutions, of the present. I am still after queer feminism. We return to these questions, these sites, because there is more work to be done.

Notes

1 R. Wiegman, 'On Being in Time with Feminism', *MLQ: Modern Language Quarterly*, 65:1 (2004), 163.
2 J. Nash, 'Love Notes from a Critic, or Notes on the Intersectionality Wars', *Stony Brook University* (6 April 2018).
3 The exceptions being primarily the Gender Department at the London School of Economics and Political Science, the Women's Studies Centre at York University, and the Centre for Gender Studies at the School of Oriental and African Studies, University of London. The Centre for the Study of Women and Gender at the University of Warwick is housed within the Department of Sociology, the Centre for Gender Studies at Sussex University is co-run by the departments of Sociology, Law, and Education, the Centre for Gender and Women's Studies at Lancaster University is housed within the Sociology Department, and the Gendered Lives research group at Loughborough University is part of the School of Social Sciences and Humanities.
4 S. Ahmed, 'Robyn Wiegman, *Object Lessons*' (review), *Feminist Theory*, 13:3 (2012), 347.
5 R. Wiegman, *Object Lessons* (Durham, NC and London: Duke University Press, 2012), 96.
6 G. Rubin, 'Thinking Sex: Notes for a Radical Theory of the Politics of Sexuality' [1984], in H. Abelove, M. A. Barale, and D. M. Halperin (eds.), *The Lesbian and Gay Studies Reader* (New York and London: Routledge, 1993), 28.
7 E. K. Sedgwick, *Epistemology of the Closet* (Berkeley and Los Angeles: University of California Press, 1990), 27 (emphasis in original).
8 H. Abelove, M. A. Barale, and D. M. Halperin, 'Introduction', in Abelove, Barale, and Halperin (eds.), *The Lesbian and Gay Studies Reader*, xv (emphasis in original).
9 See J. Butler, 'Against Proper Objects', *differences: A Journal of Feminist Cultural Studies*, 6.2:3 (1994), 1–26.

10 See J. Butler, *Bodies that Matter: On the Discursive Limits of Sex* (New York and London: Routledge, 1993).

11 E. Weed, 'Introduction', in E. Weed and N. Schor (eds.), *Feminism Meets Queer Theory* (Bloomington and Indianapolis, IN: Indiana University Press, 1997), x.

12 Butler, 'Against Proper Objects', 3.

13 Abelove, Barale, and Halperin, 'Introduction', xv.

14 B. Martin, 'Sexualities Without Genders and Other Queer Utopias', *Diacritics*, 24:2/3 (1994), 104.

15 See also A. Jagose, *Orgasmology* (Durham, NC: Duke University Press, 2012), especially chapter five 'Counterfeit Pleasures: Fake Orgasm and Queer Agency', for a discussion of the privileging of certain kinds of sex acts in queer theory.

16 J. Butler, 'Against Proper Objects', in Weed and Schor (eds.), *Feminism Meets Queer Theory*, 1.

17 The feminist and queer debates I have been tracing seemingly exclude the developments and contributions of trans theory to the theorisation of the relationship between gender and sexuality. While trans theoretical writing was emerging at the same time as queer, its institutionalisation comes markedly after: *The Transgender Studies Reader* (eds. Susan Stryker and Stephen Whittle) was published over twenty years after *The Lesbian and Gay Studies Reader*. Yet, Butler's invitation to keep the relationship between gender and sexuality open and transforming seems especially pertinent now, given how the relationship between gender and sexuality is re-conceptualised and reimagined via trans theory. See, for instance, A. L. Chu, 'On Liking Women', *n+1 magazine*, 30 (2018).

18 A. Jagose, 'Feminism's Queer Theory', *Feminism & Psychology*, 19:2 (2009), 160.

19 M. Gregg, 'Book Review: *Feminism's Queer Temporalities*', *Feminist Review*, 113 (2016), e2.

20 V. Hesford, in S. McBean, *Feminism's Queer Temporalities* (London and New York: Routledge, 2016), ii.

21 Personal correspondence, 3 February 2017.

22 Of course, this is one of the ways that the timing of academia is tied up with the timing of feminism; the publication of a book inevitably produces invitations often bound to the topic of the book. The production of more writing on the book's topic is one way of building an academic profile, of advancing my position in the field. There is therefore something to be gained by revisiting, repeating, and retreading, and it sits in a complicated relationship to my intellectual desires to keep writing about this topic – or, rather, my being 'stuck' with a topic produces an accumulation that is the stuff of an academic career.

23 E. Freeman, 'Still After', *South Atlantic Quarterly*, 106:3 (2007), 495.

24 C. Colebrook, 'Stratigraphic Time, Women's Time', *Australian Journal of Feminist Studies*, 25:59 (2009), 13–14, emphasis in original.

25 T. G. Atkinson, *Amazon Odyssey* (New York: Links Books, 1974), 83.

26 See V. Hesford, *Feeling Women's Liberation* (Durham, NC and London: Duke University Press, 2013).

27 C. Hemmings, 'Is Gender Studies Singular? Stories of Queer/Feminist Difference and Displacement', *differences: A Journal of Feminist Cultural Studies*, 27:2 (2016), 95.

28 R. Wiegman, 'The Times We're In: Queer Feminist Criticism and the Reparative "Turn"', *Feminist Theory*, 15:1 (2014), 19, en. 1.

29 E. K. Sedgwick, 'Paranoid Reading and Reparative Reading; or, You're So Paranoid, You Probably Think This Essay is About You', in E. K. Sedgwick (ed.), *Novel Gazing: Queer Readings in Fiction* (Durham, NC and London: Duke University Press, 1997), 1–37.

30 C. Hemmings, 'The Materials of Reparation', *Feminist Theory*, 15:1 (2014), 28.

31 Hemmings, 'Is Gender Studies Singular?', 84.

CHAPTER 10

Social Reproduction: New Questions for the Gender, Affect, and Substance of Value

Marina Vishmidt and Zöe Sutherland

Since the global financial crisis of 2008, there has been a resurgence of Marxist feminist critique, with many writers and activists reformulating its theoretical and political adequacy for the present conjuncture. It is in this context that social reproduction theory has increasingly come to be a rallying point.[1] Central to this theory is the claim that the sustenance of life and human relationships – whether or not it is recognised as (waged) labour – is fully integral to capitalism as a mode of production. For many feminists, this sustenance is understood more specifically as the reproduction of labour-power. As it remains disproportionately 'women' who are tasked with responsibility for this sustenance – in or out of the household – social reproduction theory positions gender, and gendered labour, as central to the reproduction of the capitalist mode of production. It thus follows historical trends in Marxist feminism which analysed the structural role of social distinctions such as gender or race in capitalism, rather than seeing them as 'superstructural' (ideological or cultural) phenomena. While we would generally align ourselves with this political tendency, we also want to think critically about the concept of social reproduction, to analyse its conceptual clarity, and to evaluate its ability to explain the process of devaluation of gendered labour within capitalist societies.

Social Reproduction

But first, what is social reproduction? Why is it an important concept for feminists? As Rada Katsarova notes, social reproduction theory has multiple lineages, popularised in the 1960s–1980s through a range of critiques of orthodox Marxism – including Marxist, Italian autonomist, postcolonial and Third World feminisms, as well as debates around slavery, race, and urban development.[2] But social reproduction is already at stake as

143

soon as the reproduction of capital is formulated. In the first volume of *Capital*, Marx states:

> Whatever the social form of the production process, it has to be continuous, it must periodically repeat the same phases. A society can no more cease to produce than it can to consume. When viewed, therefore, as a connected whole, and in the constant flux of its incessant renewal, every social process of production is, at the same time, a process of reproduction.[3]

And a few pages later:

> Capitalist production, therefore, under its aspect of a continuous connected process, of a process of reproduction, produces not only commodities, not only surplus-value, but it also produces and reproduces the capital relation; on the one side the capitalist, on the other the wage-labourer. (p. 724)

Here Marx is noting a continuity and unity between production and reproduction, considered from the viewpoint of the 'social totality' or total social capital, and its ability to maintain itself and expand.

In the 1970s and 1980s, feminists used formulations such as these to theorise the oppression of women in capitalist societies. Since Marx was using the concept of reproduction at a high level of abstraction – including production and consumption per se – feminists worked to concretise it politically, as well as analytically. Hence, when feminists spoke about social reproduction, they often meant something quite specific: the production and reproduction of labour-power. This formulation can be seen in the 1970s interventions of Italian Marxist feminists such as Mariarosa Dalla Costa, Leopoldina Fortunati, and Silvia Federici, and later in the work of Lise Vogel.[4] At the very heart of the conditions of possibility of the reproduction of capitalism is labour-power, that is, people with the potential to be waged workers. Due to the central role of labour-power in producing surplus value for capital, its reproduction is a necessary condition for capitalist accumulation.

A key insight of Marxist feminism has thus been that the vast wealth produced through capitalist accumulation has been possible only at the expense of the invisible and unpaid labour of over half of the population. Not only is it women who have largely reproduced labour-power, that is, maintained and cared for the past, present, and future workforce, but these activities have been systematically devalued within capitalist societies. Historically, not only has reproduction been construed as unpaid work, but it has also been made invisible *as* work through both its privatisation and its naturalisation onto certain bodies. As a result, the positioning – and to some extent construction – of 'women' within such relations can have significant implications over a single lifespan, stretching far beyond the work itself: financial dependence, reduced opportunities, and participation in the public sphere or in value-producing labour activities, greater levels of poverty in old age, increased vulnerability to domestic violence, and so on. By insisting upon identifying these 'reproductive' tasks as 'labour', feminists of this period brought to light the sheer extent and structural importance of unpaid work done by women working both for a wage outside the home and without a wage inside the home: the renowned 'double shift'. At the same time, they demonstrated the centrality of this work to communist and socialist politics. If the labour of women – now defined as 'reproductive workers' – was key to the vast wealth of capitalist accumulation, their political agency must equally be key to its revolutionary overthrow.[5] Yet as the capacity for childbearing was often considered to be the minimal – for some, ineradicable – basis of women's oppression, feminist struggle of that era often focused on the refusal, minimisation, or else socialisation, of all *other* reproductive tasks.[6] This was a stance that cut across the Marxist-feminist controversies about whether reproduction, then mainly discussed as 'domestic labour', was considered to be directly value-producing or simply as constituting the condition of possibility of the production of value.

In analyses that came to the fore in the 1970s–1980s known as the 'domestic labour debate', reproduction was often equated with a specific set of gendered tasks. As feminists sought to extend Marx's category of 'labour' beyond the productive sphere, reproduction was too simply conflated with those tasks that were associated with the 'reproductive sphere' or private household. As the Endnotes collective have argued, the consequence of this was that certain activities came to be read as reproductive, some of which were not, in fact, confinable to unpaid work in the home.[7] Defining reproduction in terms of a preconceived set of gendered tasks had the consequence of naturalising what was in fact a historically and geographically specific division of social labour. This has become increasingly evident as capital has restructured recently to commodify more and more activities associated with reproduction, which has effectively led to their redistribution to precarious, low-paid, and often informal service workers, such as (undocumented) immigrants.

In the attempt to concretise the place of gender within Marx's analysis of capital as a social relation, feminists produced an understanding of social reproduction that aimed at precision, yet one whose meaning remained indeterminate. And this understanding formed the basis for later work, as is evident in Johanna Brenner and Barbara Laslett's 1991 essay, which explicitly distinguished 'social' reproduction from Marx's notion of the reproduction of the 'societal' per se.[8] The concept of social reproduction thus captures one dimension of Marx's social totality: the reproduction of labour-power, or the further 'hidden abode' before and beyond the workplace, in which the worker's 'instinct for self-preservation' finds a social articulation.[9] Yet, even with the specification made by anchoring reproduction to labour-power, the indeterminacy inherent within the concept of social reproduction was not fully dissolved. Rather, the application of the concept can be stretched almost indefinitely, being made to signify not only something as capacious as the reproduction of a mode of production, or the capital-labour relation, but the reproduction of life per se.[10] As such, it becomes almost impossible to distinguish social reproduction in any determinate sense, which can pose political, as well as conceptual problems. As labour-power is a special commodity – composed of both the commodity and its bearer – it is difficult to distinguish where the worker-product ends and the 'person' begins.[11] And what counts as the reproduction of labour-power is open to further specification, given what Marx called the 'historical-moral element', that is, the historically and socially determined minimal conditions of the reproduction of labour-power in specific places and times for specific categories of people.[12]

In addition to this, many theorists of the 'domestic labour debate' were prone to falling back into conceptualising patriarchy and capitalism as two semi-autonomous systems, even as they tried to offer a unifying theory. This was largely due to the difficulty of developing an account which would imbricate the logic of capitalist exploitation of labour-power and class division with the logics of socially effective subordination through gender. To be able to grasp the process of the devaluation of certain forms of labour, the significance of reproduction needed to be thought from a more totalising viewpoint, situating it within its relation to capital accumulation – as well as the 'social reproduction' of gender as such.

Social Reproduction Theory Today: Intersectional or Ontological?

Contemporary social reproduction theory draws upon aspects of the work of Lise Vogel and Silvia Federici and attempts to develop an account that takes on board the criticisms of second-wave feminism, while remaining committed to developing a unitary theory. While Marxist feminism has been critical of dominant formulations of 'intersectionality' for their lack of materialist rigor, contemporary social reproduction theory aims to produce a more materialist intersectionality. This is one that would not only anchor gender, but also racialisation, and other categories of subordination, within a thinking of 'totality', and generate a form of politics that would take the imbrication of all these into account, albeit not as independent variables or the contingent outcomes of multiple interacting systems of oppression.[13]

Yet social reproduction theory itself faces obstacles in theorising social relations through the abstract but totalising matrix of the capitalist social form. While composed of relatively diverse voices, a general tendency within social reproduction theory is to posit the stratification, division, and 'multiplication' of labour – what Sue Ferguson calls the 'integrative ontology of labour' – as the keystone of this totality:[14]

> At the heart of social-reproduction feminism is the conception of labour as broadly productive – creative not just of economic values, but of society (and thus of life) itself . . . This is not 'labour' as it has been understood in mainstream economics and vulgar Marxism. Rather, it is the 'practical human activity' that creates all the things, practices, people, relations and ideas constituting the wider social totality–that which Marx and Engels identify as 'the first premise of all human history'. (p. 14)

For Ferguson, social reproduction theory also aims to link this totality to experience, through an analysis of embodied subjects in a 'socio-geographical spatialisation'.[15] Within such an expanded framework, it is thought that a more global picture of the diverse concrete positions of – especially, but not only – women might be theorised.

The concept of an 'integrative ontology of labour' would seem to answer the call for a 'unitary theory' made by earlier thinkers such as Vogel, and reiterated by Cinzia Arruzza and others, one that would overcome the dualisms of previous Marxist-feminist programmes.[16] But in so doing, it runs the risk of erasing important distinctions and lines of causality, subsuming all kinds of activities, forces, and dynamics to the category of 'labour'.[17] Crucially, the 'workerist' basis of social reproduction theory does not tend to draw an analytic distinction between activities that might merely appear reproductive in their concrete characteristics and those that are socially validated by the wage. As a result, it risks assuming an affirmative stance towards the labour associated with reproduction, valorising it politically *because* it is devalued.[18] This is often cast in feminised terms of 'nurturing' and 'survival' which occlude effective social divisions.[19] The recent currency of discourses of 'care', as they devolve to the often consumerist focus of 'self-care', is a case in point, putting a radical gloss on discredited liberal feminist idioms of empowerment. Social reproduction theory's focus on an often undifferentiated notion of 'labour' thus becomes problematic insofar as it can reinscribe gender and labour as positive values to be affirmed within a fundamentally violent and destructive system of the *reproduction* of capital. At the same time, its indeterminate concept of reproduction has proven effective at expanding both the field of social struggle and the solidarities that can be practised within it.

In light of these considerations, more work needs to be done to attend to the theoretical and political consequences of those formulations of social reproduction that bracket questions around global value chains, finance, and politics in order to frame the *labour* of reproduction as their key term.[20] A consequence of this tendency in the social reproduction framework is that it often cannot escape its need to reinscribe the split between the productive and reproductive for analytical purposes, often leading indirectly to the political and ethical valorisation of the latter over the former, or directly translating the latter into the former.[21] This acts to obscure the messy unity that exists between them today, resulting from the privatisation, commodification, and financialisation of social reproduction. While the privatisation (as in the confinement of 'housework' to individual domestic units) and commodification (in the form of the waged labour of outsiders to those units, that is, 'the help') of social reproduction are relatively ubiquitous in human societies and pre-date capitalism, it is financialisation which perhaps is more historically distinct and linked to the social divestment and financial extraction strategies driving today's political economics.

Other Approaches to the Reproduction of the Social

Neither gender nor race can be adequately explained as ranks in the labour market.[22] Instead, we need to look at how gender and race differentially pose an 'outside' to the reproduction of capitalist class relations that enable them to function. This implies that value is not only an 'economic' term, but also – if we take up Marxian concepts of value analysis – a primarily social form that pervades all kinds of relations in a capitalist society, as the lived reality of the abstractions such as money, competition, and private property. It operates not only by perpetuating hierarchies in the workplace, but also by propping up these hierarchies – often brutally – in access to resources and infrastructure that affect life chances on every level.[23]

This 'outside' is taken up by the Endnotes collective, who present a totalising account of the persistence of gender and gendered labour in capital which does not produce an ontology of labour.[24] Contra the association of gender with certain kinds of unwaged, reproductive tasks, they use a value-form approach to concretise the definition of gender in a way that can account for the shifting relation of different tasks to the process of capitalist accumulation over time. Defining gender as 'the anchoring of a certain group of individuals in a specific *sphere of social activities*' allows them to distinguish between activities that appear reproductive in their concrete characteristics and those that are socially validated by the wage, a distinction that is itself the product of a specific historical and form-determined gendered configuration. This avoids the reduction of gender to an overly simple association with specific tasks, locations (the home), or bodies (feminised). As the collective convincingly argues, these reductions do not explain why and how gender is produced and reproduced, and how this occurs over time, through geographical space, and through differential positionings within the same location. Rather, their theory holds the tension between the interior and exterior via the category of the abject. It argues that gender *appears and is felt as* an external constraint precisely at the point at which capital expels some tasks that had become interiorised to its 'exterior', and drags us along with it in that abjection. As an example, most carework, unwaged and waged, physical and emotional, still devolves upon feminised subjects even after the pre-destination of 'women' for this kind of work has been ideologically discredited, and formal equality has been legislated in many places. To this extent, the authors locate the feminist fight in a rejection of those processes of (our) exteriorisation.[25]

Likewise, we could also look to some of the more materialist and feminist exegeses of Foucauldian biopolitics. Biopolitical accounts developed in parallel to the social reproduction framework and sought to analyse the 'reproduction of the relations of production' from a totalising standpoint, one that could take into account the production of gendered and racialised divisions of social labour and relations of power.[26] Reading social reproduction through biopolitics problematises the terrain of social reproduction as a plenum of activities and tasks positively coded as reproducing life tendentially *in itself*, and only contingently within and for the capital relation. In the paradigm of biopolitics, life, and notions of 'life', cannot be separated from the mode of production and the subjects, docile and/or entrepreneurial, suitable to it. It also implies a de-normalisation of the gendered dimension of social reproduction, as gender and sexuality, like the wage relation, are seen to be part and parcel of the system of production.

In light of these perspectives, we would suggest that it is crucial not to collapse social reproduction and the reproduction of capital into an ontology of labour, and that the analysis of the abstractions of value as well as the concrete situatedness of historical social formations are key in order not to end up with an affirmative account of gendered labour. In this regard, the reproduction of gender itself has to be put into question. If we are to put this gendering itself at stake, it is essential that we also address the question of why the family form has so persistently served as its basis, not merely as a historical holdover from prior social formations, but also through a capitalist epoch that constantly seems to threaten that form, and which we are told is essentially gender-blind. While this is not the place to develop such claims, we might venture a hypothesis: that the enduring centrality of gendering logics within capitalist accumulation may be inscribed in the capitalist form of value itself. Such a grounding for the reproduction of gender as such might provide some basis for overcoming the terms of the opposition between them. As Francesca Manning writes:

> If we are truly committed to a rigorous and unifying theory of capital, we must *consider the possibility* that race and gender are as logically necessary as class is to this mode of production. We must follow this hypothesis as far as it takes us. There has not yet been any good reason established as to why we should turn back from it.[27]

Some Concluding Reflections

The centring of the category of labour, and its indefinite expansion, is a major source of indeterminacy in the social reproduction perspective. Conversely, defining reproduction too narrowly, in terms of a set of gendered tasks, runs the risk of naturalising a historically and geographically specific division of social labour. The separation of reproductive labour as a political matrix from its position in the reproduction of capital is a common *telos* of the way political implications are drawn from social reproduction theory, one which can generate unwelcome effects, such as the moralisation of care, particularly in times of social crisis, and the inadvertent confirmation of existing gender roles. Some examples of this can be found in voices that enunciate the feminist stakes of the 'reproductive commons', whose proposal to resolve the current crises of reproduction is the self-management of reproduction, staking all on the transvaluation of subsistence into practices of autonomy.[28]

Approaches taking issue with this particular type of focus on reproductive labour have started to emerge, engaging the abiding issue of indeterminacy of the category in a variety of ways. Some of these deal with the concept of social reproduction as a status mediated by legal forms and stratifications of personhood in Western capitalist modernity. Others focus on the implicit normativity of social reproduction's focus on the family as a site of the production of use values that can be turned into the material bedrock of revolutionary subjectivity. Others still reassess the social formation of 'the family' from a queer Marxist and transfeminist standpoint and open up the notion of 'social reproduction' in light of the cultural and biopolitical specificities of transfem existence under austerity conditions.[29]

To better understand the reproduction of gender in capitalism, it is important to avoid reinscribing the dichotomy between reproduction and production, and to insist upon situating them in a continuum, while analysing how it is that gendered, racialised and sexualised forms of exploitation and domination are the infrastructure of that continuum, logically and materially.[30] The hard question remains why it is that various forms of devalued labour continue to be naturalised onto certain kinds of bodies, despite the major fragmentations and shifts in the social structure presented by global migration, the (re-)commodification of domestic labour, and the increasing porousness of gender.

Notes

1 Social reproduction theory draws upon a range of work, including L. Vogel, *Marxism and the Oppression of Women: Toward a Unitary Theory* (Leiden: Brill, 2013 [1983]); S. Federici, *Revolution at Point Zero: Housework, Reproduction, and Feminist Struggle* (Oakland: PM Press, 2012). Recent literature includes T. Bhattacharya (ed.), *Social Reproduction Theory: Remapping Class, Recentering Oppression* (London: Pluto Press, 2017); M. E. Gimenez, *Marx, Women, and Capitalist Social Reproduction: Marxist Feminist Essays* (Leiden: Brill, 2018). In November 2015 *Viewpoint* magazine published a special issue on social reproduction, available at viewpointmag.com.

2 Katsarova notes that within the history of feminist theory, these distinct registers often overlap, producing a range of meanings of social reproduction, often left unarticulated. See R. Katsarova, 'Repression and Resistance on the Terrain of Social Reproduction: Historical Trajectories, Contemporary Openings', *Viewpoint*, 5 (31 October 2015), viewpointmag.com.

3 K. Marx, *Capital: A Critique of Political Economy*, Vol. I, trans. B. Fowkes (Harmondsworth: Penguin Books, 1976), 711.

4 M. Dalla Costa and S. James, *The Power of Women and the Subversion of the Community* (Bristol: Falling Wall Press, 1972); L. Fortunati, *The Arcane of Reproduction: Housework, Prostitution, Labor and Capital*, trans. H. Creek (New York: Autonomedia, 1995) (originally published in Italian as *L'Arcano della Reproduzione: Casalinghe, Prostitute, Operai e Capitale*, Marsilio Editori, Venezia, 1981); Federici, *Revolution at Point Zero*; Vogel, *Marxism and the Oppression of Women*.

5 This was a key argument of the Wages for Housework campaign. See Federici, *Revolution at Point Zero*; L. Toupin, *Wages for Housework: A History of an International Feminist Movement, 1972–77*, trans. K. Roth (London and Vancouver: Pluto Press and the University of British Columbia Press, 2018).

6 An exception was Shulamith Firestone's proposal for the detachment of reproduction from the body. See S. Firestone, *The Dialectic of Sex: The Case for Feminist Revolution* (London: Verso Books, 2015 [1970]).

7 Endnotes Collective, 'The Logic of Gender', *Endnotes 3: Gender, Race, Class and Other Misfortunes* (2013), 56–91.

8 J. Brenner and B. Laslett, 'Gender, Social Reproduction and Women's Self-Organization: Considering the US Welfare State', *Gender & Society*, 5:3 (1991), 314.

9 For 'hidden abode of reproduction' see K. Weeks, *The Problem With Work: Feminism, Marxism, Antiwork Politics, and Postwork Imaginaries* (Durham, NC and London: Duke University Press, 2011), 24–5. For 'workers' instinct', see Marx, *Capital*, 718.

10 This capacity for slippage is encouraged within theories that assume some idea of the 'total subsumption' of life under capital. If the global triumph of capital over its previous antagonists in the last few decades has generalised capital's domination to all spheres of social life, it confronts us as the sole basis of our very reproduction, making the link of social reproduction to the totality somewhat tautological.

11 While 'life' may be oversaturated by the wage relation, it cannot be completely subsumed by it.

12 Although Marx was discussing the living standards of the waged worker, the symptomatic extension of this question to the 'sphere' of reproduction – how living standards were maintained, and by whom – defined the mapping of the gendered division of labour in Marxist feminism during the latter half of the twentieth century.

13 For many Marxist-feminists, 'intersectionality' wrongly conceives of gender, race, and sexuality as coherent and autonomous – yet somehow comparable – locations of identity, which coincide contingently. For Sue Ferguson, while it describes how specified social locations shape experience and identity, it cannot explain how they interact as part of a dynamic set of social relations in which processes, ideas, and institutions reproduce and challenge these identities. See S. Ferguson, 'Canadian Contributions to Social Reproduction Feminism, Race and Embodied Labour', *Race, Gender & Class*, 15:1–2 (2008), 42–57.

14 S. Ferguson, 'Intersectionality and Social-Reproduction Feminisms: Towards an Integrative Ontology', *Historical Materialism*, 24:2 (2016), 38–60. For 'multiplication of labour', see B. Neilson and S. Mezzadra, *Border as Method, or, the Multiplication of Labor* (Durham, NC and London: Duke University Press, 2013).

15 Ferguson draws on David Harvey's elaboration of this concept. See 'Canadian Contributions', 51–4.

16 C. Arruzza, 'Remarks on Gender', *Viewpoint* (2 September 2014), viewpoint mag.com. See also C. Arruzza, 'Functionalist, Determinist, Reductionist: Social Reproduction Feminism and its Critics', *Science & Society*, 80 (2016), 9–30.

17 Recent work in the social reproduction debate deals with this issue by theorising these activities as 'reproductive' in the historically determinate framework of capitalist societies in specific eras and places. Yet the indeterminacy in social reproduction theory is only secondarily one of taking a 'trans-historical' view of reproductive tasks. Rather, it is often vague about how reproduction is to be distinguished from production, and produces a tautological relation between the devalued labour of feminised (and, at times, racialised) bodies and subjects and the designation of this labour as 'reproductive'.

18 The abstract character of an analysis that imputes resistant subjectivity to the most disregarded and oppressed social subjects can, we suggest, be linked to the abstraction of an analysis that recuperates the political significance of various kinds of activities under the rubric of labour. These moves share a reluctance to engage the historical and political or ideological mediations that enter into the composition of social forms.

19 This observation is intended not as a homogenising criticism of all social reproduction theory, but as a specific criticism of a tendency in the 'applied' uses of social reproduction in organising milieus, wherein a vitalist continuum is often established between the human necessity and the recognition of devalued labours and activities, and the bodies or communities that perform them. For a counterpoint, see J. Gibson, 'Fire This Time: Notes on the Crisis of Reproduction', *LIES: A Journal of Materialist Feminism*, 2 (2015), 143–55.

20 Bhattacharya's edited collection *Social Reproduction Theory* does not fore-ground discussions of global value chains or situate social reproduction within systemic patterns of global accumulation, extraction, and expulsion, unlike older work, for example, by Federici. While Nancy Fraser, Emma Dowling, Salar Mohandesi, and Emma Teitelman discuss the financialisation of social reproduction, most contemporary social reproduction theorists, following Vogel, stick to the labour involved in the reproduction of labour-power.

21 This has been likened to the tendency of orthodox Marxism to focus on the autonomy of use value vis-à-vis exchange value, rather than seeing use value as one side of the total form of value in capitalist society, a move that risks naturalising gendered forms of social labour. See M. Gonzalez, 'Two Debates, One Solution: Rethinking the Essential Categories of Social Reproduction

Theory', presentation at the 15th Annual Historical Materialism conference, London (11 November 2018).

22 See C. Chen, 'The Limit Point of Capitalist Equality', *Endnotes*, 3 (2013), 202–23.

23 See R. Scholz's work on 'value dissociation' and the need for an 'outside to value' in capitalist modernity and its ontologies of gender, race, and humanity in 'Patriarchy and Commodity Society: Gender without the Body', in N. Larsen, M. Nilges, J. Robinson, and N. Brown (eds.), *Marxism and the Critique of Value* (Chicago and Alberta: M-C-M, 2014), 223–42.

24 See *Endnotes*, 3 (2013).

25 Conversely, it could be suggested that the psychoanalytic category of the 'abject' is too ambiguous.

26 See M. Foucault, *The History of Sexuality, Volume One: The Will to Knowledge*, trans. R. Hurley (London: Penguin, 2008) and *The Birth of Biopolitics: Lectures at the College de France, 1978–1979*, trans. G. Burchell, (Basingstoke: Palgrave Macmillan, 2008). For an attempt to bridge Marx, Althusser, and Foucault, see F. Guery and D. Deleule, *The Productive Body* [1972], trans. P. Barnard and S. Shapiro (Winchester: Zero Books, 2014). See also P. Macherey, 'The Productive Subject', *Viewpoint* (31 October 2015), viewpointmag.com. For a combination of Foucauldian analysis with feminist and black studies approaches, see S. Hartman, *Wayward Lives, Beautiful Experiments: Intimate Histories of Social Upheaval* (Durham, NC and London: Duke University Press, 2019) and *Scenes of Subjection: Terror, Slavery and Self-making in Nineteenth-Century America* (New York: Oxford University Press, 1997).

27 F. Manning, 'Closing the Conceptual Gap: A Response to Cinzia Arruza's "Remarks on Gender"', *Viewpoint* (4 May 2015), viewpointmag.com.

28 S. Federici, 'Feminism and the Politics of the Commons', *The Commoner* (2011), www.commoner.org.uk.

29 Gonzalez, 'Two Debates'. See also: A. Mitropoulos, *Contract and Contagion: From Biopolitics to Oikonomia* (Wivenhoe, New York, Port Watson: Minor Compositions, 2012); M. Cooper, *Family Values: Between Neoliberalism and the New Social Conservatism* (New York: Zone Books, 2018); N. Raha, 'Queering Marxist [Trans]Feminism: Queer and Trans Social Reproduction', paper delivered at Marxism in Culture seminar, Institute of Historical Research, London (28 April 2017).

30 However, we suggest that the indeterminacy we have outlined as an ongoing problematic for social reproduction theory can be addressed with closer attention to the legal, financial and political determinations that shape the conditions of social reproduction. Gimenez queries the use of 'social reproduction' in Marxist feminist theory and suggests we should instead be talking about 'capitalist social reproduction', which makes it a historically delimited category rather than an indeterminate one. See Gimenez, *Marx, Women, and Capitalist Social Reproduction*, 278–308.

III

Forms

Feminist Dwellings: Imagining the Domestic in the Twenty-first-century Literary Novel

Karen Schaller

On 27 October 2016, Pussy Riot released 'Make America Great Again', a video that asked an America then heading to the polls, 'What do you want your world to look like? / What do you want it to be? / Do you know that a wall has two sides? / And nobody is free?'¹ Partway through, the lyric shifts address, from a national 'you' to a specifically feminised body. Pussy Riot ask: 'Do you want to stay in the kitchen? / Is that where you belong?'² Here, the coherence of a national body at the level of geopolitical borders is, also, indivisible from the zoning of labour, marginalisation, and retreat embodied in the threat of a return to the domestic.

What kind of scene does the domestic offer twenty-first-century feminism? And how can the literary novel, whose history is imbricated with the classed, raced, and gendered politics of the domestic, help us to read and think its possibilities for a feminist imaginary now? Pussy Riot invoke the domestic as the threat of a regressive future. This tells us something about the temporality of the domestic as a site for questions about where feminists find ourselves now: if feminist orientations to the domestic ask us where we are going, such questions are also asked from the perspectives of where we are from, and where we imagine we are. Charged as much with the diversity of our attachments as it is the range of our disaffections, asking 'Is this where you belong?' yokes a supposed consensus about the limits of the domestic to a narrative about feminism as transformation, capable of arriving at a place and time defined against, indeed articulated as beyond, the domestic we are past. It is a threat that brings home our investments in and orientations to the material possibilities of a feminism capable of deciding how, where, or with whom you make your home and do your homemaking. As a threat it works on an implied agreement that we can distinguish this home-work from the constraints of a domestic that is behind us, out-of-place in the twenty-first century.

In this chapter I consider three novels spanning our century so far: Zadie Smith's 2005 *On Beauty*, Deborah Levy's 2011 *Swimming Home*, and Miranda July's 2015 *The First Bad Man*.[3] Each is given shape by and develops textual strategies arising from questions about the domestic. Critical responses to the home frequently imagined by nineteenth- and twentieth-century feminist writing might suggest that the domestic is too compromised for a twenty-first-century feminist imaginary. As other chapters in this volume show, we are increasingly alert to the politics of the domestic, not only in how it intersects with economies of gender, race, and class, but also in how resistant it has been to feminist intervention or transformational politics. Our everyday vocabularies are now inflected by concepts of affective labour, the mental load, and institutional or academic housekeeping, which identify gendered, raced, and classed distributions of devalued labour that underwrites our economies and name how concepts of care mask that labour and naturalise these ascriptions. These terms also point to how bodies are tracked as domestic outside the homeplace, enabling us to politicise the fatigues of domestic labour in the workplace as well as the home. These economies engage a range of precarities and privileges that are not always reducible to the identity of a body historically zoned for the domestic. But bodies *are* worn differently depending on their historic, as well as contemporary, proximity to it. Despite the inventiveness with which we might represent and perform our subjectivities, economies of the domestic can verge on the totalising in their persistent essentialism.

But we have also seen a proliferation of work interested, and perhaps even invested, in the domestic's generative potential for feminism. As well as writers such as Maggie Nelson and Rachel Cusk or, more recently, Carolyn Jess-Cooke's collection on motherhood and creativity, we can also think about critical engagements with the language of the domestic to articulate feminist practice, such as Sara Ahmed's use of metaphors of 'home' – of bricks, of houses, and of dwellings – in *Living a Feminist Life* (2017). I am curious about these (re)turns, which suggest that even if the domestic resists feminist transformation, it also continues to supply feminism with a capacity for, or promise of, resistance. Indeed, this is also a crucial part of the twenty-first-century critical inheritance for feminist thinking. As Nancy Kang and Silvio Torres-Saillant observe, the 'habit' of thinking about the domestic as 'inherently oppressive … correlates with a typical reading that concentrates on the travails of white middle-class women'.[4] It is a critique perhaps most notably articulated by bell hooks in her 1990 essay 'Homeplace (a site of resistance)', in which she discusses the radical potential of black homemaking – how giving care has and can constitute resistance to racist domination – and the erasures of that radical work by models of the domestic that see it as a site from which women need to be freed.[5] Kang and Torres-Saillant observe that women who turn to the home are still frequently judged as wasting their talent, intellect, or ambition, and their decisions perceived as 'capitulation to patriarchal expectations of the past, and as a source of future regret' (p. 133). Similarly, Andrea O'Reilly argues that such habits of opposition risk 'an ambivalent relationship' between feminism and motherhood, in which homemaking and mothering is irrecuperable from heteronormativity.[6] For Kang and Torres-Saillant, the key question is 'whether a woman can embrace the domestic space while remaining able to discern, achieve and pursue other options as well' (p. 136). But the novels I discuss remind us that it is not only about the extent to which we can move within, through or around the domestic: as Sara Ahmed's work on orientation observes, the domestic we feel at home *in* tells us about what we are at home *with*.[7] The ideological density of the domestic textures its scenes with those we come from – not only our own, but also those we inherit from our cultural, critical, and feminist imaginaries.

Smith's *On Beauty* explicitly addresses these inheritances. It is remarkably preoccupied with houses, the stories they tell and the fictions they construct, and the women whose work makes these houses a home. Rendered with an indivisibility between the domestic scene and its ideological contours, Kiki and Howard's house is explicitly articulated as a means of social mobility whose capital is both currency (rental income pays Kiki's nursing tuition) and cultural (tenants value its heritage). Its homely affects are overtly gendered (its expansive cosiness and warmth are contrasted with the cold cramped interior of Howard's father's terraced house in England). And it provides the language for Kiki and Howard's intimacy in the 'mansion of their marriage' (p. 15) – just before she moves out, they have sex: the language of his coming is 'Home!' (p. 396).

Yet critical responses demonstrate how comfortably twenty-first-century literary scholarship can still position the domestic, as both a literary form and a literary scene, in a binary fashion: one critic calls *On Beauty* a campus novel combining 'a deeply emotional domestic drama with the public performances of the so-called culture wars'.[8] Interest in the domestic tends to concentrate on Monique, the Haitian cleaning woman who makes Kiki 'nervous of what this black woman thought of another black woman paying her to clean' (p. 11). But there is nothing implicit about Kiki's feelings, which read almost like a quotation from hooks's essay. The citational quality of the novel's representation of the domestic produces an attention to the house as a literary institution that explicitly addresses the debates it inherits from twentieth-century feminism.

This allows us to think differently about the novel's 'homage' to E. M. Forster's *Howards End* (1910). Kiki and Carlene's relationship has been read as a 'bond' over art, in which the Haitian painting Carlene bequeaths Kiki enables a thinking of the social.[9] But the painting is Smith's version of the house in *Howards End*, and just as Howards End puts Margaret Schlegel into uncomfortable proximity with Mrs Wilcox's domesticity, Kiki is unsettled by coming into contact with Carlene's. This contact makes Kiki feel 'the same sorrow she had felt when a hitherto perfectly nice cabbie began to tell her that all the Jews in the first tower had been warned beforehand' (p. 95). Yet Kiki finds Carlene's orientation to her own domesticity compelling because it cannot be written off as mere ignorance. When Carlene declares 'I don't ask myself *what* did I live for ... That is a man's question. I ask *whom* did I live for', Kiki opposes: 'I don't believe you believe that .... I *know* I didn't live for anybody and it just seems to me it's like taking us all, all women, certainly all *black* women, three hundred years backwards if you really – ' (p. 176). Carlene interrupts: 'I lived for love ... I can't make a case for my life, but it *is* true' (p. 176). In refusing to justify her life to a greater authority, to argue *for* her life, Carlene resists the demand that the domestic be accounted for: it is only possible to ask her to explain her life if we believe it has no value.

Carlene's appraisal re-orients Kiki: she sees that her own life has and is a domestic scene, and not the scene she imagined. Her way of loving, despite the choices she thinks she has made, may not be so different from Carlene's. Not because of her own values, but because of how these are received. Howard believes his infidelity 'broke that splendid circle of Kiki's love, within which he had existed for so long, a love (and it was to Howard's credit that he knew this) that had enabled everything else' (p. 109). All he sees is the life she enabled for him. But for Kiki this is a betrayal of her own life's work: 'I staked my *life* on you. I staked my *life*' (p. 207). Kiki realises that because her labour of love has not been recognised as a politicised choice, the value of her politicisation has been erased. Kang and Torres-Saillant call for a 'complementary domesticity' – a paradigm of empowerment that 'reiterates the need for women's self-definitions of the homespace and affirms [her] right to determine how, when, and where she will enter or exit the doors and borders that constitute it' (p. 134). While Kiki moves across the thresholds of her domestic scene, she also returns to it. It is unclear whether this return is a sign of her complementary domesticity, or a diminishment of her volition. But what we can see is that even owning her home does not guarantee her empowerment: Kiki's agency in the domestic is still coupled to her husband's value for it.

By making the house of *Howards End* an artwork, *On Beauty* articulates the proximity between domestic scenes a hundred years apart. But making a house an artwork also speaks forward to the question of whether feminism's critical orientation to the domestic can be a creative one. If a house can become an artwork, can housekeeping be art? Late in *On Beauty*, Kiki takes stock of her life through the 'scattered possessions' her children have left behind: 'She had not become Malcolm X's private secretary. She never did direct a movie or run for the Senate. She could not fly a plane. But here was all this' (p. 424). What is the difference between what Kiki has made, and art? The novel ends with a close up of Howard's picture of Rembrandt's 'Hendrickje Bathing' (a very different kind of painting to Carlene and Kiki's). Instead of speaking Howard looks at the detail of the painting, its 'intimation of what is to come' (p. 442). Is this a promise of reparation? Or is it a scene of return based on the value of one domestic body for the other – Hendrickje's for the painter, Kiki's for Howard – and the subjecthood he wishes to invent for himself? Through Carlene's painting Kiki encountered the question of whether a homemaker is, themselves, enabled to confer value to their own making. Perhaps the most telling thing about the ending is that Kiki does not answer; instead she smiles and looks away, while Howard gazes at this representation of a domestic scene.

In 1990, Patricia Yaeger called for feminist analyses of the domestic to 'move beyond fragmenting analyses of class and gender that insist on legitimating one form of oppression over another. We need to construct multiple models of "power" that recognise the overdetermination of class, gender and race oppressions'.[10] *On Beauty* works over this call. If Kiki cannot ascribe value to her work, then she is subject to the confines of a middle-class feminism that views the domestic scene as irreparably oppressive. Yet we cannot be too quick to name her homemaking the kind of resistance imagined by hooks. Kiki imagines 'making another speech to the Black American Mother's Guild: *Well, you just have to offer them encouragement and the correct role models, and you have to pass on the idea of entitlement. Both my sons feel entitled, and that's why they achieve*' (p. 424). Her daughter's absence from this fantasy is startling, especially given how frequently Zora is framed as *too* entitled. If Kiki has gifted entitlement to her children, this gift does not offer equal purchase on the institutions they navigate, the homes they can make for themselves in the world. Zora uses all her advantages to secure a place for herself in academia, but although she works hard, and is able to quote all the important works, she is not at home in the academy. It is a different version of women's work: Zora's academic potential is reduced to the accumulations of foot-notes that do not add up to authority nor to creative or intellectual originality, and her home in the university is limited to a kind of tenancy. The resistances domesticity might furnish are utterly contingent on how its bodies can wear it. Like Kiki's relationship to her ownership of house and home, tenancy is neither powerless, nor transformative: it is a kind of dwelling in and with the compromised politics of the domestic. Tenancy is there, from the beginning: 'homage' is the tribute a tenant vassal makes to their lord. As an homage to *Howards End*, *On Beauty* engages the house as a literary institution where our imaginings of domestic empowerment and agency are already imbricated with the ideologies that furnish its scenes.

Deborah Levy's *Swimming Home* (2011) is equally at home with the critical inheritances that write the domestic. And *Swimming Home* also recognises that the homes we make are not our own: as Alison Blunt and Ann Varley observe, the home is 'a space of belonging and alienation, intimacy and violence, desire and fear'.[11] Ambi-valenced, the domestic does not present us with a problem of how it can hold such oppositional relations, but rather the need to recognise that the domestic works through the indivisibility of these feelings. The domestic is unhomely: its sphere of care or protection is the threat of violence, and its feelings of security require precarity. But what Blunt and Varley also evoke is the extent to which we do not want to see our domestic scenes in this way: when we are at home we do not want to see what we are, also, at home with.

What do we know about the domestic? What do we not want to know? And what do we wish we could un-know? Feminist knowledge about the domestic is one way of thinking about how the novel's setting orients us to the domestic: rather than attempt to transform or rehabilitate the domes-tic, *Swimming Home* is not set in a family home but in a rented tourist villa in the Alpes-Maritimes, where the Jacobs (Joe, a poet, Isabel, a war-reporter, and their daughter Nina) share their holiday with family friends Mitchell and Laura and the mysterious interloper Kitty Finch. Un-homing the domestic does not resolve its ambivalences, however: it accentuates these. Indeed, the use of 'villa' rather than 'home' immediately points us to how the novel's architexture disturbs a distinction between the flows of power and kinds of subjectivity described by residency and property ownership in the antiquated past and those imagined to be (or not to be) inhabited in the present. We are, in the first few pages, asked to see each body here intimate with shifting iterations of globalisation, and entangled with expressions of the colonialisms we think we are 'post'. We can see this in Joe's shirt, for example, which is not merely a raw silk but 'the shirt his Hindu tailor had made for him from a roll of raw silk' (p. 5). It is even more urgent in the explicit casualness of Laura and Mitchell's droll response to Kitty's interrogations about their shop:

> 'So what do you and Mitchell sell at your "Cash and Carry"?'
> '"Emporium"', Laura corrected her. 'We sell primitive Persian, Turkish and Hindu weapons. And expensive African jewellery.'
> 'We are small-time arms dealers', Mitchell said effusively. 'And in between we sell furniture made from ostriches.' (pp. 37–8)

Here the colonial affects of acquisition and appropriation are translated into the 'global' or 'tribal' aesthetic marketed for the decorative self-fashioning of the homes and bodies of the British middle-classes. The flows of exploitation and appropriation at work in this aesthetic are uncomfortable reminders of the histories of colonialism at work in the global traveller/tourist economy, and while Laura's correction ('Emporium') pointedly ignores the classed charge of Kitty's remark, it belies the architexture of empire underwriting such domestic aesthetics. In case we miss the point, Mitchell's 'effusion' gets off on that association, putting the consumer of 'exotica' in gross contact with civil war.

Swimming Home surfaces these contacts but also observes how easily they slide out of view. While we hear about the immigrant cleaners who work at the tourist villas and the strike they are organising, we also know that the tourists do not see this as their responsibility, because these are not 'their' homes. When Laura hears 'how the North African cleaner who mopped the floors for a pittance in the villa was apparently on strike' she is conscious of who the woman is (she 'wore a headscarf' and 'was more skilled with electrics' than the caretaker) but not conscious of why she should matter to her: 'This woman had been on her mind for some reason and just as she was wondering why she had been so preoccupied by her she remembered what Isabel had said [about] Laura opening a separate account from the one she shared with Mitchell' (p. 100). Such moments suggest a way of thinking about the politics of our domestic consciousness, of asking how willing we are to consider our own complicities and implications, that what or whom we care for also implies the bodies we do not care about: as

Maria Puig de la Bellacasa writes, 'our cares also perform disconnection. We cannot possibly care for everything, not everything can count in a world, not everything is relevant in a world – there is no life without some kind of death.'[12] Moments such as Laura's are not unconscious: the novel spends time showing us how Laura's thoughts move between cares until they cohere around what matters to her most. Her carelessness enacts the geopolitics of the domestic.

Swimming Home is a novel that trains our attention on how easily things can slip out of view, and of how costly our cares, and carelessness, can be. Yet among the many things we might miss, the doubleness of our desires for the domestic might be the most dangerous. Late in the novel Nina looks for Kitty's poem under her father's bed: 'There was something else under the bed too but she did not have time to find out what it was' (p. 117). What she finds but does not want to know she found is the gun her father will later use to kill himself. The 'thing' is not only a gun but the historical effects of not being able to go home, of being un-homed: although hinted at throughout the novel, after his death we find out that while he was smuggled into Britain in 1942, his family were deported to Chelmno death camp (p. 153) and that 'the thing, the threat was lurking there in all his words' (p. 152). The domestic here is multivalenced. Jozef's loss of home is unequivocal, but it does not mean he does not also exploit the domestic he has in his own ways – his infidelity in the home his wife supports, his daughter Nina's too-early induction into the role of mother/wife, or the way he tries to use Kitty sexually and emotionally. In the holiday villa, the home away from home, we encounter the contiguities between these domestic violences and the carelessness towards the cleaners. But will we care? James Duncan and David Lambert observe that the concept of home is 'inextricable from that of self, family, nation, sense of place, and sense of responsibility towards those who share one's place in the world'.[13] It is important, then, that Jozef's story contextualises our desire to habilitate the domestic within the historical traumas effected by the domestic policies and practices of Nazi lebensraum, or 'living room'. In doing so the novel puts the history we know in disturbing contact with the histories we deny our homes are making.

In his essay following the novel, 'Tom McCarthy writes that while the setting and plot of Swimming Home are 'borrowed, almost ironically, from the staid English-middle-class-on-holiday novel, all similarities end there' (p. 160). It is not quite true: the novel also borrows the domestic politics of that literary form, the familiar pleasures of the domestic scenes of the reader who is on holiday from home. Un-homing the domestic surfaces the ambivalences that we are both familiar with, yet would rather pretend we did not know: it is a way of answering the desire for home with the geopolitics of its call. *Swimming Home* offers an imagining of the domestic that reminds us that these ambivalences are as much a part of its scene as its pleasures. No imagining – even imagining it elsewhere – can un-home them from the domestic scene.

If the politics of the domestic cannot be un-homed, can they be reimagined? In July's *The First Bad Man* Cheryl, a single woman in her early forties, develops an elaborate system that minimises the labour of looking after herself. She eats out of a pan to prevent washing plates, keeps her cutlery to one setting, and avoids moving household items so that they never need to be put away: 'Like a rich person I live with a full-time servant who keeps everything in order – and because the servant is me, there's no invasion of privacy. At its best, my system gives me a smoother living experience' (p. 22). Cheryl's system appears to facilitate a version of the domestic that resists its politics. But her reflections on her system are strangely depoliticised: the promise of an alertness to the politics of domestic labour is undermined by her sense that this is about 'privacy'. Her reasons for her system, however, help us to understand that the novel's orientation to the domestic is not un-critical, even if Cheryl herself seems to be. Even at its smallest unit, the domestic is still a site of precarity. Underwriting Cheryl's system is an anxiety about the potential for her body to fall out of the domestic scene and into homelessness:

> Let's say a person is down in the dumps ... Soon the dishes are piled ... So the person starts eating with dirty forks out of dirty dishes and this makes the person feel like a homeless person ... . So they stop bathing. Which makes it hard to leave the house ... The person begins to throw trash anywhere and pee in cups ... We've all been this person, so there is no place for judgment, but the solution is simple. (p. 21)

Cheryl's system is sustaining – it protects her from being unable to function within, or for, domesticity: her house, she remarks, 'was perfectly in order, as it always is, thanks to my system' (p. 20). Yet this protection is also a form of erasure: 'At its best', she tells us, 'it's as if I don't exist' (p. 22). Cheryl is not critically orientated to heteronormativity, rather she performs it within her single-home. Indeed, her pride in her system, her descriptions of how it works, and her cheery clipped advice ('Stop moving things around' (p. 21)) sound like domestic manuals rather than critique. She practises heteronormativity outside her home as well: she describes her boss calling her 'ginjo', which she 'thought meant "sister" until he told me it's

Japanese for a man, usually an elderly man, who lives in isolation while he keeps the fire burning for the whole village' (p. 19). Yet Cheryl does not protest or resist: 'I made myself very still so he would continue. I love to be described' (p. 20). Her agency here is not reducible to an active/passive binary, but can instead be read as a means by which she orients herself to heteronormativity with the hope for flourishing within it. She is, after all, acutely aware of her diminished, and diminishing, use-value. When prescribed a chromotherapy solution to take each morning before urinating, for example, she comments: 'If I had been in my early thirties instead of my early forties would he have said before first urination or sexual intercourse? That's the problem with men my age, I'm somehow older than them' (p. 4).

The First Bad Man attends to Cheryl's practice of heteronormativity, a practice expressed through the domestic labours she performs regardless of boundaries between work and home. Philip, a board member she is attracted to, wants her to guide him in his relationship with a younger woman. Her bosses send their daughter Clee to live with her. Clee destroys her system, begins a violent intimate relationship with Cheryl, and after she becomes pregnant leaves her baby with Cheryl. And, from the beginning, Cheryl is on the lookout for the baby she has always felt is hers. Despite the configurations of Cheryl's relationships, their potential queerness, what this narrative of becoming-through-caring materialises is the violence of heteronormativity. We can think here of Cheryl and Clee's intimacy (long before they have sex with each other), which takes the form of 'simulating' the women's self-defence videos Cheryl's company sells. These scenes enable intimate bodily contact: beating each other up vibrates with beating off. But they also enable Cheryl's domestic scene, every room and furnishing, to be saturated and smeared with the charge of sexual domination that they borrow from misogyny. The misogyny that underwrites the threat of sexual assault is redistributed from the parking lot, the driveway, the park, into the heteronormative textures of the domestic scene. Lest Cheryl be confused by their intimacy, Clee declares her orientation: '"I guess I'm 'misogynist' or whatever." [Cheryl had] never heard the word used like this, like an orientation' (p. 76). Later in the novel Cheryl talks to her therapist: '"it might not be a game, it might be real. She's a 'misogynist' or something. That's her thing." I described the wolfish intensity that came over [Clee] when she simulated' (p. 93). If orientation, as Ahmed argues, is a feeling of 'being at home', then recasting misogyny as orientation not only reminds us how at home we are with its structures in the domestic, but also unsettles the possibility for heteronormativity to imagine a version of itself, and of its domestic scene, not textured by the threat of violence that accompanies the labour, or service, of care. While reviewers might be right to describe Cheryl as transformed by love, that transformation takes the form of a coming more fully into heteronormativity, not a veering from it.[14]

Rather than transcend or transform heteronormativity, Cheryl's story finishes with her becoming mother/wife. It is a fabrication that she tells us institutes her erasure: 'I hoped to retain a tiny corner of the old me, just enough to warn other women with. But I knew this was unlikely; when the process was complete I wouldn't have anything left to complain with, it wouldn't hurt anymore, I wouldn't remember' (p. 220). Rather than discover a new way of being, Cheryl's becoming is, unexceptionally, heteronormativity's cruel promise of a happy ending for its domestic labours. *The First Bad Man* does not depart from heteronormativity, nor does it present a feminist imagining of domesticity that can transcend or transform its economy. Instead the novel reimagines heteronormativity, that is, imagines it for us all over again, such that its care/threat, its erotics of violence, are materialised.

The novel closes on another simulation as Cheryl and her son run towards each other, fifteen years into her future: 'He ran toward her and she ran toward him … They were laughing and laughing and running and running and running and music played, brass instruments, a soaring anthem, not a dry eye in the house, the credits rolled. Applause like rain' (p. 276). Cheryl has come into being. But she is no longer in this scene. She has become merely a 'she', the image of a mother, the figure of a woman coming. And what an image it is – supposedly redeeming in its singularity, it is utterly like every moment in which a novel or film has narrated the value of domesticity in terms of the lives brought into being, consolations commensurate with the women's lives that have been erased. Imagination has not controverted narrative destination. But that does not mean it is compliant. The literary novel here is not tasked with the improbability of imagining a transformation of the domestic; instead it works through its capacity to simulate it. Clee's declaration that 'I'm misogynist' reads like a misquote, but it is a pretty good citation of heteronormative domesticity.

Quotation is, perhaps, worth dwelling on. Each of these novels has employed forms of citation that hold open the proximity between their domestic scenes, and those we might think we have left behind. That holding open is important – it finds room for these texts to feel for us the politics of those scenes, the tensions and contradictions, without resolving into an erase/sustain binary. In doing so, each of these novels dwells on and with the domestic in ways that work over its politics without recourse to a conversion narrative of transformation, or the domestic as a scene where we can arrive. Sara Ahmed writes that citation 'can be feminist bricks: they are the materials through which, from which, we create our dwellings'.[15] The novel in the twenty-first century is still making sense of how it inherits, and inhabits, the domestic. In the novels I have discussed, citing that domestic offers a form of dwelling that is not resolvable into departure or reinstitution. Dwelling can feel like a failure to move on, or disappoint with its sense of retreat. But it can also be a form of remaining that is neither permanent nor simply letting be – to 'dwell' is also to practise a form of fixed attention, a kind of careful orientation in which, for the time being, we can inhabit the domestic without letting its politics slide out of view.

Notes

1 Pussy Riot, 'Make America Great Again' (26 October 2017), youtube.com.
2 Ibid
3 Z. Smith, *On Beauty* (London: Hamish Hamilton, 2005); D. Levy, *Swimming Home* (Sheffield: And Other Stories, 2011); M. July, *The First Bad Man* (Edinburgh: Canongate Books Ltd, 2015).
4 See N. Kang and S. Torres-Saillant, *The Once and Future Muse: The Poetry and Poetics of Rhina Espaillat* (Pittsburgh: University of Pittsburgh Press, 2018), 133.
5 b. hooks, *Yearning: Race, Gender and Cultural Politics* (Boston: South End Press, 1990), 41–50.
6 A. O'Reilly, *Matricentric Feminism: Theory, Activism, Practice* (Bradford: Demeter Press, 2016), 162.
7 S. Ahmed, *Queer Phenomenology: Orientations, Objects, Others* (Durham, NC: Duke University Press, 2006), 9–12.
8 C. Green, 'The Droves of Academe', *Missouri Review*, 31:3 (Fall 2008), 183.
9 See C. Moraru, 'The Forster Connection or, Cosmopolitanism Redux: Zadie Smith's *On Beauty*, *Howards End*, and the Schlegels', *The Comparatist*, 35 (May 2011), 144.
10 Yaeger, 'Beyond the Fragments', *NOVEL: A Forum on Fiction*, 23:2 (Winter, 1990), 208.
11 A. Blunt and A. Varley, 'Geographies of Home', *Cultural Geographies*, 11 (2004), 3.
12 M. Puig de la Bellacasa, 'Nothing Comes Without Its World': Thinking With Care', *The Sociological Review*, 60:2 (2012), 204.
13 J. Duncan and D. Lambert, 'Landscapes of Home', in J. Duncan, N. Johnson, and R. Schein (eds.), *A Companion to Cultural Geography* (Oxford: Blackwell, 2003), 395.
14 See the inside cover matter, especially from *New York Times*, *Daily Beast*, and Dana Spiotta.
15 S. Ahmed. *Living a Feminist Life* (Durham, NC: Duke University Press, 2017), 16.

CHAPTER 12

Who Rules the World? Reimagining the Contemporary Feminist Dystopia

Sarah Dillon

Feminist dystopian writing powerfully emerged in the science fiction of the Anglophone West at the height of second-wave feminism in the 1970s and 1980s with texts such as Suzy McKee Charnas's *Walk to the End of the World* (1974), Joanna Russ's *The Female Man* (1975), Marge Piercy's *Woman on the Edge of Time* (1976), and later, Margaret Atwood's *The Handmaid's Tale* (1985) and Octavia Butler's *Parable of the Sower* (1993). But the reinvigoration of feminism in the twenty-first century has seen a resurgence of feminist dystopian imaginings. In fact, it could be described as a tidal wave. Contemporary feminist dystopias written in English or readily available in English translation, include Sarah Hall's *The Carhullan Army* (2007), Joanna Kavenna's *The Birth of Love* (2010), Hilary Jordan's *When She Woke* (2011), Jane Rogers's *The Testament of Jessie Lamb* (2011), Eugene Fischer's 'The New Mother' (2015), Johanna Sinisalo, *The Core of the Sun* (2016), Helen Sedgwick's *The Growing Season* (2017), Lidia Yuknavitch's *The Book of Joan* (2017), Jennie Melamed's *Gather the Daughters* (2017), Louise Erdrich's *Future Home of the Living God* (2017), Leni Zumas's *Red Clocks* (2018), Sophie Mackintosh's *The Water Cure* (2018), Christina Dalcher's *Vox* (2018), and Joanne Ramos's *The Farm* (2019). Young adult author Kiran Millwood Hargrave's adult debut, the historical dystopia *Vardø*, was recently secured by Picador for a six-figure sum after a fiercely contested thirteen-publisher auction.[1]

These texts' concerns echo those of their twentieth-century predecessors, exploring dominant themes of control of reproductive rights, sexual and other forms of violence against women, and the balance of power between the sexes. Some changes in the genre are beginning to emerge: Pat Schmatz has begun to expand the field in new directions with her transfeminist dystopia, *Lizard Radio* (2015); and young adult feminist dystopian fiction is flourishing.[2] But there is perhaps surprising consistency between the themes of this new wave and their ancestors, indicating that feminism as a tool for political and social change has not come as far as we might wish to think. In fact, such works have become even more relevant to contemporary Western society, in particular North America, since the election of President Donald Trump. On 21 January 2017, over five million people worldwide and over one million in Washington DC joined the Women's March in protest at Trump's inauguration. Two days later, on Monday 23 January, surrounded by white men, Trump signed an anti-abortion executive order that has far-reaching consequences for women's reproductive rights worldwide. This was his first act as president. The following day George Orwell's *1984* hit number 6 on Amazon's bestseller list. But it was not Orwell's dystopian classic that was most heavily referenced on the Women's March, it was *The Handmaid's Tale*, with protestors carrying posters bearing slogans such as 'Make Margaret Atwood Fiction Again!', 'The Handmaid's Tale is NOT an instruction manual!', and 'nolite te bastardes carborundorum'.[3] All of this was no doubt unanticipated but welcome publicity for the streaming service Hulu, whose television adaptation of Atwood's novel, commissioned before Trump's election, premiered in April 2017.

I share with many feminist cultural commentators in the media an uneasiness regarding this proliferation of feminist dystopias, an uneasiness which has led Anna Silman in *The Cut*, for example, to describe the first two episodes of the second season of *The Handmaid's Tale* as 'a ceaseless cavalcade of grisly feminist torture porn to rival our greatest misogynist auteurs'.[4] Hulu originally ordered one series of ten episodes closely following the original novel, but of course immediately capitalised on the success of the first series – in no part due to its unsettling reverberations with contemporary political change in America – by renewing it for a second season just a month after the premiere and for a third season one year later, in May 2018. That same month, Sarah Ditum published a piece in *The Guardian* entitled 'Never-ending Nightmare: Why Feminist Dystopias Must Stop Torturing Women' in which her criticism of the proliferation of feminist dystopias is two-fold. Ditum's first criticism is that the worlds of such novels are now too closely aligned with that of the real world to offer any sort of critical perspective on it. In fact, they simply amplify the horror of reality. 'The world as it is', she says, 'offers such a rich variety of nightmares for women that it seems superfluous for fiction to devise ever more horrifying worlds that could be'.[5]

What Silman and Ditum are responding to here is a lack of critical perspective in contemporary feminist dystopias. To phrase this within the terms of the theory of the genre, contemporary works have become merely 'dystopias', not 'critical dystopias'. The latter term was coined by Lyman Tower Sargent in 1994 to define a work that 'takes a critical view of the utopian genre'.[6] Crucially, the critical dystopia has its origins in feminist dystopian writing. Sargent chooses Marge Piercy's *He, She and It* (1991) as his example of this subgenre. Rafaella Baccolini adopted the term in 2000, using it retrospectively to define Katharine Burdekin's *Swastika Night* (1937) and *The Handmaid's Tale*.[7] Tom Moylan develops it further in *Scraps of the Untainted Sky* (2000), again locating its origins in feminist dystopian writing.[8] According to Moylan, critical dystopias, 'burrow within the dystopian tradition in order to bring utopian and dystopian tendencies to bear on their exposés of the present moment and their explorations of new forms of oppositional agency' (pp. 198–9). Critical dystopias are neither simply utopian nor bleakly anti-utopian; rather, they construct a careful balance between the two, 'albeit generally, and stubbornly, utopian, they do not go easily toward that better world. Rather, they linger in the terrors of the present even as they exemplify what is needed to transform it' (p. 199). In order to fulfil its purpose of providing 'imaginative sustenance and inspiration' for political activism, this careful balance between the utopian and the dystopian must be maintained (p. xv). As Andrew Milner notes, critical dystopias partake in 'the central political dilemma of dystopian fiction, that, if its serious purpose is in its warning, then the more grimly inexorable the fictive world becomes, the less effective it will be as a call for resistance'.[9] This theoretical framing explains Silman's and Ditum's response to feminist dystopias of the contemporary moment. In failing to balance the utopian and the dystopian, these works are simply anti-utopias, rather than critical dystopias, and as such they lose their political motivational power. As Moylan explains, these texts 'readily remain in the camp of nihilistic or resigned expressions that may appear to challenge the current social situation but in fact end up reproducing it by ideologically inoculating viewers and readers against any forms of anger or action, enclosing them within the very social realities they disparagingly expose' (p. 196).

Ditum's second criticism of contemporary feminist dystopias is that such works are multiplying, and escalating imaginatively, because of the market value of female misery: 'suffering sells, especially when it's women who are doing the suffering, and as with any trend, the pressure is for each new iteration to outdo what came before'.[10] Both of Ditum's points are crucial, but Ditum omits a third important criticism, one rooted in the history and present experiences of women of colour. Writing 'as a Black woman who has an intimate understanding of

Black American History', Jenn M. Jackson observes that Hulu's *The Handmaid's Tale*, 'feels less like entertainment, horror, or even dystopic nightmare. Instead, it just seems like appropriation, the stealing of not only Black experiences but our deepest pains too.'[11] Jackson outlines the parallels between some of the show's most supposedly 'dystopian' moments, and the lived experiences – past and present – of Black women, including the history of Black mothering and, part of that history, desperate decisions to kill one's own children to protect them from re-entering slavery, and also female circumcision and the forced sterilisation of Black women.[12] For Jackson, 'shows like *The Handmaid's Tale* don't honor those histories or even acknowledge them. Instead, they retell our experiences using whiteness as the subject and entertainment value as the backdrop.'[13]

So, there is a problem with contemporary feminist dystopian imagining. First, Hulu's *The Handmaid's Tale* commodifies Black pain in particular and, more broadly, such works imaginatively exploit female suffering for commercial gain. Second, many such works have lost the essential balance between utopia and dystopia necessary to function as powerful critical dystopias within the feminist tradition. Third, given the recent rapid incursions upon the freedoms that women have gained, the imagined worlds we find in them are no longer so far removed from a potential reality for Western women in the twenty-first century as they might have seemed a few decades ago, further lessening the possibility for critical distance without full immersion in horror. More specifically, if one takes an international perspective, such worlds have never in fact been very different from the reality of life for many women across the globe. How, then, might we go about reimagining the feminist *critical* dystopia from an intersectional twenty-first-century perspective? I want to take two approaches to answering this question: first theoretical, then, literary critical. In the first section, I situate the feminist dystopia within the context of Darko Suvin's theory of science fiction, in order to identify the necessity of estrangement, and of balancing utopia and dystopia, so as to retain the politically motivating power of the critical dystopia. I then interrogate Suvin's concept of the 'zero world' from a feminist perspective, in order to suggest that contemporary feminist critical dystopias might be most empowered and empowering if mapped in relation to the (almost) universal zero world of women *not* in power. In the second section, I analyse Naomi Alderman's *The Power* (2016) as an example of a contemporary feminist dystopia that performs these theoretical requirements.

Problematising the Zero World: When Women Rule

Within science fiction theory, Utopia (a category that includes utopias, anti-utopias, dystopias, and critical dystopias) is understood to be a subgenre of science fiction. As Suvin defines it, 'strictly and precisely speaking, utopia is not a genre but the *socio-political subgenre of science fiction*'.[14] Suvin's theory of science fiction therefore encompasses and applies to dystopian works. Suvin defines SF, including the dystopia, as the literature of cognitive estrangement. This attitude of estrangement is at once creative and cognitive, with cognition significantly implying 'not only a reflecting *of* but also *on* reality' (p. 10). SF is, therefore, defined as

> a literary genre whose necessary and sufficient conditions are the presence and interaction of estrangement and cognition, and whose main formal device is an imaginative alternative to the author's empirical world. (p. 8)

As a subgenre of science fiction, the critical dystopia can be effective as a genre of social and political critique because the novum (the dominant innovation or novelty) produces an estrangement from reality which causes the reader to reflect critically back upon it, and be prompted as a result to act for change. Suvin argues that SF, dystopias included, thus serves a crucial literary-political function as 'a diagnosis, a warning, a call to understanding and action, and – most important – a mapping of possible alternatives' (p. 12). Here we see how Suvin's theory elucidates one of the major criticisms of contemporary feminist dystopias outlined above – they are no longer sufficiently distant from our present reality to serve as a politically motivating form of cognitive estrangement, nor do they serve as maps of possible alternatives. We do not need fiction right now to warn us how precarious women's rights are, and the imaginative indulgence in female suffering we find in such works offers no viable alternatives to our lived experiences. Such works lack estrangement, *and* the necessary critical balance between utopia and dystopia.

Another critique of contemporary feminist dystopias I have outlined above – blindness to the problematic universality of this first-person plural, 'we', and to the different realities of women depending on race, class, ability, and more – offers a site for an intersectional feminist development of Suvin's theory. He argues that one of the main characteristics that differentiates SF from other literary genres is the nature of its relationship to the 'real' world, what he calls 'the "zero world" of empirically verifiable properties around the author'.[15] For Suvin, naturalistic fiction has a straightforwardly reflective relation to the zero world, along Shakespearean lines: such works, he says, 'create a significant statement about the human condition by holding a mirror to nature' (p. 18). In contrast, the reality of an SF world is radically estranged from the zero world of the author, but for this to serve a cognitively estranging function, the *reader* must share the norms of reality of the author. As we know, this is neither the case in SF nor in fact in so-called 'naturalistic' fiction. With regard to the latter, this is usually the source of arguments for literature's empathetic function – that we read about people and worlds different from us and so become better people as a result.[16] With regard to SF, and to dystopias, we need to move beyond Suvin's theories on two specific points: the first is to recognise that effective cognitive estrangement depends on the relationship between the world of the text and the zero world of the *reader*, not the *author*; the second is to recognise in turn that the readerly zero world, while being no less empirically verifiable, differs from person to person, further complicating any claim that SF as a genre, dystopias as a subgenre, or even a single text, might be universally estranging.

How can an engagement with contemporary feminist dystopias move beyond Suvin's theories on these two points, and yet retain his basic premise, that dystopias have social and political power because they function, as their parent genre does, as a literature of cognitive estrangement? I suggest that we can do so by focusing on a specific category of feminist critical dystopias – those in which women rule the world. While women across the world are subject to varying degrees of suppression and freedom, the majority of societies, even the supposedly most 'advanced' ones, are still patriarchal. While some matrilineal societies do exist across the globe, the idea that women might rule the world is, I propose, sufficiently alien to a sufficient majority of women as to provide a generative site of intersectional cognitive estrangement for a new wave of feminist dystopian imaginings. Women not in power provides a common, if never universal, readerly zero world in relation to which a new body of transnational transmedial feminist dystopias can flourish. The novum of women in power can be used to reimagine questions of gender, femininity, masculinity, reproduction, sex, and power in ways which produce texts that balance the utopian and the dystopian and are therefore indeed able to serve as 'a diagnosis, a warning, a call to understanding and action, and . . . a mapping of possible alternatives'.[17]

There is of course a pre-twenty-first-century history of stories in which women rule. Outside of the SF genre, such a history would begin in Ancient Greece, where the idea that women might be in power was so laughable it was the subject of one of Aristophanes' most ribald comedies, *Assembly-Women*. When discussing this play briefly in *Women & Power* (2017), Mary Beard uses it to illuminate the simple but important point that 'as far back as we can see in western history there is a radical separation – real, cultural and imaginary – between women and power'.[18] Interrogating this radical separation, two utopian texts from the early twentieth century mark the beginning of the exploration within modern Anglophone science fiction literature of worlds in which women rule. In 1905 Begum Rokeya Sakhawat Hossain published 'Sultana's Dream', which inverts standard gendered power relations in India – women rule and it is the men who are kept in purdah. A decade later, in the USA, Charlotte Perkins Gilman published *Herland*, in which a utopian all-female society has arisen in an isolated community. There is also a significant body of twentieth- and twenty-first-century texts exploring matriarchal worlds on other planets perhaps because, as Naomi Alderman notes, 'it's so much easier to do thought experiments about an alien world, it's clean and isolates precisely the problem you want to talk about'.[19] Such works include Joan Slonczewski's *A Door into Ocean* (1986), Nicola Griffith's *Ammonite* (1992), David Brin's *Glory Season* (1993), Ursula Le Guin's 'The Matter of Seggri' (1994), N. Lee Wood's *Master of None* (2004), and Kameron Hurley's *The Stars Are Legion* (2017).

There are far fewer twenty-first-century novels exploring when women rule on Earth. Such imagining can be found in recent graphic novels, though, of which two successful series stand out. Brian K. Vaughan's *Y: The Last Man* (2003–8) explores a world in which one man and his pet monkey survive a global plague which targets only those with a Y chromosome. Moving beyond anglophone fiction, Fumi Yoshinaga's *Ōoku: The Inner Chambers* (大奥 Ōoku), an ongoing manga series begun in 2005, is based upon the same premise of a male-only virus which leads to the establishment of a matriarchal society led by a female shōgun. An exploration of both series would require more space than remains here, but scholarly work on each is amassing.[20] In the rest of this chapter, I want to look at a twenty-first-century novel that explores what a matriarchy on Earth might look like, how it might arise, and what its consequences might be. This work is the heir to two important late twentieth-century predecessors: Pamela Sargent's *The Shore of Women* (1986) and Sheri S. Tepper's *The Gate to Women's Country* (1988). Both of these novels explore terran matriarchies with heightened awareness of the tension therein between utopia and dystopia, thereby achieving the balance required to function as critical dystopias; in both, the novum of a world in which women rule enables the exploration of how and why gender power relations have been reversed, and the consequences thereof for questions of reproduction, education, value systems, sex (both hetero and homo), violence, and the use of technology. The contemporary text I want to analyse here,

Alderman's *The Power*, takes its place in this tradition. It provides a feminist critical dystopia for our times through its complex balancing of utopia and dystopia; its self-reflexivity on the power and importance of writing; its radical imagining of violent revolutionary change; and its global plurivocality.

A Contemporary Feminist Critical Dystopia: *The Power*

The Power's novum is introduced in its frame narrative which is set in a world in which women rule. The text opens and closes in epistolary form, with an exchange of letters between Naomi and Neil. Neil is a historian and aspiring male writer, whose letterhead signals his membership of 'The Men Writers Association'.[21] He is sending the manuscript of his first novel to Naomi for feedback. The book is his attempt to convince the contemporary public that the status quo has not always been as it is now, and that at one time men had ruled and women had had to go to violent lengths to overthrow them. Neil is using the dystopian mode precisely for, in Moylan's terms, its power to 'challenge contemporary perceptions of a closed social reality as well as the perceived inability to do anything to change it' (p. 194): 'it's not "natural" to us to live like this. It can't be', he writes to Naomi, 'I can't believe it is. We can choose differently' (p. 338). The novel-within-the novel, and its framing, thus perform the self-reflexivity inherent in the critical dystopia. As Moylan notes, 'an inherent part of the critical dystopia's textual resistance lies in its meditation on the very act of writing "as itself an act of hope"' (p. 192).[22] But Naomi is merely titillated by the idea of a work of imagination which includes such novel ideas as 'male soldiers, male police officers and "boy crime gangs"' – she struggles to take it seriously (p. x). In her first letter after reading Neil's manuscript, Naomi confirms that there has indeed been a moment in ancient history where there was a violent shift, one which erased all earlier records – called the Cataclysm – but she remains unconvinced by Neil's interpretation of what actually happened then, and what society might have been like before it. From her comments, it is clear that her world is a mirror image of our own, with her stereotypes about what a world run by men would look like reflecting our zero world stereotypes about what one run by women might be like: 'I think I'd rather enjoy this "world run by men" you've been talking about', she writes, 'Surely a kinder, more caring and – dare I say it? – more *sexy* world than the one we live in' (p. x). Neil and Naomi's world represents a *radical* feminist utopia. It is not a society in which everything is perfect, but one in which it is men, not women, who suffer most from its violence and inequities. Alderman is therefore not imagining an all-encompassing utopia, but through inverted realism she *is* imaging a utopian future for women in which we, not men, rule. She creates, in Suvin's words, an *'imaginary community . . . in which human relations are organized more perfectly than in the author's community'*, at least, perhaps, from the perspective of a female reader (p. 45).

This radical utopian future offered to the reader of *The Power* is located in the frame narrative, just as the 'Historical Notes' at the end of *The Handmaid's Tale* offer a utopian horizon in contrast to the anti-utopian force of the body of Offred's tale. But it is also offered within the first half of the novel-within-the-novel – Neil's novel 'The Power' – maintaining, as Baccolini and Moylan say the critical dystopia must, 'the utopian impulse *within* the work'.[23] For Naomi and readers in the zero world of the future, the novum of 'The Power' is that men were once in power. For readers in our world, the novum of 'The Power' is that teenage girls have developed the ability to discharge electric shocks through their hands, powered by a new skein across their collarbone which has grown after a WWII anti-gas drug caused DNA changes. Whereas most contemporary feminist dystopian fiction imagines female disempowerment, usually as a result of the violation of reproductive rights, Alderman's novel imagines radical female empowerment, not through control of those rights nor through imagining a world entirely empty of men but through this new 'power'. Alderman's novel is not concerned in fact at any point with reproduction – this is both a startling and a refreshing break from tradition, taking the novel's exploration of female subjugation and empowerment beyond this single focus of concern. At first, for the reader in our world, 'The Power' represents a triumphant utopia in which women's newly acquired power allows us to stand up to men and overturn the systems of dominance entrenched in societies the world over. This reversal of women's fortunes is exhilarating. Even when the power leads to violent retaliation, it is felt that it is deserved, for instance, in the murder of a sexually abusive stepfather by the girl he is in the act of raping. As the character Tunde observes, 'justice is being meted out – although it's not considered good form to say so' (p. 132). In the utopian opening of the novel-within-the-novel, the power is both a literal force for change, and functions as a conceit, an extended metaphor for female empowerment itself.[24]

However, halfway through the novel-within-the-novel, there is a tipping point – the power does not just mean freedom and equality for women, a balance of power. Instead, the empowerment of the women leads to violent revolution and radical disempowerment of men. First, they are simply displaced from positions of power and authority, for instance as lead presenter on the news, or governor of the state, or head of a crime family. But then violence and abuses escalate: men are domestically and sexually abused; they are gang raped; violence against them is not investigated; unfettered sexual violence is perpetrated in war zones; the mainstream media will not broadcast the atrocities and in some countries the internet is controlled and censored; men's freedom of movement is curbed; 'curbing' is in fact the name for the male genital mutilation now practised; men have to be registered to a woman in order to shop, travel, exist. Inverted gender stereotypes abound – men are better at diplomacy, advertising tells women that their fortunes in life depend upon their strength. With this turn in the tale of 'The Power', Alderman's novel introduces the balance between utopia and dystopia so essential to a feminist critical dystopia. For it confronts its feminist reader with the dystopian possibility that, given greater physical power and the means to exercise it, women would act no differently to men. It imagines that power and abuse are systemic and endemic. In this sense, it fits into Fredric Jameson's category of the 'if this goes on' type of dystopia, such as George Orwell's *1984*, in which 'the force of the text . . . springs from a conviction about human nature itself, whose corruption and lust for power are inevitable, and not to be remedied by new social measures or programs, nor by heightened consciousness of impending dangers', nor, it seems, by giving women power.[25] *The Power* offers a radical utopian hope for the eradication of female subservience and persecution, but only at the dystopian expense of violent revolutionary change and the redistribution of that subservience and persecution onto men, rather than it being eradicated entirely.

Mirroring the inverted realism of the frame narrative, nothing that happens to men in the novel-within-the-novel is not happening to women right now in our world. Alderman states this again and again in interviews:

> Nothing happens to men in the novel – I explain carefully to interviewers – that is not happening to a woman in our world today. So is it dystopian? Well. Only if you're a man. That answer's too simple, of course. It's pat, and gets a laugh from an audience, but the relationship between our world and utopias or dystopias of all stripes is a complicated one.[26]

To unpack that complexity in a scholarly way, *The Power*'s effect of cognitive estrangement may in fact be more powerfully dystopian for a male reader, who experiences the most extreme difference between his zero world and the world of the novel, rather than for the female reader, many of whom will see their lived experiences reflected in it, even if the gendering is reversed. At the same time, the novel accounts for the fact that the zero world of women – both those within the novel-within-the-novel before the power emerges, and its female readers – is empirically different across the world, yet united by a universal subjugation to men. There is a significant difference of degree here, of course: the power enables Margot, an American politician, merely to stand up to the misogynistic Governor of her State, whereas it enables women held as sex slaves in Moldova to violently overthrow their captors and rapists. But the internationalism of the novel and its plurivocality, weaving together as it does the narratives of multiple women, points to the unity in difference that must drive twenty-first-century intersectional feminism, and the truly *critical* dystopias that might power it.

Notes

1 See 'Picador to publish Kiran Millwood Hargrave's debut adult novel' (10 April 2018), panmacmillan.com.

2 See, for instance, Neal Shusterman's *Unwind* (2007), Ally Condie's *Matched* (2010), Caragh O'Brien's *Birthmarked* (2010), Teri Hall's *The Line* (2010), Megan McCafferty's *Bumped* (2011), Anna Carey's *Eve* (2011), Lauren DeStefano's *Wither* (2011), Dan Wells's *Partials* (2012), and Louise O'Neill's *Only Ever Yours* (2014).

3 This latter phrase appears in Atwood's *The Handmaid's Tale* (London: Vintage, 2017), 62. It is mock Latin for 'don't let the bastards grind you down'.

4 A. Silman, 'The Most Traumatizing Moments from *The Handmaid's Tale* Season Premiere', *The Cut* (25 April 2018), thecut.com.

5 S. Ditum, 'Never-ending Nightmare: Why Feminist Dystopias Must Stop Torturing Women', *The Guardian* (12 May 2018).

6 L. Tower Sargent, 'The Three Faces of Utopianism Revisited', *Utopian Studies*, 5:1 (1994), 9.

7 See R. Baccolini, 'Gender and Genre in the Feminist Critical Dystopias of Katherine Burdekin, Margaret Atwood, and Octavia Butler', in M. Barr (ed.), *Future Females, the Next Generation: New Voices and Velocities in Feminist Science Fiction* (Boston: Rowman and Littlefield, 2000), 13–34.

8 See T. Moylan, *Scraps of the Untainted Sky: Science Fiction, Utopia, Dystopia* (Boulder: West View Press, 2000), esp. 183–99.

9 A. Milner, *Locating Science Fiction* (Liverpool: Liverpool University Press, 2012), 121.

10 Ditum, 'Never-ending Nightmare'.

11 J. M. Jackson, 'It's Even Harder to Watch *The Handmaid's Tale* When You Know Black Women's History', *Water Cooler Convos* (12 June 2017), water cooolerconvos.com.

12 Toni Morrison's *Beloved* was inspired by the Margaret Garner incident of 1856 recorded in S. Weisenburger, *Modern Medea: A Family Story of Slavery and Child-Murder from the Old South* (New York: Hill and Wang, 1998). On female circumcision, see M. A. Watson, 'Female Circumcision from Africa to the Americas: Slavery to the Present', *The Social Science Journal*, 42:3 (2005), 421–37. On the history of American eugenics, see A.M. Stern, *Eugenic Nation: Faults and Frontiers of Better Breeding in Modern America* (Berkeley: University of California Press, 2005), M. Chávez-Garcia, *States of Delinquency: Race and Science in the Making of California's Juvenile Justice System* (Berkeley: University of California Press, 2012), and N. Molina, *Fit to Be Citizens?: Public Health and Race in Los Angeles, 1879–1939* (Berkeley: University of California Press, 2006). For similar criticisms of *The Handmaid's Tale* to Jackson's, see also N. Gorrie, 'Why *The Handmaid's Tale* Is Not Dystopian for Black women – It's Real Life', *SBS* (10 July 2018), sbs.com.au.

13 Jackson, 'It's Even Harder to Watch'.

14 D. Suvin, *Metamorphoses of Science Fiction: On the Poetics and History of a Literary Genre* (New Haven and London: Yale University Press, 1979), 61. This is an accepted and commonly held position. See also F. Jameson, *Archaeologies of the Future: The Desire Called Utopia and Other Science Fictions* (London: Verso, 2007), xiv, where he adopts Suvin's definitions.

15 Suvin, *Metamorphoses*, 11.

16 For a brief critique, see my essay 'English and the Public Good', in R. Eaglestone and G. Marshall (eds.), *English: Shared Futures* (Martlesham: Boydell & Brewer, 2018), 194–201.

17 Suvin, *Metamorphoses of Science Fiction*, 12.

18 M. Beard, *Women & Power: A Manifesto* (London: Profile, 2017), 70.

19 N. Alderman, 'Dystopian Dreams: How Feminist Science Fiction Predicted the Future', *The Guardian* (25 March 2017).

20 On *Y: The Last Man*, see L. Brown, 'Yorick, Don't Be a Hero: Productive Motion in *Y: The Last Man*', *Image TexT: Interdisciplinary Comic Studies*, 3:1 (2006), n.p.; M. C. Hill, 'Alternative Masculine Performances in American Comics: Brian K. Vaughan and Pia Guerra's *Y: The Last Man*', *Studies in Popular Culture*, 38:2 (2016), 79–98; D. L. Khng, 'Philosophising Gender Politics in *Y: The Last Man*', *Journal of Graphic Novels and Comics*, 7:2 (2016), 167–77; D. Adesola Mafe, '"We Don't Need Another Hero": Agent 355 as an Original Black Female Hero in *Y: The Last Man*', *African American Review*, 48: 1–2 (2015), 33–48. For English language scholarship on *Ōoku*, see H. Hori, 'Views from Elsewhere: Female Shoguns in Yoshinaga Fumi's *Ōoku* and their Precursors in Japanese Popular Culture', *Japanese Studies*, 32:1 (2012), 77–95.

21 N. Alderman, *The Power* (London: Penguin, 2017), ix.

22 Moylan is citing Ildney Cavalcanti's unpublished dissertation 'Articulating the Elsewhere: Utopia in Contemporary Feminist Dystopias', diss. University of Strathclyde, 1999, 202.

23 R. Baccolini and T. Moylan, 'Introduction: Dystopia and Histories R. Baccolini and T. Moylan (eds.), *Dark Horizons: Science Fiction and the Dystopian Imagination* (London: Routledge, 2003), 7.

24 On *The Power* in relation to different conceptions of power and contemporary progressive politics, see my chapter, 'Empowerment Under Threat: Naomi Alderman's *The Power*', in R. Hertel and E.-M. Schmitz (eds.), *Empowering Contemporary Fiction* (Leiden: Brill, forthcoming).

25 Jameson, *Archaeologies of the Future*, 198.

26 Alderman, 'Dystopian Dreams', n.p.

CHAPTER 13

Transnational Feminism and the Young Adult Novel

Jill Richards

What would it mean to take up the young adult novel as a source for transnational feminist theory? This question is somewhat unexpected, in part because scholarly considerations of young adult fiction have most often surveyed the blockbuster success of North American series adapted into movie cycles, including *The Twilight Saga* (2005–8), *The Hunger Games Trilogy* (2008–10), and *The Divergent Series* (2011–13). Across these novel-to-film franchises, the centrality of a female heroine has spurred a number of critical debates about the feminism or anti-feminism of the young adult genre. Some critics saw young adult fiction as an extension of older sensational or melodramatic traditions in writing devoted to women; others positioned the rise of the sexualised female heroine as a statement about neoliberal consumption.[1] However, these debates have neglected young adult fiction written outside the USA, thus positing the national context as the appropriate and necessary backdrop for literary historical analysis. These conversations look very different when we begin to consider feminism in a transnational landscape, to include conflicts between Western and non-Western conceptions of agency, international development policy directed towards youth populations, an international division of gendered labour practices, and diasporic perspectives on the family as a unit of social reproduction.

In this chapter, my sense of the transnational looks to emphasise comparison and circulation, rather than a unified global identity. This distinction relies on the work of Inderpal Grewal and Caren Kaplan, who have argued that transnational perspectives on gender and sexual identity are necessary to account for the increasingly global arc of capitalist development without levelling the asymmetries between extra-national sites. If a consideration of global sexuality threatens to homogenise cultural identities or colonise non-Western traditions under the wider rubric of Western norms, the turn to the transnational can offer a strategy to account for the workings of sexuality across borders, all the while attending to the historical specificity of the nation state. As Grewal argues in *Transnational America*, this more comparative, interdisciplinary focus looks to account for a particular conjuncture in neoliberalism wherein it is not necessarily the territorially bounded rights but practices of international consumption that afford a sense of full citizenship.[2] In this account, struggles for consumerist practices stand in as a model of freedom and choice that creates modes of affiliation and belonging across national borders. Methodologically, this focus highlights relations between national and imperial sites; as Jacqui Alexander and Chandra Talpade Mohanty argue, 'to talk about feminist praxis in global contexts would involve shifting the unit of analysis from local, regional and national culture to relations and processes across cultures'.[3]

An increasingly extra-territorial notion of citizenship and feminist praxis often coincides with a turn to universal or human rights, through both new social movements and international development. In her consideration of international development policy, Michelle Murphy tracks the ways in which foreign investment has focused on the racialised figure of the 'third-world girl' as a key site of intervention.[4] While economic development policy in the 1980s often represented women and children in need of rescue, the language around the girl's future is much more optimistic, presenting the teachable girl as a national security solution. Per Lawrence Summers, chief economist for the World Bank, 'educating girls quite possibly yields a higher rate of return than any other investment available in the developing world'.[5] Since the 1990s, the World Bank and UN-affiliated programmes frequently position the 'third-world girl' in terms of her future-oriented value as a potential mother, whose education will coincide with lower fertility rates and a higher GDP.

The 'Invest in a Girl' campaign and like ventures of philathrocapitalism securely link the biopolitical futures of a nation to the future value of a racialised 'third-world girl'.[6] Therein is a developmental model based on the girl's reproductive future. Murphy translates the anticipatory mode of investment as a biopolitical expansion: '*some children must be invested in so that the future others might not be born, so that rates of return increase, so that future adults are worth more, so others live more prosperously*' (p. 114). As Murphy notes, this expansion reanimates a familiar imperial concern for non-Western women and children as victimised subjects awaiting rescue. However, it also securely connects the matter of population with the female adolescent as a future-oriented subject particularly primed for intervention. In the context of US media cultures, Julia Passante Elman takes up the matter of intervention as a governmental disposition towards the category of adolescence more generally. What Elman calls the 'chrono-social category of adolescence' signals a range of not-yets: the subject not yet pathological, not yet normative, not yet a citizen, not yet an adult.[7] However, as Elman notes, adolescence is often theorised as a universal psychology or hormone-addled bodily stage, neglecting the ways in which the adolescent is socially constructed as a subject of knowledge and national governance, not only within the nation but also according to the racial, class, and ability status of the youth undergoing intervention.

By focusing on the future-oriented, not-yet subjectivity of the adolescent, I do not mean to hypothesise a universal mode of experience across Western and non-Western sites. Instead, I want to consider the ways in which youth functions as a discourse in the public sphere and international law. This discursive analysis takes up the ways in which adolescence articulates a position of rightlessness, for a subject neither fully adult nor child; how this subject is gendered as a masculinised threat, feminised victim, or future mother of the nation; and how undocumented adolescents and underage workers complicate a strictly territorial account of the intersections between age, gender, and sexuality.

This chapter will outline how a transnational perspective changes the way we articulate both gender and adolescence, using the young adult novel as a literary site wherein these intersecting identities are catalysed. Though the existence of the genre arguably extends into the nineteenth century, I focus on twenty-first-century novels marketed to a young adult audience. In each case, these texts situate the adolescent girl as a key site of invention in the nation's biopolitical future. Indeed, the young adult genre departs most notably from modernist and contemporary narratives geared towards adults not for its existence of a teen protagonist; any number of novels marketed to adults feature a coming-of-age adolescent narrator. What might be the most defining feature of the genre is the way in which it animates a biopolitical logic, wherein the future of the population is endangered through its governance. That this population is 'youth', rather than marked otherwise, renders the adolescent subject problematically universal as a site of identification and interestingly collective as a form of identity linked to chronology, wherein adolescence marks a threshold stage and site of knowledge production that prefigures adulthood.

The International Problem Novel

The young adult problem novel generally offers a realist consideration of a wider social ill, individualised through the perspective of a confessional, first-person narrator. Sheila Egoff locates the rise of the genre in the 1970s USA, with the blockbuster success of S. E. Hinton's *The Outsiders* (1967), Paul Zindel, *The Pigman* (1968), Anonymous, *Go Ask Alice* (1971), and Robert Cromier, *The Chocolate War* (1974). In Egoff's account, the early problem novels were 'strongly subject-oriented with interest primarily residing in the topic rather than the telling. The topics – all adult-oriented – sound like chapter titles from a textbook on social pathology: divorce, drugs, disappearing parents, desertion, and death.'[8] If children's literature had before sheltered its subjects, these works presented teenagers enmeshed in a fully adult, often cruel world. Falling somewhere between true-to-life narratives and cautionary tales, the international problem novel positions young persons as suffering, worldly subjects.

Moving into an international context, the realist young adult novel on social problems is probably the most populated genre subcategory of young adult fiction; some notable selections include Andrew Salkey's *Riot* (1967), based in Kingston, Jamaica; Shyam Selvadurai's *Swimming in the Monsoon Sea* (2007), on queer romance in 1980s Sri Lanka; Fatima Sharafeddine's *The Servant* (2010), an account of a young girl sent away to work as a live-in maid in Beirut; Angie Thomas's *The Hate U Give* (2017), on the police murder of a black teenager and the subsequent riots in the USA; Florenz Webbe Maxwell's *Girlcott* (2017), a historical fiction focused on the Bermuda cinema boycott of 1959; and Vivienne Ndlovu's *Waste Not Your Tears* (2018) on the HIV/AIDS crisis in Zimbabwe.

Notable in this canon is the work of Faïza Guène, whose *Kiffe Kiffe Tomorrow* (France, 2004) focuses on the everyday life of Doria, a Moroccan immigrant living with her mother in the Paradise Projects on the outskirts of Paris. The novel is set amid debates about the adolescence crisis in the Paris *banlieues*. At the time, these discourses centred on the youth protests linked to the deaths of two young, immigrant men, who were electrocuted when running from the police. In the coverage of the riots, the international press fixated on the threat of a racialised, masculine youth subject. The *New York Times* account begins sensationally: 'The images are unnerving: hooded, swift-footed youths infiltrating protest rallies in the heart of tourist Paris, smashing shop windows, setting cars on fire, beating and robbing passers-by and throwing all sorts of objects at the riot police.'[9]

Kiffe Kiffe focuses on a subject often left out of these debates, the immigrant girl. If the novel's first-person narration offers a singularly individualised portrait of Doria, any number of logics put her into a wider framework. The reader encounters Doria through a network of

social services: food stamps, a school-appointed psychiatrist, social workers checking in on their apartment. In this landscape, Paradise Estates
affords certain forms of sociality and care (the neighbours that bring food
and gossip), but also persistent physical and economic immobility. Doria
begins one chapter, 'In my building, there's a girl being held prisoner on
the tenth floor. Her name is Samra and she's nineteen.'[10] Here the
language of fantastic capture becomes literalised in a realist vignette, to
articulate the ways that gender, ethnicity, religion, and citizenship status
become tied to domestic violence for subjects invisible to the news cycles
covering the ongoing riots. In this way, *Kiffe Kiffe* departs from the
traditional problem novel framework: here it is not one singular social
problem that motivates the story, but a network of interlocking sites, to
include violence internal to the family, police violence, and the racialised
surveillance of the welfare state.

Magical Nations and Colonial Governance

If the problem novel positions social problems against an individual's story,
a turn to the schoolroom offers a broader narrative of an imagined community, often in alliance with the nation state. Regarding this tradition, we
might ask: Why is the magical salvation of the nation so often set at the feet
of teenagers? Why is the boarding school for magic such a seductive
location for their collective sociality? These questions emerge, in part,
through the success of the *Harry Potter* franchise, wherein the magical
school, Hogwarts, ensures the national future of both England and
humanity. However, *Harry Potter* marks only one site in a wide body of
literature that relocates the primary development of young persons from
the family to the school. These works summon up the common trope of
children's literature, wherein parental figures need to be killed off to enable
juvenile independence. However, in this case the school replaces the absent
family, offering an alternative space of both intimacy and intervention for
the developing adolescent. Most widely, what follows considers rewritings
of the traditional boy's schoolroom tale that centre a female protagonist.
Here what is important is not so much the matter of female identity as
such, but the ways in which it allows for a reconsideration of what Wendy
Brown has called the 'masculinism of the state' as 'the features of the state
that enact, sustain, and represent masculine power as a form of
dominance'.[11] For Brown, this dominance can be understood along two
trajectories as 'the power to describe and run the world *and* the power of
access to women; it entails a general claim to territory and claims to, about,

and against specific "others'" (p. 167). What follows considers a range of attempts to reconsider the schoolroom as a feature of the state that produces inequality, as understood by subjects lacking territorial claims and gendered forms of national belonging.

There are any number of non-magical boarding school novels directed at young adults, including Melina Marchetta's *Jellicoe Road* (2010), which begins with parental death and then chronicles the adolescence of its female protagonist at a boarding school in Australia. Emily M. Danforth's *The Miseducation of Cameron Post* (2012) situates its orphaned protagonist in rural Montana, where she is sent away to a boarding school/penitentiary devoted to conversion therapy. These novels all afford the establishment of community through institutions beyond the family; this sense of alternative sociality is only increased in the more fantastic subgenre of the boarding school plot, wherein students are drawn together through their magical abilities. Now published in over thirty countries, Sara Elfgren and Mats Strandberg's *The Engelsfors Trilogy* (Sweden, 2013–15) narrates the unlikely convergence of depressive, drug-using, bullied, and generally ne'er-do-well high schoolers drawn together to fight an ancient evil. Meanwhile, Rainbow Rowell's enormously popular *Carry On* (2015) is a queer fan fiction of *Harry Potter*, set in a magical boarding school wherein the young male wizards fall in love with each other.

However, the magical schoolroom appears in young adult fictions beyond the USA and Europe, sometimes as an explicit rewriting of the blockbuster franchises in a more feminist vein. Published in 2011, Nnedi Okafor's *Akata Witch* locates this magical landscape in Nigeria, where protagonist Sunny Nawazue discovers that she is part of a secret population who possess inherited magical powers. Already, Sunny is a misfit in a number of ways: 'You see why I confuse people?' she begins. 'I'm Nigerian by blood, American by birth, and Nigerian again because I live here. I have West African features, like my mother, but while the rest of my family is dark brown, I've got light yellow hair.'[12] As in *Harry Potter* or *Carry On*, the genetic inheritance of magical ability summons a range of allegorical effects. Here, magic, like blood or racial lineage, creates vulnerability at the level of the population. Sunny's gender and albinism already make her vulnerable to suspicions of magic powers: 'People say stuff about people like you. That you're all ghost, or a half and half, one foot in this world and one foot in another' (p. 23). Okafor literalises these fears, but makes a number of careful distinctions between West African spiritual practices and the Leopard people – Okafor's magic crosses tribal modes of belonging and eschews the practice of marking out children as witches responsible for illness or accident.

While *Akata Witch* relocates the magical schoolroom to Nigeria, Maria Turtschaninoff's *Maresi* (Finland, 2014) transforms the student body, moving away from a tradition largely intent on young male cohorts to consider a separatist society of women and girls. Now translated into Chinese, German, French, and English, *Maresi* is the first volume chronicling the Red Abbey, an isolated retreat for women and girls fleeing domestic violence or poverty. Men are not allowed to step foot on the island; breaking this taboo unleashes a vengeful magic born out of the mountains and the women's hair. The first book of an incomplete trilogy, *Maresi* ends with the titular protagonist leaving the protection of the all-female Abbey in order to change the lives of women who live outside of its confines.

In this way, neither *Akata Witch* nor *Maresi* follows the more traditional arc of schoolroom literature, in which refractory children are trained to become proper inheritors of the nation. Opposed to *Tom Brown's Schooldays* or even *Harry Potter*, these texts broach a number of new questions: What about youthful subjects who do not possess this national future, for reasons of gender, ethnicity, or birth right? What about indigenous youth, who possess a very different historical relation to both educational institutions and settler colonialism? In *Prairie Rising: Indigenous Youth, Decolonization, and the Politics of Intervention* (2016), Jaskiron Dhillon considers the ways in which indigenous youth in Canada are targeted for the maintenance of the settler colonial state under the rubric of participation. Dhillon focuses on the governance of everyday indigenous life through tactics of state intervention, particularly in child welfare, health, criminal justice, and education systems in Saskatoon. In so doing, Dhillon tracks a shift in the settler colonial governance, from the overt violence of the systematic removal of indigenous youth from their communities and placement in the residential school system, to a newer, more liberal politics of mutual recognition and participation that nevertheless reproduces colonial state authority. In so doing, Dhillon draws upon a wider tradition of anti-racist indigenous feminism that places gendered forms of violence at the centre of an anti-colonial analysis.

Dhillon's work takes up the scene of governmental intervention as a contact point between the settler colonial state and indigenous youth. A number of young adult novels stage this encounter in more fantastic terms, including Cherie Dimaline's *The Marrow Thieves* (Canada, 2017) and the graphic novel series *A Girl Called Echo* (Canada, 2018) written by Métis author Katherena Vermette, illustrated by Scott B. Henderson and coloured by Donovan Taciuk. In *Vol. 1 Pemmican Wars* of *A Girl Called Echo*, Métis teenager Echo Desjardins finds herself transported out of her history class and into the period of the Pemmican Wars of 1814. Echo goes back and forth: between her foster home and a Métis camp on the fur-trade route. Primarily told through images, *A Girl Called Echo* uses the magic of time travel to stage a particular incommensurability that makes up the everyday life of indigenous teens such as Echo, but can also be pictured as a magical landscape, caught between liberal pluralist claims for mutual recognition through social welfare reform and the persistence of the settler colonial state.

Insurgent Youth

In 'Youth as Peril and Promise: The Emergence of Adolescent Psychology in Postwar Egypt', Omnia El Shakry situates discourses of 'youth crisis' as a critical response to the student protests of the 1930s and new understandings of adolescence as a distinct psychological stage in the 1940s. El Shakry chronicles the ways in which the social scientific category took shape within the discipline of psychology, such that adolescence came to be understood as a period of untamed, sometimes threatening sexual energy. Though postwar perspectives on adolescent psychology vary, most focus on the prevalence of unconscious sexual impulses that might produce new social types such as the juvenile delinquent. El Shakry thus localises and historicises 'youth as an insurgent subject of politics', often positioned as a figure in need of social regulation and control.[13]

If the problem novel offers a realist account of the adolescent against widespread social ills, a different, much more violent strain ratchets up this conflict into an adolescent *battle royale*, or a fight among many combatants. Early instances of the genre courted scandal by opening with male youth in need of protection. In William Golding's *Lord of the Flies* (1954), the schoolboys' plane capsizes in the Pacific Ocean as they escape the danger of an unspecified war in England; in Richard Hughes's *High Wind in Jamaica* (1929) the youth are sent *to* England, from the Caribbean, after a hurricane destroys their home. More recently, these battle scenes have become increasingly co-ed, allowing for a vexed overlap between romantic love, sexual violence, and *battle royale*. Here again, the addition of female protagonists do not automatically make these texts feminist; instead, the gendering of the subjects involved in battle renders the novels a site to consider the ways in which an authoritarian state produces and controls forms of adolescent sexual difference across national borders.

Anglophone accounts of the seemingly recent popularity of young adult fiction often leave aside one of the most internationally successful franchises in this vein, Koushun Takami's *Battle Royale* (Japan, 1999). In the novel, which Takami adapted into a popular Manga and movie series, the Japanese government sends junior high students to a deserted island and forces them to murder one another so that the last might survive. Part live action magna, part colonial outpost fantasy, *Battle Royale* has been credited as one of the key predecessors of the recent American boom in serial teen dystopias that feature an overlap between co-ed *battle royale* and love story, including *The Hunger Games*, *The Divergent Series*, *The Legend Trilogy*, *The Maze Runner*, *The Uglies Series*, *The Delirium Trilogy*, and *The Unwind Dystology*.

However, *Battle Royale* also has a sustained influence on Japanese literature for adolescents into the present day. Natsuo Kirino's novel *Real World* (Japan, 2003) pointedly refers to *Battle Royale*, but the novel is also based on the 1997 murders of a fourteen-year known as Sakakibara Seito, who sent a letter to the police that claimed his actions were the result of the overly competitive Japanese school system. Sakakibara's crimes sparked off Japanese fears of a rise in juvenile delinquency as a result of undue academic pressures placed upon adolescents. If *Battle Royale* and its successors render the enemy the authoritarian state, in *Real World* it is the competitive pressures of multinational capitalism and the increasing precarity of youth in a moment of high unemployment and governmental austerity.

The *battle royale,* however, does not have to be a reaction to an oppressive or totalitarian society. In Janne Teller's *Nothing* (Denmark, 2000), adults are largely off-stage, as the youth become increasingly violent when left to their own devices. Winner of the Printz award, the novel is a narrative so spare it seems like a fable or fairy tale, minus the magic. *Nothing* might be a sinister counterpart to *Potter*, or a Dutch version of the *Hunger Games*, all black humour and scatology. In this instance, the school children's lottery-like selections for violence are entirely self-imposed. At the outset of seventh grade, in the provincial town Tæring, Pierre Anton perches in a tree and claims that life has no meaning. Over the course of the school year, in response to his taunts, Pierre's classmates each sacrifice a meaningful object to a 'heap of meaning' in order to prove Pierre wrong.[14] The additions to the heap become increasingly grotesque, to include a murdered pet, a disinterred body, and a severed finger. The students' undoing is the work of Sophie, who gives her virginity to the heap in an off-stage gang rape, then instigates further acts of group violence. What is so particularly disturbing about *Nothing* is the way that its prose relies so closely on a form associated with children's books: the sing-song, counting, chime-like repetition.[15] Often relegated to a blank page, these moments return like a refrain: 'Scared, more scared, most scared' (p. 6); 'One stone, two stones, many stones' (p. 21); 'A bad Muslim! No Muslim! No one!' (p. 101); 'Thirteen, fourteen, adult. Dead' (p. 198).

In children's books, counting refrains are for reading together, to make juvenile readers feel like part of the story. In *Nothing*, this inclusion is a horror, but the novel is interesting for the way in which it positions youth as a threat to itself, seen from afar and with some horror. This particular horror is an inversion of expected innocence, and certainly the spectre of horrible youth has a long genealogy. However, the recent surge in dystopian adolescent fictions can also be understood as a response to the transnational rise of anti-authoritarian youth movements, and with them reactionary fears of criminalised gangs, thugs, hooligans, or feral children taking to the streets. In an essay focused on youth participation in the Arab Spring, Paul Amar surveys this response through the rise of both NGOs and security states focused on policing insurgent youth: 'these campaigns are infused with paternalism and moralism that condition liberals to see *horror* – not agency or history or politics – when confronted with the labor practices, mobility circuits, and sexual expressions that constitute the material and social conditions of young lives.'[16] In this way, Amar relocates where we might expect to find horror in relation to adolescent subjects: not through youth's vulnerability to injury, but for the ways that these subjects increasingly look like adults. What is threatening, in this context, is the youth that works like an adult, the sexual youth, the migrant youth, and the insurgent youth. Responses leaning heavily on paternalism do not necessarily look to protect these subjects from external threats, but to limit the political agency and influence of a growing and seemingly unpredictable youth population.

Conclusion

The genre terms broached by this chapter are only provisional, and can scarcely account for the range and scope of transnational young adult literatures today. For instance, where in this grouping might one put Kai

Cheng Thom's *Fierce Femmes and Notorious Liars: A Dangerous Trans Girl's Confabulous Memoir* (Canada, 2016)? A combination of prose, poetry, drama, and DIY manual, *Fierce Femmes* is the story of a Chinese-Canadian trans girl who runs away from home to the Street of Miracles, where she joins the Lipstick Lacerators, a vigilante gang of mostly runaways, mostly sex workers, and all trans women. The book is a faux-memoir, a fairy tale, series of vignettes, and an account of a pitched battle against the police. Like many of the other texts considered, *Fierce Femmes* chronicles a growing surplus population, the runaway trans sex workers who are drawn to the Street of Miracles. Early in *Fierce Femmes*, the narrator acknowledges that she comes at the end of a wider literary tradition, one that tends to feature the trans girl as 'this sort of tragic, plucky-little-orphan character who is just supposed to suffer through everything and wait'.[17] 'I decided then and there that someone had to write us girls a dangerous story', she continues, taking the narrative into a quite different direction. 'I wanted something kick-ass and intense with hot sex and gang violence and maybe zombies and lots of magic' (p. 3).

Neither genre-bending fictions such as *Fierce Femmes* nor the more familiar young adult franchises have received much academic attention in any scholarly discipline. However, across a wide range of genres and national traditions, these works do offer an uncannily apt site to rethink transnational feminist theory, including global divisions of labour, sex work, and development, as fantastic and future-oriented enterprises directed towards the reproductive capacities of the adolescent girl. In their negotiations with the wider biopolitical governance of adolescence as a site of intervention, these works are perpetually reinventing themselves to account for the experience of the present.

Notes

1 For the relation to melodrama, see J. C. Richards, 'Women, Weepies, and the Fault in Our Stars', *Post45: Contemporaries* (10 February 2014), post45 .research.yale.edu; for consumerism, see O. Koffman and R. Gill, '"The Revolution Will Be Led by a 12-year-old-girl": Girl Power and Global Biopolitics', *Feminist Review*, 105 (2013), 83–102 and E. Morrison, 'YA Dystopias Teach Children to Submit to the Free Market, Not Fight Authority', *The Guardian* (1 September 2014).

2 I. Grewal, *Transnational America: Feminisms, Diasporas, Neoliberalisms* (Durham, NC: Duke University Press, 2005), 10.

3 M. J. Alexander and C. T. Mohanty (eds.), *Feminist Genealogies, Colonial Legacies, Democratic Futures* (New York: Routledge, 1997), xix.

4 M. Murphy, *The Economization of Life* (Durham: Duke University Press, 2017), 113–24.

5 Qtd in M. Murphy, 'The Girl: Mergers of Feminism and Finance in Neoliberal Times', *The Scholar and Feminist Online*, 11:1–11:2 (2012–13), n.p.

6 See girleffect.org and also L. Hayhurst, 'Corporatising Sport, Gender and Development: Postcolonial IR Feminisms, Transnational Private Governance and Global Corporate Social Engagement', *Third World Quarterly*, 32:2 (2011), 531–49.

7 J. Elman, *Chronic Youth: Disability, Sexuality, and U.S. Media Cultures of Rehabilitation* (New York: New York University Press, 2014), 2.

8 S. Egoff, 'Beyond the Garden Wall', in Z. Sutherland, *The Arbuthnot Lectures 1970–1979* (Chicago: American Library Association, 1980), 196. See also M. Cart, *Young Adult Literature: From Romance to Realism* (New York: American Library Association, 2010).

9 E. Sciolino, 'Violent Youths Threaten to Hijack Demonstrations in Paris', *New York Times* (30 March 2006).

10 F. Guène, *Kiffe Kiffe Tomorrow*, trans. S. Adams (New York: Harcourt, 2006), 83.

11 W. Brown, *States of Injury: Power and Freedom in Late Modernity* (Princeton: Princeton University Press, 1995), 167.

12 N. Okafor, *Akata Witch* (New York: Viking, 2011), 3.

13 O. El Shakry, 'Youth as Peril and Promise: The Emergence of Adolescent Psychology in Postwar Egypt', *International Journal of Middle Eastern Studies*, 43:4 (2011), 592.

14 J. Teller, *Nothing*, trans. M. Aiken (New York: Atheneum, 2010), 38.

15 See S. Lerer's *Children's Literature: A Reader's History, from Aesop to Harry Potter* (Chicago: Chicago University Press, 2009), 4.

16 P. Amar, 'The Street, the Sponge, and the Ultra: The Queer Logics of Children's Rebellion and Political Infantilization', *GLQ*, 22:4 (2016), 570–1. For the Anglo-American reaction to global representations of childhood, see K. B. Stockton, 'The Queer Child Now and Its Paradoxical Global Effects', *GLQ*, 22:4 (2016), 505–39.

17 K. Cheng Thom, *Fierce Femmes and Notorious Liars: A Dangerous Trans Girl's Confabulous Memoir* (Montreal, QC: Metonymy Press, 2016), 2.

CHAPTER 14

Feminist Manuals and Manifestos in the Twenty-first Century

Jennifer Cooke

'There is no manual for becoming a woman', declares Caitlin Moran in *How to Be a Woman* (2011), a manual on negotiating contemporary womanhood that brims with advice and guidance in digestible lists and anecdotes.[1] Moran's is one of many in a new, extremely popular, twenty-first-century subgenre of the 'feminist blockbuster' that I am calling the feminist manual.[2] This chapter will be the first to outline the characteristics of the contemporary feminist manual and assess its contribution to feminism in comparison with another feminist form that has seen a recent marked rise, the manifesto, that older, energetic staple of second-wave agitation. Insofar as both manifesto and manual envision the transformative potential of a feminist future, there is commonality but, as I shall argue, while contemporary feminist manifestos envision a collectively achieved radical politics, feminist manuals are neoliberal phenomena where change is achieved individually even when the politics advocated by the writer are revolutionary. These genres illuminate the tension between two different forms of present-day feminism, one that overwhelmingly advocates personal, individual change, as the manuals do, and another that argues primarily for structural and institutional change, collectively achieved, as the manifestos declare is necessary.

Twenty-first-century Feminist Manifestos

The rhetorical mode most readily deployed by feminist manifestos is that of the demand. Manifestos are performative texts that aim to affectively move their readers and ultimately to influence the course of history. In Kathi Weeks's words, they are 'an exemplary literature of provocation' that seek 'to bridge the divide between writing and acting'.[3] Laura Winkiel concurs, defining manifestos as 'activist texts that seek to generate urgent, immediate action'.[4] The era of the feminist manifesto's flourishing is famously the 1960s and 1970s, the time of Valerie Solanas's *The Scum Manifesto* (1967) and Shulamith Firestone's *The Dialectic of Sex* (1970), with their demands for the end of wage-labour, the abolition of money, and the reorganisation of childcare and reproduction.[5] Weeks notes that after this period, 'the early 1980s witnessed a decline of feminist utopian literature, matched by a comparable retreat from the utopian in feminist theory' (p. 182), which she attributes to a newly pragmatic bent within US feminism as it responded to an 'increasingly hostile political environment' (p. 183) and desired to avoid being dismissed as unrealistic, strident, and extremist in the popular imagination. Weeks concludes that in this period, 'anticapitalist agendas were overshadowed by the urgency of rear-guard actions and more purely defensive efforts to mitigate the impact of structural adjustment policies' (p. 184). The twenty-first century has seen a reinvigoration of the manifesto form, perhaps stimulated by the turn of the millennium but certainly consolidated by growing political urgency over increasing wealth disparities and environmental degradation, both of which intersect with gender inequality and are being inadequately addressed by governments worldwide. The consensus that we are facing a series of serious global crises – from climate change to migration, from threats to democratic processes to the rise of the far-right, from the growing power of social media corporations to dwindling natural resources – produces an environment ripe once again for thinking that seeks to fundamentally restructure the way we live.

I want to focus on contemporary feminist manifestos that issue specific radical demands for institutional, structural, and social change, all of which have revolutionary potential: Sara Ahmed's 'Killjoy Manifesto' in *Living a Feminist Life* (2017); the online document, 'Xenofeminism: A Politics for Alienation' (2015), published by the collective Laboria Cuboniks and contextualised by Helen Hester's *Xenofeminism* (2018); and the 'Trans Health Manifesto' included in the 2017 issue of the *Radical Transfeminism* zine.[6] Together, these manifestos represent a new direction in political demands and spring from a twenty-first-century feminist politics that is particularly attentive to the power institutions have to shape our lives.

Published after her resignation from Goldsmith's, University of London, in condemnation of the ongoing sexual harassment cases the institution was failing to deal with transparently and decisively, Ahmed's 'Killjoy Manifesto' builds upon the figure of the feminist killjoy that she first outlined in *The Promise of Happiness* (2010).[7] Even if we have not heard the term before, we all know how to recognise the feminist killjoy:

she is the one who points out a sexist or misogynistic problem, who 'ruin[s] the atmosphere' in the room; she robs the joke of its humour and the group who laughs at it of their warm feeling of shared sociality.[8] It is thus not surprising to find that Ahmed's killjoy manifesto entails being prepared to make others unhappy. The manifesto is framed as a series of ten commitments (as opposed to commandments) that she calls principles. Certain of these are particularly uncomfortable demands because what is asked of the feminist killjoy has deeply personal and potentially professional repercussions, including 'I am willing to cause unhappiness' (p. 258), 'I am willing to support others who are willing to cause unhappiness' (p. 259), and 'I am willing to snap any bonds, however precious, when those bonds are damaging to myself or to others' (p. 266). These uncompromising demands require a high degree of solidarity. Ahmed admits that breaking a friendship or family relation 'can take psychic and political work to be ready to snap that bond' (p. 267). Her uncomfortable demands are intended to root out pragmatic compromises, many of which can be witnessed in institutional settings, especially the university, where for the sake of their career, their students, or sometimes through sheer exhaustion, lecturers and professors accept situations they nevertheless know are unethical and unfeminist. Ahmed asks that feminism not simply be a cloak, a nomination, or a research specialism but a practical and performative enactment: you will know me through my deeds.

Where Ahmed's principles concern social refusals through which the here and now is actively made uncomfortable, a more traditionally utopian vision of future change is provided in the online xenofeminism document, which, while it does not call itself a manifesto, is full of demands, definitely 'an activist text', and has been received as a manifesto.[9] Nevertheless, its opening section proclaims that 'XF is not a bid for revolution' (p. 1). It aims instead to be protean and appropriative, claiming '[o]urs is a transformation of seeping, directed subsumption rather than rapid overthrow; it is a transformation of deliberate construction, seeking to submerge the white-supremacist capitalist patriarchy in a sea of procedures that soften its shell and dismantle its defences, so as to build a new world from the scraps' (p. 10). Nature's waters are subverted to turn against its guests, complementing a xenofeminist commitment to an anti-naturalism that also entails dismantling nuclear domestic spaces. Further, they propose to repurpose technology 'for progressive gender political ends' that put 'women, queers, and the gender non-conforming' at the forefront (p. 2). An example of such repurposing is explored in *Xenofeminism* by Hester, a member of Laboria Cuboniks. Perhaps surprisingly, given the digitally sophisticated inflection of many of the manifesto's claims, Hester turns to the Del-Em, a home-made device designed by 1970s American feminists, that 'suction[s] the endometrial lining from a human uterus' and can thus be used not only to regulate periods – by quickly removing menstrual blood – but also to prevent 'the establishment of early-term pregnancies, up to seven weeks after a person's last monthly period' (p. 71). Calling this a 'partial, imperfect, but hopeful example of what a xenofeminist technology might look like', Hester is drawn to the Del-Em because it empowers people to take control of their own repro-ductive cycles, and, like testosterone sold on the black market, evades the gatekeeping of medical practitioners (p. 70).

XF makes reference to the global, political problems of the contemporary: 'the ultimate task', the authors declare, 'lies in engineering technologies to combat unequal access to reproductive and pharmacological tools, environ-mental cataclysm, economic instability, as well as dangerous forms of unpaid/underpaid labour' (p. 2). Laboria Cuboniks laments the 'excess of modesty in feminist agendas of recent decades' (p. 3), proposing instead commitment to a new universalism that is thoroughly intersectional and 'must guard against the facile tendency of conflation with bloated unmarked particulars – namely Eurocentric universalism – whereby the male is mis-taken for the sexless, the white for raceless, the cis for real, and so on' (p. 6). This is a Marxist-inflected feminism that has absorbed the warnings that Black, brown, working-class, and trans feminists have long been delivering to their white cis-sisters.[10] Xenofeminism is smart, digitally alert, and unafraid to resurrect political categories that have rather fallen out of favour, such as universalism. Its commitment to DIY repurposing, upskilling, hacking, and wetware are all uncompromisingly contemporary. Yet, the manifesto remains at points tantalisingly abstract, such as in the claim that Xenofeminists will operate as 'collective agents capable of transitioning between multiple levels of political, material, and conceptual organization' (p. 3) and at other points somewhat evasive, such as in nominating XF 'a platform' not a 'programme', a distinction that sounds digitally judicious yet collapses if we return to the Del-Em as an example, since it can be thought of as both a platform for bodily autonomy and part of a programme for achieving it (p. 10).[11] Xenofeminism is promising but not always fully fleshed out in the manifesto, necessarily restricted by the requirements of the form, which is why Hester's book is a crucial companion.

My final example in this mode is the 'Trans Health Manifesto', published in the first issue of the zine *Radical Transfeminism* and authored by the activist group Edinburgh Action for Trans Health. A defining

feature of transfeminist theorising and thinking is its ability to intercon-
nect different forms of oppression, from medical pathologisation to carceral cruelty, from labour precarity to sex worker and mental health
discrimination.[12] Precarious work is more prevalent among trans people,
who frequently suffer workplace discrimination.[13] Mental health difficulties, linked not only to body dysmorphia but also the problems of social
isolation caused by discrimination, are common too.[14] Thus the faultlines
that might seem to separate different but negative life experiences are rather
seen by trans theorists to be networks bound by the same institutional and
state-supported logic. The 'health' in the title of both the activist group and
the manifesto refers, then, not simply to the wellness of the physical body
or even a combination of physical wellness and good mental health, but
instead has a far wider conception that is interested in the social, medical,
and state structures that make some people more able to achieve bodily and
mental health while others are stigmatised, interrogated, pathologised,
and, at worst, locked out by the system.

The 'Trans Health Manifesto', like XF, seeks more potential for DIY
self-creation, demanding the availability of 'medical training to enable us
to safely carry out medical procedures & research for each other' and fully
funded 'research centres and libraries of knowledge' curated by and for
trans people (p. 60). The authors demand free access to safe hormones, and
proper information about different drugs and dosages so that trans people
can self-medicate; voice coaching that avoids pressuring people into gender
normative patterns; resources for hair removal; and education about being
trans for children, designed and led by trans people. Like Laboria
Cuboniks, they are gender abolitionists, but they articulate specific concrete demands, such as 'an end to birth certificates and to legal gender'
(p. 61). They make clear, too, that the problems these documents pose are
not confined to those within the trans community, writing, 'Birth certificates are not just a violence against trans people, they are a material to the
state's oppression of "undocumented" immigrants and asylum seekers'
(p. 61). They call for amnesty and the right to remain for all 'trans, lesbian,
gay and bisexual, immigrants and asylum seekers' because, echoing
a political slogan seen in protests against detention centres for migrants
in the UK, 'no one is illegal' (p. 61). They note that the development of
trans medicine is part of a longer and more global history of discrimination
against vulnerable sections of society, from the eugenics of the Nazi camps
to 'the sterilisation & birth control trials forced on the women of Puerto
Rico, to the thousands of Black and brown people who have died on NHS
psychiatric wards, from the denial of the reproductive rights of disabled

people, to the denial of access to abortions' in Northern Ireland (pp. 57–8). Their very first set of demands is both concrete and uncompromisingly utopian: 'We demand nothing less than the total abolition of the clinic, of psychiatry, and of the medical-industrial complex. We demand an end to capitalist & colonial "medicine"' (p. 58). The 'Trans Health Manifesto' clearly demonstrates how demands that stem from experiences with a system that makes life difficult for one community can open out to thinking how other sections of the community can be included in demands for change.

We observe three different approaches in these manifestos. Ahmed asks us to change ourselves in order to challenge the system, to jam its operational underpinnings. XF asks us to subvert the system, using its own tools against it, dismantling the master's house from within. Finally, the 'Trans Health Manifesto' demands that the system fundamentally change so that it is in the service of its users, even created by them. What the manifestos share, though, is notable: a properly intersectional thinking through of and demand for solidarities; an emphasis on knowledge, the need to know our histories and how they continue to be sustained; and the need to upskill and inform ourselves. 'The Killjoy Manifesto', 'Xeno-Feminism: A Politics for Alienation', and 'The Trans Health Manifesto' together demonstrate that not only is the feminist manifesto alive and well, reviving the interest shown by its second-wave predecessors in sharing skills and knowledge, but it is also attentive in new twenty-first-century ways to building opportunities for solidarity, gender abolition, and lessening the power institutions currently have over our lives.

Feminist Manuals

A very different kind of writing is evident in feminist manuals, which operate on the rhetorical plane of persuasion precisely in order to avoid accusations of stridency, utopianism, and the identification of feminists as killjoys. If Moran was among the first tranche of recent feminist manual writers, many subsequently followed suit. A range from 2014 to 2015 includes Laurie Penny's *Unspeakable Things: Sex, Lies and Revolution* (2014), Roxane Gay's *Bad Feminist* (2014), Chimamanda Ngozi Adichie's slim adaptation of a Ted Talk, *We Should all be Feminists* (2014), and Emer O'Toole's *Girls Will be Girls: Dressing Up, Playing Parts and Daring to Act Differently* (2015). There is diversity of nationality and ethnicity, here, and of political positions on the spectrum from liberal to radically left, but in terms of content and tone the manuals are remarkably homogenous. As

Moran's is, they are frequently grounded in personal experience, with a confessional bent that echoes the feminist memoirs of the 1980s.[15] O'Toole, Penny, and Moran begin with or quickly move to recount difficult relationships with weight and food, whether through over-eating, anorexia, or bulimia.[16] There is an emphasis on relationships and romance, sex, gender, clothing and the trappings of femininity, and what the feminist relationship to men should be. Even if their authors admit to exploring same sex relationships, the books are primarily heterosexual. Black feminists such as Gay and Adichie underline the intersections between misogyny and racism; the white feminists, bar Penny, are quieter on this front. All of them dedicate space to confronting the negative connotations that the word feminism has accrued and reassuring their readership that feminism is a rational matter of achieving equality with men.[17] If individual books have blind spots and compositional weaknesses, they nevertheless represent a mainstream popular platform for the disse-mination of feminist principles.

Tone is telling; it is a text's 'affective bearing, orientation or "set towards" its audience and world', Sianne Ngai suggests.[18] In these manuals, the style of writing seeks to convert or confirm rather than issue a call to arms. To this end, humour is often evident: readers are repeatedly invited to chuckle at the authors' errors, insecurities, and poor choices as universal and recognisable experiences of girl- and womanhood. The authorial voice is that of an older sister or cool auntie: a woman who understands what her readership are encounter-ing because she too has faced the same challenges and can offer advice from the position of experience, as one who has learned and is stronger for it, as one who can look back and interpret her previous behaviour or that of others with the benefit of feminist hindsight. Crucially, 'becoming-feminist' is represented as a journey of self-realisation rather than a result of encounters with feminist literature. 'It took me years', writes Penny, 'to understand that pretty privilege comes with its own set of problems' (p. 35); 'I was well into adulthood', admits O'Toole, 'before I became aware that I was in a carefully scripted show [called womanhood]' (p. 12). The implied reader imagined by these texts is thus not necessarily just a teen, as their titles and jacket designs may suggest. In that contemporary extension of the term which has stretched far into adulthood, she is a 'girl' who is confused or uncer-tain how to conform – or wants to jettison conforming – to the contradictory prescriptions of Western culture's highly commercialised conceptions of successful womanhood.[19]

Dedications are the blunt tool of tone, nominating figures with whom readers can easily identify. Penny's manual was created in conversation, she says, with young, cool, and excitingly edgy types: 'teenage runaways, radical feminists, anarchists, hipster kids, sex workers, mad artists, convicted criminals, transsexual activists and sad young women in small towns longing for adventure', although the last is closer to the reader the book imagines (p. 4). The opening dedication is crafted to appeal to those who like – or would like – to see themselves as dissatisfied with the status quo:

> This book is for the others, as one of the others, as one of those who will never be satisfied with good enough, with free enough, with equality for some. This is for the unspeakable ones, the unnatural ones, the ones who upset people. Who do not do as they are told. Who speak when they shouldn't and refuse to smile when they are supposed on demand. Who are weird and always want too much. (pp. 4–5)

However, it is tame in comparison to a longer dedication it uncannily echoes, penned a few years earlier by Virginie Despentes in her feminist volume *King Kong Theory* (2006), which begins, 'I am writing *as* an ugly one *for* the ugly ones: the old hags, the dykes, the frigid, the unfucked, the unfuckables, the neurotics, the psychos, for all those girls who don't get a look in the universal market of the consumable chick.'[20] Next to this feisty list that deliberately deploys the language used to dismiss those it addresses, Penny's version pales, the placatory logic informing her flattery of her reader – who is smart enough to want equality, freedom, things to be *better*, who refuses to play by the social rules governing women's behaviour – laid bare. Unsurprisingly, Despentes's text is not in fact a feminist manual – it is not interested in offering guidance – but a series of essays based on her lived experience.[21] The feminist manuals share with Despentes the conviction that fulfilling perfect womanhood or femininity is a fiction. Taken to its logical conclusion, this renders all women misfits to a lesser or greater extent since the model to which they are encouraged to culturally and socially aspire is unobtainable.

Overall, feminist manuals seek to reassure women and girls that if they object to, resist, or are simply wearied by the demands of contemporary womanhood, then they are not alone; that wearing lipstick and similar expressions of femininity are compatible with feminism; and that patriarchy does not only adversely affect women but also negatively limits how men relate to the women in their lives. The readership of feminist manuals can be considered to be part of what Lauren Berlant calls 'an intimate public': 'a market [that] opens up to a bloc of consumers, claiming to circulate texts and things that express those people's particular core interests and desires' and helps them feel connected and understood.[22] Berlant identifies 'women's culture' as the first US intimate public, and we can see feminist manuals as aimed at a specific subset of this, one less invested in sentimentality but still bound together by female complaint. To position feminist manuals within the context of trends in contemporary publishing, Leigh Gilmore's work on the rise of neoliberal life narratives is helpful.[23] Gilmore tracks the ascendency of women's memoir in the twentieth century, the suspicion it then attracted, and finally its displacement by the neoliberal life narrative, a form which she describes as typically 'featur[ing] an "I" who overcomes hardship and recasts historical and systemic harm as something an individual alone can, and should, manage through pluck, perseverance and enterprise' (p. 89). These narratives offer pleasing redemption stories whereby the 'individual transforms disadvantage into value' but they also 'absolve readers of the requirement to do anything other than follow the writer's advice in their own lives because the writer has relieved readers of history's ethical claims on us' (p. 89).[24]

Feminist manuals are clearly not cut from exactly the same cloth as neoliberal life narratives: while they might involve stories of personal pluck and enterprise, they locate these in a patriarchal society that must be challenged, thus recognising and naming a historical and systemic harm which neoliberal life narratives in contrast cast as possible to transcend through individual striving. Nevertheless, there is a history largely missing from feminist manuals, and that is the history of feminism itself, both as an account of activist interventions and as a developing trajectory of thought. Remarkably, feminist manuals tend not to engage much with, and sometimes not even to mention, other feminist thinkers, especially those who have made original contributions to the field. The only one in my sample who engages in any depth with feminist theory is O'Toole, whose book road-tests Judith Butler's ideas of gender performance and includes quotes from theoretical thinkers and extrapolations of their ideas, making it by far the most intellectually rich of the five. Penny namechecks various iconic feminist authors and texts but mostly only briefly and in summary, although she does provide footnotes and a fulsome bibliography. Gay reviews a handful of other popular feminist writers, including criticising Moran for producing a 'feminism [which] exists in a very narrow vacuum, to everyone's detriment' (p. 104). In *How to be a Woman*, Moran mentions Germaine Greer several times, but only in passing, while Adichie admits that 'each time I try to read those books called "classic feminist texts", I get bored, and I struggle to finish them' (p. 10).[25]

The result of these books' lack of sustained engagement with the history of feminist thinking is a stark repetitiveness: each one repeats insights that feminism has long been delivering. This is not lost on their readership. The website *Goodreads*, which hosts readers' reviews, reveals that feminist manuals disappoint many of their readers who, even if they have enjoyed the humour, agreed with the content, or appreciated the honesty of the writers, nevertheless often complain that these texts offer nothing new in the way of feminism.[26] One rather bleak conclusion to draw from this could be that feminism itself is stuck, another that these writers lack the imagination to move feminism forward. However, the problem is more emmeshed with the authors' public and publishing profiles than allowed for by these explanations. Penny and Moran are journalists; O'Toole also writes opinion pieces for the press; Adichie is a novelist, as is Gay, who is also a writer of memoir and had a large Twitter following before the publication of *Bad Feminist*. These authors have public personas and specific audiences, even fanbases, that are a result of the other writing and books they have produced.[27] Their feminist manuals are likely to be commercially successful because their names are recognisable and their other writing well-liked. In some cases, such as Gay's *Bad Feminist* or Moran's later *Moranifesto*, the texts collect together short think pieces initially published elsewhere, thus repeating what they have already produced.[28]

The year 2014 was an ideal time to publish a feminist manual: it was glibly declared by the media to be 'the year of feminism', a premature claim precipitated by events involving prominent popular culture figures, including Beyoncé performing in front of large letters spelling out 'Feminist' at the Virgin Music Awards and Emma Watson's impassioned speech about gender equality at the UN.[29] Individually, these feminist manuals have elements that may be appreciated: for O'Toole's attempt to make theory a practice, for the clarity with which Adichie gives her examples, or for the importance of Gay's insistence on intersectionality. There is value in how they are readable introductions to broad feminist principles. Appraised collectively, however, they reproduce a series of repetitive and well-worn feminist assertions. The feminist manual is a profitable venture for publishers, who are confident about publishing what sells and so have backed shelves full of such texts. But the accompanying risk for feminism is that as a genre these texts make it feel stale, repetitive, and stuck. Moreover, they showcase women in competition with each other in the publishing marketplace – crudely typified by Gay awarding Moran only a two-star rating on *Goodreads* – rather than in deep and productive feminist dialogue with either their forebears or with each other. Feminist manuals are thus a perfect neoliberal publishing phenomenon. Repeatedly, they validate that it is the self that delivers feminist understanding, which is sometimes then confirmed by a brief invocation of a classic feminist text. Learning is presented as the result of personal experience rather than of engaging with the history of feminist thought and activism, even while, paradoxically, these books are presented as sites of learning for their readers. The model presents feminism as a personal journey, rather than a collective set of actions and insights that have unfolded over a specific time period. The self as our primary tutor, as responsible for our orientation to the world, is a thoroughly neoliberal conception and not one of much value for feminist social justice.[30] It is not so much that feminist manuals have nothing to offer their readers, although the complaints I mention certainly testify to a dissatisfaction among some, but that they have little to offer each other or the histories they mostly silently rely upon, and therefore nothing to offer to the debates, arguments, and ideas that move feminist thinking and action forward.

While feminist manuals confirm what we already know about the challenges of living as a woman in the twenty-first century, it is this century's feminist manifestos that are so far providing new strategies to disrupt the current systems and institutions that maintain inequality and deliver discrimination. Because the manifestos tend to circulate in forms and forums that are more commonly frequented by academics and activists, their ideas are not reaching mainstream audiences. There is clearly a thirst for new feminist thinking among some of the manuals' readership, the women motivated enough to write and post reviews of these texts online, and yet the models of neoliberal publishing and the authors it favours are unlikely to deliver to them this necessary rethinking of feminist futures. There is a lacuna at the centre of the mainstream distribution and circulation of feminist ideas effected by the manual and, given that it is the manifestos that are rethinking how to structure the world and its resources, it is to them we should be turning instead.

Notes

1 C. Moran, *How to Be a Woman* (London: Ebury Press, 2011), 11.
2 See A. Taylor, *Celebrity and the Feminist Blockbuster* (London: Palgrave Macmillan, 2016). Taylor traces the history of the feminist blockbuster to

begin with Helen Gurley Brown, Betty Friedan, and Germaine Greer. She admits her study is 'not primarily focused on the formal aspects of these texts' (p. 4) whereas my reading is particularly attentive to tone, structure, how these texts insert themselves (or not) into the feminist canon, and how they embody politics. Taylor's definition is broad; mine far less so since it is confined to books that are dedicated to teaching their readers how to be feminists through memoir and confessional anecdote. Taylor also discusses Roxanne Gay, as I do here.

3 K. Weeks, *The Problem with Work: Feminism, Marxism, Antiwork Politics, and Postwork Imaginaries* (Durham and London: Duke University Press, 2011), 214.

4 L. Winkiel, *Modernism, Race, and Manifestos* (Cambridge and New York: Cambridge University Press, 2008), 12.

5 V. Solanas, *Scum Manifesto* (London and New York: Verso Books, 2015), 43; S. Firestone, *The Dialectic of Sex: The Case for Feminist Revolution* (New York: Farrar, Straus, and Giroux, 1970), 185. The twentieth century's first feminist manifesto was by Mina Loy in 1914.

6 S. Ahmed, *Living a Feminist Life* (Durham, NC: Duke University Press, 2017), 251–68; Laboria Cubonkis, 'Xeno-feminism: A Politics for Alienation', available at laboriacuboniks.net and as a downloadable PDF, to which my page numbers refer; H. Hester, *Xenofeminism* (Cambridge: Polity, 2018); and Edinburgh Action for Trans Health, 'Trans Health Manifesto', in N. Raha et al. (eds.), *Radical Transfeminism* (Leith, 2017), 56–61.

7 Ahmed blogged about her reasons for leaving. See 'Resignation is a Feminist Issue' (27 August 2016), feministkilljoys.com.

8 S. Ahmed, *The Promise of Happiness* (Durham, NC: Duke University Press, 2010), 65.

9 Hester, one of its co-authors, calls it a manifesto in *Xenofeminism*, 2; Annie Goh recalls that it was launched as a manifesto. See A. Goh, 'Appropriating the Alien: A Critique of Xenofeminism', *Mute* (29 July 2019), metamute.org.

10 See Goh, 'Appropriating the Alien' for a divergent view which interprets the XF commitments to intersectionality, especially class and race, as 'add ons'. Goh sees troubling affinities between xenofeminism and accelerationism, and even the neoreactionary figure Nick Land. She also critiques the manifesto's contradictory uses of alienation, which she sees as linked to a problematically white 'us' still resident within the text's advocacy for universalism.

11 Ibid. Goh also calls the text 'vague and elusive'.

12 For attention to sex work, medical pathologisation and gatekeeping, capitalism and feminism, see Paul B. Preciado's *Testo Junkie: Sex, Drugs, and Biopolitics in the Pharmacopornographic Era*, trans. B. Benderson (New York: Feminist Press, 2013).

13 D. Spade, *Normal Life: Administrative Violence, Critical Trans Politics, and the Limits of the Law* (Durham, NC: Duke University Press, 2015), 50–93.

14 N. Raha, 'Transfeminine Brokenness and Radical Transfeminism', *The South Atlantic Quarterly*, 116:3 (July 2017), 632–46.

15 For a description of 1980s feminist confessional writing, see R. Felski, *Beyond Feminist Aesthetics: Feminist Literature and Social Change* (London: Hutchinson Radius, 1989), 86–121.

16 E. O'Toole, *Girls Will be Girls: Dressing Up, Playing Parts and Daring to Act Differently* (London: Orion Publishing, 2015), 1–7; L. Penny, *Unspeakable Things: Sex, Lies and Revolution* (London: Bloomsbury, 2014) 25; Moran, *How to Be a Woman*, 8. Moran's promotional video for the book starts by discussing comfort eating. Available at youtube.com.

17 R. Gay, *Bad Feminist: Essays* (New York: Corsair, 2014), x–xiv; C. Ngozi Adichie, *We Should All Be Feminists* (London: Fourth Estate, 2014), 8–11; Penny, *Unspeakable Things*, 5 and 9; O'Toole, *Girls Will be Girls*, 38–41; Moran, *How to Be a Woman*, 71–88.

18 S. Ngai, *Ugly Feelings* (Cambridge, MA: Harvard University Press, 2005), 43.

19 The use of 'girl' or 'girls' to refer to women is so prevalent that a recent multi-media advertising campaign by Sport England to encourage activity among women and girls in the UK is called 'This Girl Can'. Available at: thisgirlcan .co.uk.

20 V. Despentes, *King Kong Theory*, trans S. Benson (New York: Feminist Press, 2009), 7.

21 Chapter 1 of my monograph, *Contemporary Feminist Life-Writing: The New Audacity* (Cambridge: Cambridge University Press, 2020), discusses *King Kong Theory* alongside other feminist autobiographies that recount rape.

22 L. Berlant, *The Female Complaint: The Unfinished Business of Sentimentality in American Culture* (Durham, NC: Duke University Press, 2008), 5.

23 Gilmore defines neoliberalism as follows: 'the state benefits from abandoning "the individual" to his or her own care and promotes that exposure as the freedom to choose in the absence of a safety net of appropriate support' in *Tainted Witness: Why We Doubt What Women Say About Their Lives* (New York: Columbia University Press, 2017), 8.

24 Gilmore's chosen neoliberal life narratives are Jeanette Walls's *The Glass Castle* (2005), Elizabeth Gilbert's *Eat, Pray, Love: One Woman's Search for Everything Across Italy, India and Indonesia* (2006), and Cheryl Strayed's *Wild: From Lost to Found on the Pacific Crest Trail* (2012).

25 For instance, the chapter on feminism begins, 'In *The Female Eunuch*, Germaine Greer suggests that the reader take a moment to taste their menstrual blood . . . Well I cannot help but agree' (p. 71) and then moves on.

26 *Goodreads* enables users to search reviews by book and view statistics on how many stars it has been awarded. For instance, Moran's *How to Be a Woman*, on 24 August 2018, had received 25,214 5-star, 29,439 4-star, 20,337 3-star, 7,709 2-star, and 4,202 1-star ratings. A typical 3-star review by poster Samadrita notes the enjoyable humour but concludes, 'Do not read this in the hopes of enriching your repertoire of feminist perspectives.' See goodreads.com.

27 O'Toole, whose book is also the most engaged with feminist thought, is rather an exception here: *Girls Will be Girls* draws on the theory she studied for her PhD in theatre studies. Her journalism dates mostly from after the publication of *Girls*.

28 Moran has capitalised on the manifesto form here, although her short, humorous 'Moranifesto' is provided only at the end. Others use the term 'manifesto' without meeting the definitions provided above, for example,

Adichie's *Dear Ijeawele: A Feminist Manifesto in Fifteen Suggestions* provides sensible advice for child-raising; Jessa Crispin's *Why I Am Not a Feminist: A Feminist Manifesto* (2017) admonishes feminists for ruining the kind of feminism she advocates; Mary Beard's book, *Women & Power: A Manifesto* (2017) comprises two public lectures that historically contextualise the vitriolic misogyny aimed at women in the public eye, especially online. Using 'manifesto' in the titles of these books is canny but misleading marketing.

29 *The Guardian, Time, Slate, The Telegraph, Huffington Post*, and others declared 2014 'the year for feminism'. For a sample of why, see *The Guardian* editorial, 'The Guardian View on a Year in Feminism: 2014 was a Watershed' (31 December 2014).

30 Natalie Cecire makes a similar point in her 21 August 2018 blog post, 'New at This': 'If we want to talk about "neoliberalism," perhaps we can look at the model of learning that sees *only* that learning which is immediately applicable to oneself as valid or real, in which YouTube plumbing videos are good but reading *Gender Trouble* is unnecessary and maybe even self-indulgent.' See natalie.cecire.org.

CHAPTER 15

'This is not a memoir': Feminist Writings from Life

Kaye Mitchell

As Rita Felski argues, confessional writing – a term she applies quite broadly, 'to specify a type of autobiographical writing which signals its intention to foreground the most personal and intimate details of the author's life' – 'poses in exemplary fashion the problem of the relationship between personal experience and political goals within feminism as a - whole'.[1] This 'problem' persists; how is it formulated and confronted and problematised by the diverse forms of life writing by women appearing since the turn of the century? This chapter considers the forms and functions of feminist writings from life (a rather broader category than 'confessional writing', admittedly) in the twenty-first century, illuminating a perceived shift in the conception of *the personal-as-political*, by examining both memoirs of the feminist movement which seek to memorialise a period and a collective experience, thereby doing history as autobiography; and more experimental forms of life writing which juxtapose stories of self with stories of others, and which presume neither the existence of a knowable self nor the necessary desirability of self-knowledge as the outcome of the act of autobiographical writing. As I will suggest, however, various shared features resurface, even in quite different kinds of life writing: an anxiety about individual identity and the construction of the written 'I'; a suspicion of the autobiographical genre itself as a vehicle for feminist politics; a belief (despite this anxiety, this suspicion) in the positive personal and political benefits of self-narration; an emphasis on affect, particularly the negative kind, and the revisiting of scenes of suffering.

As Lynne Segal has claimed, the 'vigorous insertion of personal lives into the political sphere ... was for a while the hallmark of 1970's women's liberation, epitomised in Sheila Rowbotham's classic text *Women's Consciousness, Man's World* (1973), and triggering such slogans as "the personal is political"'; Segal traces a line between this 'feminist conscious-ness-raising' and the later 'cultural flowering of women's autobiographical/

semi-autobiographical fiction'.[2] Feminism of the 1960s and 1970s, then, had at its heart, and as one of its key political strategies, self-narration and the marshalling of apparently 'personal' and 'private' experiences and feelings in the service of determinedly structural, sociopolitical change. It also, if we follow Segal's line of thinking, had a direct influence on the literary and publishing trends of recent years, helping to fuel what Leigh Gilmore has described as a 'surge in life narratives published in the late twentieth century', with 'women's life stories' a prominent part of this 'boom'.[3]

And yet, the kinds of texts emerging from and expressive of this apparent autobiographical impulse might leave something to be desired. So, in Segal's view, 'from the closing decades of the twentieth century, self-narration has tended to conform to a Zeitgeist largely disdainful of *any* broader analysis of the social and economic underpinnings of selfhood' (p. 125); and thus the 'confessional novels' of the 1990s onwards 'were . . . no longer journeys of shared hope, embarked upon with others in pursuit of collective goals, but rather narrated tales of individual triumph over trauma' (p. 126). The shift she identifies is away from a focus on 'what we had quickly diagnosed as our *shared*, rather than unique or *individual*, personal woes', away from the search for 'collective solutions for what we diagnosed as shared female afflictions', and towards a much more individualising notion of 'trauma' (p. 126).

In what follows, I consider whether the feminist writings from life appearing in the twenty-first century confirm or complicate this trend of individualisation, whether they do indeed reduce political, structural, and public issues to personal struggles, or whether they use personal struggle as a lens for confronting and combatting those structural injustices with which feminism has always concerned itself. The following discussion is divided into two parts. The first, 'Memoir as Memorialisation', addresses recent feminist memoirs with a focus on the feminist movement of the so-called second wave (notably Andrea Dworkin's *Heartbreak* (2002) and Lynne Segal's *Making Trouble: Life and Politics* (2007)), and asks how and to what ends past feminisms are narrated and remembered in the present. As Clare Hemmings has noted, the 'story' of the feminist 'past' is so frequently told 'as a series of interlocking narratives of progress, loss and return that', she claims, 'oversimplify this complex history and position feminist subjects as needing to inhabit a theoretical and political cutting edge in the present'.[4] How do memoirs *by feminists*, memoirs *of feminism*, tell this 'story'?

The second part, 'Hybrid Forms', turns to the emergence of generically inventive and autofictional forms of life writing by women in recent years. Mixing essay, fiction, theory, and autobiography, texts such as Kate

Zambreno's *Heroines* (2012) and Chris Kraus's *Aliens and Anorexia* (2000) tackle difficult emotions and experiences (mental illness, anorexia, anger, shame, failure), yet do so from a standpoint that troubles authenticity, authority, and the stability of the self writing, via hybrid forms whose own instability and open-endedness facilitate that troubling. These narratives displace the writing 'I' via the incorporation and assimilation of various other life stories, thereby apparently moving 'beyond the subject and towards intersubjective practices and modes of knowing' (to quote Hemmings, in relation to feminist theory) (p. 198). In my readings of Zambreno and Kraus, I assess the possibilities and limitations of this embrace of empathetic intersubjectivity as an ethical strategy of recent feminist life writing, considering how this reframes – in perhaps problematically privatised ways – earlier notions of solidarity and collectivity.

Memoir as Memorialisation

Writing in 2008, Margaret Henderson noted what she termed an '"autobiographical turn" towards feminist history', suggesting that 'a significant part of the contemporary upsurge in women's life writing has been the proliferation of autobiographies and memoirs by American feminist activists, particularly from the mid 1990s onward.'[5] A clutch of publications around the turn of the century bears this out, notably: Susan Brownmiller's *In Our Time: Memoir of a Revolution* (1999), Andrea Dworkin's *Heartbreak: The Political Memoir of a Feminist Militant* (2002), Betty Friedan's *Life So Far: A Memoir* (2000), Robin Morgan's *Saturday's Child: A Memoir* (2001), and *The Feminist Memoir Project: Voices from Women's Liberation* (1998; 2nd edn 2007), the anthology edited by Rachel Blau DuPlessis and Ann Snitow, with contributors such as Kate Millett, Joan Nestle, Vivian Gornick and Barbara Smith. Moreover, this phenomenon is not limited to the USA, with UK-based feminists such as Lynne Segal (*Making Trouble*, 2007), Michèle Roberts (*Paper Houses*, 2007), and Sheila Rowbotham (*Promise of a Dream*, 2001) similarly publishing, in the twenty-first century, books of an autobiographical nature focusing on the period of the second wave. Collectively, these publications express a desire both to memorialise and to re-assess a particular period of feminist history. Generically, these books test the boundaries between autobiography and history, offering highly personal perspectives on a very public movement. At the same time, they reveal the continuing importance for feminism of telling these stories of self as a way of telling much 'bigger' stories of a particular period, a movement, a shifting set of ideas and ideologies, allegiances and conflicts.

Henderson, however, warns against what she calls 'the *Bildung* of the exceptional woman', which is:

> [A]n ideal vehicle to narrate the acceptable feminist subject and feminist past in and for postfeminist times. Such a form offers us the memories and making of a highly individualistic, successful, powerful, entrepreneurial, and famous female self who is circumspect about the revolutionary past of feminism. This characterization overlaps with that of the ideal female subject of late capitalism. (pp. 166–7)

Can the feminist memoir/memoir of feminism avoid reproducing this 'ideal female subject of late capitalism'? Can the self be written into its historical and political contexts in ways that resist this neoliberal imperative? I will consider two contrasting examples here.

Heartbreak opens with the claim that: 'I have been asked, politely and not so politely, why I am myself. This is an accounting any woman will be called on to give if she asserts her will.'[6] What follows reads, above all, as an assertion of (individual) will, as Dworkin repudiates the wisdom/tyranny of adults (teachers and parents), and distances herself from possible allies and co-conspirators. She proclaims that, 'I was an exile early on, but exile welcomed me; it was where I belonged', and much of her narrative reinforces this picture of her as a rebel, an outsider, a loner; she is 'exceptional', though arguably not in the way that Henderson intends (p. 42). While Dworkin seems rather distant from 'the acceptable feminist subject … for postfeminist times', her memoir is nevertheless highly individualistic, ego-driven, and less optimistic about sisterhood than comparable works. Personal experiences are to the fore – her rebellions at Bennington, the fact that she is a battered wife (in her first marriage) who has 'prostituted' herself while on the run from her husband and trying to survive (p. 121) – and there is little sense, for most of the book, of her being part of a collective endeavour.

Thus, although she declares herself 'grateful … to the women's movement – to the women who had been organising and talking and shouting and writing, making women both visible and loved by each other' (p. 121), she says little about the workings of that movement, and her anecdotes about encounters with various forms of collective activism generally hinge upon a disagreement or argument and culminate in her distancing herself from the group or organisation in question. In a chapter titled 'my last leftist meeting' she asserts that 'the women's movement had outclassed the peace movement' – implicitly placing them in competition – and walks out of the meeting because of the 'woman-hating' in evidence there (p. 129). When she speaks out about male violence at a memorial service for Petra Kelly, a murdered feminist, anti-pornographer, and pacifist, she claims that 'no pacifist woman stood up to support me' (p. 136); and when one woman does thank her on the way out, she insists, 'That's enough; it has to be enough – one on-site person during a conflict showing respect' (p. 137). She damns the National Organization for Women – 'this duplicitous feminist organiza-tion' – for their 'milksop politics' (pp. 172, 171).

What emerges from these stories is a vision of Dworkin as a lone crusader – the woman who other women approach in the street to tell of their experiences of rape and abuse. She becomes a vehicle and repository of their stories: 'I became responsible for what I heard. I listened; I wrote; I learned' (p. 179). Yet there is little sense of how her activism informs a wider debate, and little nuance in her anecdotes about the stories offered her (in the telling of which, child abuse, rape, pornography and prostitu-tion are frequently conflated, creating a hyperbolic maelstrom of undiffer-entiated fear and horror). Ultimately, the effect of her extreme empathy, her over-identification with the suffering she absorbs, seems to be that 'I'm tired, very weary, and I cry for my sisters' (p. 180). Although she proceeds to detail the successes of the feminist movement in her lifetime – including legislation against sexual harassment and marital rape – Dworkin never-theless allows her own weariness to stand for the movement ('Feminists have good reasons for feeling tired' (p. 194)), and it feels like a crucial statement when she declares that, 'writers write alone even in the context of a political movement' (p. 185).

Is it the very genre of the memoir that compels this subsuming of the political by the personal? *Heartbreak* ends as it began with a defensive insistence on the insularity and partiality of the memoir:

> *A memoir, which this is*, says: this is what my memory insists on; this is what my memory will not let go; these points of memory make me who I am, and all that others find incomprehensible about me is explained by what's in here. (p. 211, emphasis mine)

Dworkin's plea, thereafter, that this memoir might 'serve as a kind of bridge over which some girls and women can pass into their own feminist work' (p. 211), ultimately rings rather hollow, not only because of the defeatism of the conclusion, but also because *Heartbreak* has throughout privileged militant individualism over collective endeavour.

Alert to the limitations of personal confession, and in stark contrast to Dworkin, Lynne Segal begins *Making Trouble* by asserting that, '*This is not a memoir*. At least, it is not simply a personal reckoning of my life so far.'[7] And from the outset, she stresses the necessary imbrication of the personal and political:

> [T]he personal reflections that mean most to me, which provide a certain temporal continuity and help sustain those attachments to others so necessary for our sense of self, often take me to places that are also political. They transcend the segregation between the personal and the political. (p. 1)

In turn, Segal shows how the Women's Liberation Movement provided her with 'the first secure moorings in a world hitherto largely devoid of significant meanings, morality or goals' (p. 5), while 'those I think of as "my generation" … had early on turned to Left-wing politics to help us move beyond personal anxieties' (p. 9). Joining with others in the pursuit of certain feminist and socialist goals is thus presented as motivated, at least in part, by strongly personal needs; but also as allowing those individual needs to be subsumed within/by something larger (and, by implication, more important).

In fact, Segal represents the development of her political affiliations and her adoption of 'shared collective goals' as the things that saved her from various personal anxieties and helped her to 'move beyond the needy, performing self' of her childhood (p. 17). Segal's 'unhappy family' is here refigured as part of 'the unique dynamics that might play a part in pushing a person towards politics as an anchor of identity' (pp. 24, 26). Furthermore, she argues that 'it is the historical contingencies of time, place and other unpredictable encounters' that 'determine our specific journeys' (p. 32), and chooses to read her personal experiences – with the admitted benefit of hindsight ('understanding life backwards') – in relation to bigger historical and structural shifts: 'I embarked upon sexual life in the Sixties, in the growing clamour for sexual liberation. I became a single mother in the Seventies, as feminism bloomed again' (p. 32), and in the 1980s, as those social movements of the earlier decades waned, she acquired, unexpectedly, a more settled life and career within academia. And yet, as Segal concedes 'living life forward, you see none of this' (p. 32), suggesting that this structural vision (seeing one's life, development, and decisions in the bigger contexts of social and historical change) is only possible in retrospect; and thereby indicating the particular *value* of a memoir such as this one, which can offer renewed understandings of both one's own life and the contexts in which it has been lived and from which it is, necessarily, inextricable.

Importantly, Segal does not rely only on her own memories, her own perspective, to construct her history of the period, asserting that 'many witnesses are needed to hold on to a sense of the past and our own presence within it, or else it shrinks to fit the platitudes of the present' (p. 61). So she includes first-person accounts from friends and others in the Women's Liberation Movement, and she reads 'all the autobiographical material I could find' (p. 62), interweaving this with her own thoughts and reminiscences. In the examples she cites, what emerges most strongly through her particular juxtaposition of viewpoints is the sense of the mutual reinforcement of the personal and the political, of feminism as a way of life – something that emerges from a life, from a set of personal experiences, but also something that then structures, determines (and shores up) that life in myriad ways: 'I was no longer alone', 'I learned who I was through the Women's Liberation Movement', '[it] was absolutely formative for me', 'it taught me new ways to love myself, by loving all of us'.[8] Segal's gloss on this is that Women's Liberation was 'a politics' that '[touched] upon every aspect of your life', and thus 'you were never outside your feminism, at home or abroad' (p. 68).

While Segal acknowledges, in *Making Trouble*, the forms of discord that arose within the feminist movement, the ways that feminist messages were appropriated and repurposed by more mainstream (and more ideologically suspect) bodies, and the challenges of ageing for once-idealistic radicals in particular, she nevertheless retains a certain optimism – mainly by adopting a perspective that transcends her own particular desires and experiences. *Making Trouble* is 'not a memoir' – or not merely a memoir – because its focus extends across a recent history of the UK, a history of the Women's Liberation Movement, an account of British socialism and leftist activism more generally, and a history of various prominent individuals (Ralph Steadman, Stuart Hall, Sheila Rowbotham, Doris Lessing, Simone de Beauvoir) with whom Segal crossed paths, or by whom she has been influenced. The scope and relative impersonality of *Making Trouble* – or rather, its persistent desire to historicise and contextualise the supposedly 'personal' – imply that life writing can be used as a vehicle for feminist history and feminist politics, without falling prey to the *Bildung* model of individualism and entrepreneurial selfhood against which Henderson rails.

Hybrid Forms and the Politics of Empathy

Segal's model of memoir stresses solidarity above all, while Dworkin's repudiates solidarity in favour of something that represents, at best, an attempt at empathy with the suffering of diverse women ('I cry for my sisters'). That empathetic model forms the subject of this next section, which considers the politics of empathy and the attempts at intersubjective understanding to be found in a strand of generically hybrid feminist life writing in the twenty-first century. As Hemmings has noted:

> [O]ne way in which feminist theorists have sought to extend the boundaries of the feminist subject has been through theorizing empathy as a mode of linking to others and as promoting intersubjective relations over and above individual status in relation to knowledge and practice. In this respect feminists invest in empathy because of its capacity to move the subject beyond the limits of her own vision. (pp. 197–8)

What might the effects be for feminist life writing of this attempt 'to extend the boundaries of the feminist subject' through empathy? If writers such as Segal, Brownmiller, and Rowbotham seek to move 'beyond the limits' of their own subjective 'vision' by offering a focus on the collective, on history, on the structural, and on lives lived together, then some of the more obviously experimental twenty-first-century feminist writings from life that I turn to in this section seek to move beyond the subjective by juxtaposing their own stories, experiences, and feelings with those of their contemporaries and forebears (real and fictional), and by exploring connections that are primarily *affective* – and often imagined, fantasised, or at least virtual.[9] In these texts, a performed empathy becomes 'a mode of linking to others' and, potentially, a means of extending 'the boundaries of the feminist subject', but it also begins from an individualist standpoint that is, I suggest, quite at odds with earlier feminist injunctions to solidarity.

Kate Zambreno's *Heroines*, which I will discuss in more detail in the following pages, is a case in point, but there are various other examples of twenty-first-century works that we might call 'hybrid' or 'metacritical'; works which combine memoir and critical writing in the service of a gender political argument and/or which juxtapose stories of self and other. Think of Maggie Nelson's *The Argonauts* (indeed, most of Nelson's published output), which, in Monica B. Pearl's memorable description, 'combines high theory and the everyday ... with its immingling of lofty thought, the quotidian, close attention to words and ideas and stray thoughts, and desire', and which 'blends and refuses genre' in its meditations on gendered embodiment and queer kinship.[10] As I have written elsewhere, *The Argonauts* also elaborates 'a politics and ethics of vulnerability in both its thinking and its formal qualities';[11] it treats vulnerability precisely as, in Erinn Gilson's formulation, 'a basic kind of openness to being affected and affecting in both positive and negative ways'.[12] This 'openness to being affected' is a recurrent feature of the almost-genre I am trying to pinpoint here.

Think also of Chris Kraus's oeuvre. *I Love Dick* (1997) might be read as an inaugural 'hybrid' text, mixing memoir, fiction, letter, and essay in its attempt to 'handle vulnerability like philosophy, at some remove'.[13] The later *Aliens and Anorexia* (2001) is especially notable, however, for the way in which Kraus fixes upon Simone Weil – who 'felt the suffering of others in her body', who was a 'performative philosopher' – as a vehicle for her own emotional porosity and sadness, and as a means for her both to inhabit and to transcend her self, her recalcitrant female body.[14] 'Re-reading *Gravity and Grace* by Simone Weil', writes Kraus, 'I identified with the dead philosopher completely' (p. 103). This *identification* is both method and content for Kraus, and it is legitimated, here, by Weil's own life and philosophy – or at least, the accounts of them that we get from Kraus. Thus, when Kraus asserts that, 'The child-Simone experienced the world as a rush of passionate sensations. The philosopher Simone ... came to call these sensations *knowledge*' (p. 140), she rationalises her own method of doing vulnerability as philosophy, of treating feeling as knowing. Meanwhile, her particular depiction of Weil as someone who 'was not a genius, not a pretty girl' (p. 140), but whose 'awareness of her personal imperfections made her sensitive to all the imperfections in the world' (p. 141) serves to valorise Kraus's own affective sensitivity, and to compensate for her perceived failures and inadequacies (*Aliens* is really about Kraus's failures: the film that cannot get distribution, the phone sex affair that dwindles). What Kraus calls Weil's 'will-to-decreation' (p. 147) – expressed both in her philosophical writings and through her self-starvation – becomes, paradoxically, both Kraus's way of explaining her own sense of lack (of being unseen, unrecognised, a kind of ghost or void in the world) and her way of countering this evanescence and shoring up a sense of self. It allows her, also, to make a case that anorexia might be 'an active, ontological state' (p. 162), rather than a form of feminine self-hatred: an altruistic, outward-looking, non-pathological attempt 'to *leave* the body' (p. 166).

Is this intense identification empathy or appropriation on Kraus's part? She writes of Weil that she 'was driven by a panic of altruism, an empathy so absolute she couldn't separate the suffering that she witnessed from her own' (p. 143), and again this allows Kraus to elaborate her own theory of empathy as 'not a reaching outward' so much as 'a loop. Because there isn't any separation any more between what you are and what you see' (p. 150). That absence of 'separation', however, threatens to subsume Weil's story, to obliterate the otherness of the other in exploring the porosity of imagined, affective commingling. While Kraus may assert that 'A single moment of true sadness connects you instantly to all the suffering in the world' (p. 155), this 'connection' is fantasised, unreciprocated – an 'altruism' that does not lead to action, just as the anorexia she describes only appears to offer transcendence of the body.

And so, to *Heroines* – a 'messy and fragmentary text', a kind of 'critical memoir' (in the words of one reviewer); 'a composite creature: part memoir, part criticism, part fiction, part feminist tract or call to arms or self-help manual or biography or work of literary history' (according to another).[15] While living in Chicago, where her husband is working in the Newberry library, and she is failing to write a novel and straining against her allotted roles as wife and adjunct, Kate Zambreno becomes 'enthralled' by the women she calls 'my madwomen' – principally Vivien(ne) Eliot and Zelda Fitzgerald, but also numerous other Modernist women writers and wives of writers.[16] These are the 'heroines' of her title, and she claims them as her own, averring that: 'Minus a community, I invented one' (p. 14). She calls them an 'invisible community' also because 'they too were made invisible' (p. 14), and *Heroines* becomes, therefore, an attempt to counter 'their erasure as subjects' (p. 156) – and also to counter her own sense of erasure as an unwilling wife and struggling writer. What kind of 'community' is this? It is transhistorical, affective; it functions through empathy and identification – as she writes, 'I align myself with a genealogy of erased women' (p. 157) – but in this 'alignment', is she reinstating the subjectivity and sovereignty of the 'madwomen' who haunt her, or is she appropriating them (and their experiences) to help her understand her own situation? (These options are, of course, not necessarily mutually exclusive.)

Notably, Zambreno's relations with her madwomen are facilitated by identification – an identification that comes mainly through reading: 'I am Madame Bovary as I read *Madame Bovary*. Ennui, excess of emotions. *C'est moi*. I am Zelda, I am Vivien(ne)' (p. 19). She figures this identification as both 'devouring' and 'channeling': 'I begin to cannibalize these women, literally incorporating them, their traumas, an uncanny feeling of repeating, of reliving' (p. 49). Some days she '[c]an only exist through screens, other people's lives' (p. 50), her own self displaced or voided. She represents her relationship with these women as '[a] form of possession' and figures herself as 'in communion with my ancestors' (p. 60) – 'Writing towards these women is like engaging in a séance' (p. 65). In this way, Zambreno reclaims many disavowed tropes of woman as mystic, hysteric, madwoman, monster. Her mode of criticism shirks textual analysis, literary history, and traditional literary biography; instead, Zambreno avers that, for her, '"criticism" . . . always originates in *feeling*'

(p. 138). She refuses the distance or objectivity that might seem to attend the act of critique – performing what Sheila Heti calls a 'technique of ventriloquism' – and instead treats feeling as knowing, affect as feminist epistemology.[17]

Setting aside whether this is or is not good critical practice (Zambreno is not writing for an academic press, and the book began life as, first, a blog and then a putative novel), we might ask whether it constitutes good or bad empathy, good or bad feminist praxis. As Hemmings explains the distinction: 'In bad empathy the subject's needs and expectations are projected onto the other; in good empathy the subject responds to and respects the other as a subject' (p. 200). What can result, in cases of failed or bad empathy, is 'sentimental attachment to the other, or worse, substitution of one's own interests for those of the other' (p. 199). One critical reviewer does indeed worry that 'Zambreno further commits her heroines to the marginal position of the muse'; another notices how, 'She speaks for the women and as the women in a voice that merges theirs and her own, which is what the writer-geniuses she reviles did to the same women in their great works.'[18] When Zambreno complains, of the male author (any of the male modernists she is discussing): 'He writes a book in an attempt to understand her (but really, this is an attempt to unravel himself, she is merely the shadow who haunts). He wants to crack into her interiority, her impenetrability' (p. 148), she fails to acknowledge the ways in which her actions might mimic theirs.

Zambreno's desire to 'write against the culture' (p. 251) – inspired, in part, by forebears such as Kathy Acker, Mary Gaitskill, and Kraus – involves also a writing against what she sees as a specifically *gendered* 'bias against autobiography that comes out of modernism' (p. 235), which reads the woman who writes autobiographically as 'simply writing herself, her toxic, messy self' (p. 237). And yet, writing 'her toxic, messy self' is precisely what Zambreno does here. *Heroines* is Zambreno's attempt to recuperate writing that is 'associative, emotional, messy, girly' (p. 244) (this is her paraphrased description of Fitzgerald's denigration of Zelda's *Save Me the Waltz*). Countering the injunction that 'one must discipline one's text, one's self', that one should not 'portray emotions in EXCESS (in literature or in life)' (p. 36), *Heroines* sets itself in opposition to the 'impersonality' commended by T. S. Eliot (in 'Tradition and the Individual Talent'), and refuses the idea that 'Writing should be composed. Should be transcendent. In the calm communion with and recognition of one's ancestors' (p. 65). Instead, Zambreno repeatedly indicates her preference for what she calls 'the aesthetic of the "unfinished"', which is that of the notebook, of the diary, of fragments (not the novel, which is supposed to be cultivated, worked over, finished)' (p. 136), and the hybrid, fragmentary, uneven, non-chronological, hyperbolic, digressive, confessional nature of *Heroines* is such that it enacts what it endorses.

It is perhaps unsurprising, then, that Zambreno so readily celebrates her blogging peers – her other 'invisible community' – for their willingness to write diaristically, and to engage with the 'raw material' of their lives (p. 265). For Zambreno, the diary – although it 'is often still considered an inferior form of writing by both critics and the culture-at-large' (p. 275) – is a vital form, and we should read the writings of the 'girl-diarist' 'as a theatre of potential great feeling and discovery, of experimentalism and play'; we should see diary-writing as an attempt, by girls, 'to navigate and create who they are, the distance between their private *agonistes* and the self that is supposed to smile' (p. 277); in this way, she implies, the diary reveals the performativity (but also the labour and struggle) of femininity-as-façade. Zambreno champions the confessional mode, the diary-made-public: she casts herself (despite her age, status, and education) as a girl-diarist, and in the internet age, 'we write our diaries in public for all to see' (p. 277). Blogging – in its rawness, its messiness, its emotional turbulence – is validated by Zambreno as cutting-edge praxis, allowing 'a new sort of subjectivity' to develop – and, we might note, a new kind of memoir – and facilitating 'a new, glib, casual, *entirely feminine* form of criticism that takes the form at times of heroine-worship' (p. 279, my emphasis). Perhaps most importantly, given the possible limitations of the empathetic model that I have discussed here, Zambreno claims that 'this subculture of literary blogs, fluid, amorphous, non-hierarchical, functions as *a community of solidarity*' (p. 293, my emphasis). Is this, then, the new locus, the new form, the new functionality, of feminist writing *from life* – this online space that allows the fulfilment of Zambreno's imperative to her readers, 'to write yourself, your body, your own experience', and in this way 'to understand yourself' and to 'become yourself' (p. 296)? Can the 'solidarity' it offers be more than fantasised, given this invocation to self-fashioning?

To Felski's claim – with which I began – that confessional writing 'poses in exemplary fashion the problem of the relationship between personal experience and political goals within feminism as a whole', and Segal's that 'feminist journeys breach the barriers between public and private', we might add the further factor of a virtual publishing arena where personal and political mix and merge in a space that itself breaches 'the barriers between public and private'.[19] The blog world, in its ever-altering incarnations, responds to a continuing feminist desire to tell stories of self – and stories of feminisms past and present – and provides a new arena in which to do so. It facilitates writing that is confessional, interactive, provisional, polemical; yet it also steers that writing in directions that might be sentimental, subjective, individualising, self-absorbed, *girlish*, preoccupied with 'personal experience' to the detriment or in the absence of clear 'political goals'. It has disseminated writing that reaches out to and even constructs a community, fostering new waves of activism (on- and offline); yet if the bonds of solidarity are forged through empathetic identification ('I am Zelda. I am Vivien(ne)'), rather than through (as Segal reminisces) 'collective efforts not just to wrestle with the world, but also to change it', they might prove less durable (p. 11). Although '[t]hose women who tried to change the world at the very least usually managed to change themselves', changing themselves was not the primary goal (p. 5), and for feminist writing from life the goals might be seen to extend beyond 'write yourself' and 'become yourself', even if these necessarily form part of the process.

Notes

1 R. Felski, *Beyond Feminist Aesthetics* (Cambridge, MA: Harvard University Press, 1989), 87 and 89 respectively.
2 L. Segal, 'Who Do You Think You Are? Feminist Memoir Writing', *New Formations*, 67 (2009), 125.
3 L. Gilmore, *Tainted Witness: Why We Doubt What Women Say About Their Lives* (New York: Columbia University Press, 2018), 85.
4 C. Hemmings, *Why Stories Matter: The Political Grammar of Feminist Theory* (Durham, NC: Duke University Press, 2011), 3.
5 M. Henderson, 'The Feminine Mystique of Individualism is Powerful: Two American Feminist Memoirs in Postfeminist Times', *a/b: Auto/Biography Studies*, 23:2 (2008), 165.
6 A. Dworkin, *Heartbreak: The Political Memoir of a Feminist Militant* (New York: Basic Books, 2002), xiii.
7 L. Segal, *Making Trouble: Life and Politics* (London: Serpent's Tail, 2007), 1, my emphasis.
8 The examples come from Audrey Battersby, Sally Alexander, Catherine Hall, and Sally Belfridge; quoted in Segal, *Making Trouble*, 68.
9 S. Brownmiller's *In Our Time* (New York: Delta, 1999) is subtitled 'memoir of a revolution'; she describes herself as 'a partisan-observer', attempting 'to recapture a vivid piece of radical history that changed the world' (p. 10); *Promise of a Dream* (New York: Verso, 2001), although containing more personal material – details about Rowbotham's romantic and sexual relationships – than *In Our Time*, is a memoir of a time period, the 1960s, and seeks to 'relate my subjective take on events to a wider social picture' (p. xi).

10 M. B. Pearl, 'Theory and the Everyday', *Angelaki*, 23:1 (2018), 199.

11 K. Mitchell, '"Feral with Vulnerability": On *The Argonauts*', *Angelaki*, 23:1 (2018), 194.

12 E. Gilson, 'Vulnerability, Ignorance, and Oppression', *Hypatia*, 26:2 (2011), 310.

13 C. Kraus, *I Love Dick* (Los Angeles: Semiotexte, 2006 [1997]), 208.

14 C. Kraus, *Aliens and Anorexia* (South Pasadena: Semiotexte, 2000), 48, 49.

15 E. M. Keeler, 'C'est Pas Moi: On Kate Zambreno's "Heroines"', *LA Review of Books* (16 December 2012) and S. Heti, 'I Dive Under the Covers', *LRB*, 35:11 (6 June 2013), 21 respectively.

16 K. Zambreno, *Heroines* (South Pasadena: Semiotexte, 2012), 8.

17 Heti, 'I Dive Under the Covers', 21.

18 Keeler, 'C'est Pas Moi' and Heti, 'I Dive Under the Covers', 21, respectively.

19 Felski, *Beyond Feminist Aesthetics*, 89 and Segal, *Making Trouble*, 208 respectively.

CHAPTER 16

Feminist Poetries of the Open Wound

Julie Carr

What brings us to feminism is what is potentially shattering.

Sara Ahmed[1]

I begin this chapter with where and who I am, with what I think I know, and with the desire to understand what I think I do not, for this is where poetry begins and also where feminism begins: in embodied ways of knowing that are inevitably specific, partial, and available for revision. First then, a claim generated out of my own experiences: that the poetry written by feminists (people of any gender who take on the mantle of feminism as a calling or epistemology) necessarily articulates the wounds that patriarchy so often imparts upon women's bodies. Indeed, the diverse and intergenerational group of poets I will be reading – Serena Chopra (US), Khadijah Queen (US), Aditi Machado (US/India), Lisa Robertson (Canada/France), and Nat Raha (UK) – take the woundedness of women's bodies as an under-recognised given. Patriarchal, colonial, economic, and sexual violence against women and femmes could be said to be the over-riding subject-matter of their poems.

We could say more generally that the articulation of such wounds is a central project of contemporary feminism (as it has been of prior feminisms), as evidenced by #MeToo. ('Becoming feminist cannot be separated from an experience of violence', writes Sara Ahmed (p. 22).) And yet, so too is the corresponding and equally dynamic celebration and display of women's bodies as sites of pleasure (Janelle Monae's 'Pynk' video, for example). Insofar as patriarchy's violence is often aimed at women's bodies' capacity for pleasure and desire, the expression of such pleasure becomes a form of resistance. Therefore, as much as the poems I will read here air the wounds of patriarchy, they also explore the erotic as a response to such wounds. As Audre Lorde challenged, now almost forty years ago, women must be 'brave enough to risk sharing the erotic's electrical charge without having to look away, and without distorting the enormously powerful and creative nature of that exchange'.[2] Or, as Rosi Braidotti puts it more recently, 'desire is what is at stake in the feminist politics of pursuing alternative definitions of female subjectivity'.[3]

Poetry is, in fact, one of the key aesthetic structures in which both complaint and eros have historically found voice. Yet what I find most compelling in the poems I will be looking at is how and why these two energies come together, often within the same poems. Eros (which, as we will see, Lorde and others distinguish from sexuality per se), rather than denying vulnerability or demanding that we somehow move 'beyond' our wounds, exposes desire, exposes attachment. In this sense, the erotic is not, in these poems, woundedness's antidote. Instead, eros, thought of very broadly as that which draws us towards one another, as that which motivates the permeation of boundaries, and as that which emphasises the vulnerability of people in relation, arises as a partner to woundedness, in a sense, as its twin.

Before I get to the poems, I would like to return our attention to a key text from an earlier era. In *Revolution in Poetic Language* (1974), Julia Kristeva offers one still compelling theorisation of how what I am calling the erotic is enfolded within the open wound of patriarchy in the context of poetic language. Despite what I see as the text's limitations (as discussed in the following), I return to it here because of how Kristeva thinks through the juncture between revolutionary (feminist) subjectivity and the pleasures of non-discursive language. The patriarchal 'wounding' that Kristeva explores in this work is not violence per se (though she does allude to it), but such violence's founding. Kristeva takes on the (Lacanian) myth of the 'mirror-stage', in which the developing child, gaining identification with its specular image – the 'ego-ideal' – must 'sever' its attachment to the mother's body, while also forming a sense of self that is *other* than, and more coherent than, its somatic experience.[4] In this foundational myth of separation, such 'severing' is accompanied by the child's movement into symbolic language: 'dependence on the mother is severed, and transformed into a symbolic relation to an other'.[5]

Kristeva rewrites this myth by focusing her lens on the period that precedes the acquisition of symbolic language, when the infant is still dependent upon its mother's body. Here, argues Kristeva, in this place and time she names 'the chora' (pp. 25–30), communication occurs on another plain, motivated and regulated by the somatic/psychic drives. Kristeva calls this plain of signification the 'semiotic', which she defines as 'a psychosomatic modality of the signifying process' (p. 28), and which includes sound and movement, though not verbal language necessarily.

Breaks in normative grammar, the overt use of rhythm and sound, syntactical disturbances, and the refusal or delay of meaning all constitute the semiotic in language, in contrast to (but always in combination with) the symbolic, understood as the direct delivery of semantic meaning.[6]

Kristeva thereby disrupts the patriarchal narrative of mother/infant severance. On an even more fundamental level, she replaces a narrative of self-individuation with a relational theory of subject-formation. Her contribution to literary-poetic theory is to recognise and revalue the non-representational aspects of language precisely *because* they recall the body and its drives to the scene. Thus, she not only places maternal attachment back into the process of healthy subject-formation and all consequent social relations, but also places 'pleasure' or 'the erotic' (*jouissance*) back into the signification process *as* the mark of its 'revolutionary' potential. Turning towards semiotic *jouissance*, 'the signifying process joins social revolution' (p. 60):

> [T]his semiotization of the symbolic – thus represents the flow of jouissance into language ... In cracking the socio-symbolic order, splitting it open, changing vocabulary, syntax, the word itself, and releasing from beneath them the drives borne by vocalic or kinetic differences, jouissance works its way into the social and symbolic. (pp. 79–80)

This 'semiotization of the symbolic' is, in another way of putting it, the presence of desire in language itself.

Kristeva's linguistic/psychoanalytic approach to the wounds of patriarchy universalises such wounds into a general theory of language and subject formation, while also universalising the mother/infant bond. For these reasons her theory cannot attend to the ways in which male power affects different women differently in unequal societies. Moreover, despite her radical rethinking of such, Kristeva's theory is still tied to psychoanalytic myths of the heteronormative family. Turning, then, to Audre Lorde (who is writing only shortly after Kristeva), we can find a more directly political and more inclusive reading of the revolutionary power of the erotic: 'In order to perpetuate itself, every oppression must corrupt or distort those various sources of power within the culture of the oppressed that can provide energy for change. For women, this has meant a suppression of the erotic as a considered source of power and information within our lives' (p. 53). By locating such revolutionary power within the specific lives of women, Lorde individualises, rather than universalises, patriarchal wounding. In 'Poetry Is Not a Luxury', she argues that poetry, 'the revelation or distillation of experience' (p. 37), gives voice to the very precise wounds and attachments of individual women's lives. Poetry's power, she argues, lies in its capacity to 'give name to the nameless so it can be thought', an essential step in the process of imagining 'the future of our worlds' (p. 37).

Such celebrations of eros (or *jouissance*) assume bodies in relation, bodies in some form of emotional or physical vulnerability. Vulnerability has, in fact, become a key term for some contemporary feminists who are continuing to rethink masculinist 'ideals of independence'.[7] On the one hand, vulnerability demands protection, especially for women and femmes in marginalised groups – women of colour, immigrants, migrants, poor women, queer and trans women, women in locations of increased violence or even femicide. However, without denying the need for greater protections, many feminists continue to model and theorise alternative ways of being, ways which revalue the shared vulnerability of the body, rather than seeking only its defence. In their 2016 collection, *Vulnerability in Resistance*, for example, Judith Butler, Zeynep Gambetti, and Letitia Sabsay, acknowledging that vulnerability is generally understood as tied to passivity and victimhood, ask what would change if 'vulnerability were [instead] imagined as one of the conditions of the very possibility of resistance'?[8]

In her essay for their collection 'Violence Against Women in Turkey: Vulnerability, Sexuality, and Eros', Turkish feminist Meltem Ahiska notes that, 'diagnosing and naming the structure [of male violence] is never enough', we must ask, 'how does the structure sustain and reproduce itself?'[9] Patriarchy will tend to think of its own violence as a (natural) response to vulnerable bodies (which leads both to victim-blaming and to body-shaming). It will, then, demand more protections for these bodies through paradoxically increasing paternalistic power (such as when US gun-rights proponents use the vulnerability of female bodies as evidence for the need for more guns). Such arguments often reinscribe 'masculine models of autonomy', rather than addressing the assumptions that lead to patriarchal violence in the first place.[10] How can we move beyond 'the situation in which there are [only] two opposing alternatives, paternalism and victimization?' (p. 3).

As feminists hoping to uproot, rather than underscore, paternalistic power, we must continue to value and assert the body and its desires, vulnerabilities, and attachments. Indeed, 'Feminists of different strands have long argued for a relational subject as a way to contest liberal forms of individualism, implicated as they are in capitalist concepts of self-interest and masculinist fantasies of sovereign mastery' (p. 3). This 'relational subject' is, then, necessarily alive to the erotic, when we think of the erotic

as a general category that encompasses desires and attachments of many
varieties. Moreover, Ahiska argues (in the context of the current plague of
femicide in Turkey), the erotic constitutes a form of resistance to patriarchal violence especially when that violence is aimed (as it often is) at
desire itself. Female desire *as resistance*, argues Ahiska, must be understood
as not simply sexual desire (which is already objectified and commodified),
but also as *eros*, 'the libido that extends to beauty, knowledge, creative
work, and politics' (pp. 227–8). I will turn now to the poets for how they
articulate the wounds of patriarchy (understood quite broadly as inclusive
of violent and verbal attacks on women's bodies, as well as masculinist
assertions of selfhood as 'severed' from the mother/other), and also for how
they articulate the pleasures of the body as defiant power – attached,
mobile, and erotically energised.

In American poet Serena Chopra's 'Chthonic Colony: My Body Invades
the Theory', Chopra recounts a scene of woundedness that is at once
a scene of care, pleasure, and attachment.[11] She is a child of about five.
She has been raped by a neighbourhood boy, her babysitter, and as a result
is suffering abrasions in and around her vulva. This foundational violence,
despite its horrific nature, is not the focus of the poem. Rather, the poem is
interested in thinking through the responses to such violence, those offered
by the parents, and those found, ultimately, within the self. In what are
presumably the days after the rape, the child lies down in the hallway and
her mother applies cold cream to her wounds. 'In the short hall between
our rooms, I am on my back, mom on crouched knees looks her eye
between' (p. 37). Later in the poem, she is at her father's house. The father
is unable to care for the wound and also, because ashamed, unable to speak
directly about it: 'Daughter', he says in the poem, '*Go put your thing*' (p.
38). Experiencing this double wounding, the rape and the father's distance,
the child enters the bathtub alone:

> At father's house in the bathroom alone
> With the cream and the wound, his shame of ruined
> Daughter, *Go put your thing.* (p. 38)

Having to apply the cold cream to her own body leads the child to discover
the pleasure of self-touching. In another way of putting it, the father's
rejection draws the child back to her mother as a source of pleasure and
care, and to her own hand as an extension of such: 'Chthonic touch, eyes,
see / The wounding leading to masturbation' (p. 38).

But this brief scene articulates more than the opposition between
mother-as source of pleasure/care and father-as source of pain/shame. For

in the moment of maternal care, the distinction between mother and daughter is not complete or clear. The 'short hall' (like a birth canal) mediates both the separation and the connection of mother and daughter. There, the daughter's vagina must be opened, as once the mother's had. And while at birth, the daughter's eyes first opened, here it is the mother's that must 'look'. These mirrored openings gaze at one another through the wound inflicted by the patriarchal 'neighbour', and in this moment of mutual regard, the mother/daughter relation is, as Kristeva puts it, 'a continuum' (p. 28). 'Me seriously bites her lip we go quiet as the cold cream', writes Chopra, describing her mother's application of the cream (p. 37). With this derangement of pronouns, we see the mother biting her own lip in serious contemplation of her daughter's wound, the daughter biting her own lip in pain, and both mother and daughter experiencing the 'biting' of the labial 'lip', where 'biting' indicates the sensation of cream touching the wound. What Kristeva would call 'the semiotic', here in the form of grammatical disturbance, generates or points to a transindividualism grounded in and reliant upon the mother/child relation. But there is more, for later in the poem we are given to understand that the self-pleasuring found in and through the open wound is also *writing*: 'Mother eyeing the wound, daughter evoking its haunting, harvest / Is my thesis' (p. 42). Thus, the poem as a whole can be read as a response to Lorde's call for women to become 'brave enough to risk sharing the erotic's electrical charge without having to look away, and without distorting the enormously powerful and creative nature of that exchange' (p. 59).

Khadijah Queen's 2015 collection, *Fearful Beloved*, addresses fear in relation to male violence: 'Inside easily won memories, violence overwhelms', she writes early on.[12] The wounding here is physical and sexual – as boys 'keep pulling shirts up / keep pulling shorts down / keep beating' 'no matter what the girl says' (p. 27), and as a man turns sexual play into violent attack, 'biting her nipple off' (p. 36) – and it is also psychological: 'Her skin dissolves in the heat as he invades her' (p. 100). And yet, right at the book's centre, Queen announces a shift away from fear:

> *Across from the man she loves, the fearful beloved is, at turns,*
>   *more & less fearful*
> What was between them is vanishing. She wonders why, just
>   now, she begins to feel
> the bruisable monument in her turn into a bouquet of lilies. (p. 46)

Following this moment where the open wound begins to shift from bruise to bouquet, we arrive at a scene (as in Chopra's poem) of a girl bathing, titled 'Inside a House (*Downstairs half-bath*)' (p. 46). Here a girl assesses herself in the mirror, having learned to dislike 'the messiness' of 'emotional seepage' (p. 46). The poem ends with a turn: '*One ought to be able to feel things*, the girl thought briefly before realizing she could no longer tell the difference between feeling & thought. In an instant, the tension in her body eased away' (p. 47).

This embrace of vulnerability, 'emotional seepage', as no longer distinct from thinking, returns the child/woman to her own body as a source of power, instead of fear. 'I become pregnant ▇▇▇▇ with my own rebirth' (p. 52), Queen writes just pages later in one of a series of diaristic poems that employ the black bar of redaction between sparsely arranged phrases. Towards the end of the book, Queen addresses 'fear' itself: 'I see how appetite for connection makes you disappear & the sensation of pure / movement dispels you – It makes a sound / It makes many sounds & voices approach an understanding / connected to one another' (p. 53). Again, the response to the fear of patriarchal wounding is not a retreat into the individuated self, and neither is it a call for more (paternal) protections. Instead Queen's 'I' finds respite from fear through 'pure movement' and 'sound' (the semiotic), and through the 'appetite for connection', which Lorde and Ahiska would call the erotic.

In her debut collection, *Some Beheadings* (2018), Aditi Machado explores the dialectic of woundedness and pleasure in a less narrative, but still deeply feminist, lyrical sequence. The wound these poems point to is not tied to a specific event (as in Chopra's case, a rape, or in Queen's, ongoing abuse). Instead Machado's speaker carries the primary patriarchal wounding that seeks to divide self from other, and, even more essentially, mind from body. Machado opens her collection, one could say, in a state of woundedness. 'A mirror / brightens the fascist in me' she writes in the book's first poem.[13] 'When I speak / the fascist in me speaks', she goes on (p. 3). This inner fascist (which, the book implies, lives potentially in all of us), made brighter by its own narcissism, announcing itself in speaking, is 'hard', 'cold', and 'private' (p. 3). The fascistic 'I' is a braggart ('a great book I will write', it claims), is tied to 'countries & natives', and lives inside a house (p. 3).

The fascistic self, however, is countered throughout Machado's book with another version of selfhood that seeks not separation or distance, not privacy and pride, but vulnerability and belonging, states which are directly associated in Machado's poems with the erotic, as in Chopra's and Queen's. Here is the second half of the poem 'In the Weeds' that marks the book's centre:

I am thinking now to describe what it's like to touch something.
What it is to rub off on someone.
When two matters interact should I hope to keep my skin.
Ambling in the winds, lost in perfections, those blips
along the odometer of time, my feet in the weeds –
my head capitulates to them. Little plants, little events. That's how
I think. A decapitation, a lovely guillotine wind lays my mind
in the weeds. That's how
I touch a plant. My water touches its. (p. 41)

Like Queen's girl who 'could no longer tell the difference between feeling & thought', Machado's 'I' gives over her dominating 'head' in order to think with her 'feet in the weeds'. The 'decapitating' wind is described as 'lovely'; the 'beheading' of the title becomes a metaphor for a more embodied way of knowing. 'Thinking' now with her head in the weeds allows Machado's speaker to loosen the borders of the self as 'My water touches its.', '& in the consideration of what is greater than I I / become lost in the folds of eros', she writes earlier in the book (p. 12).

As in Chopra's writing, eros here includes the pleasures of writing itself:

O copular scapular,
o joints & weddings,
your prescience, this love
of grammar I cannot
resist, this day
that will not pass
its morning, this soft
labor, delicate palate. (p. 24)

Here the semiotic is activated in the sonic slides between words: copular to scapular; delicate to palate. But it is also present in how Machado keeps us semantically off-balance as she moves between the language of the body, the language of romance, and the language of language itself. The 'joints' and 'weddings' suggest the connections and articulations between words (the 'copular' is, in fact, a grammatical joint or link), the joints of the body, and the coming together of beloveds. Enjambment allows the avowed 'love' to attach first to the 'you' (which might be the speaker's body or another's) and second to grammar, which like a lover cannot be resisted. If you speak the final line out loud, you'll find your tongue delicately pulsing your palate such that the pleasures of language physically manifest. In this poem, then, pleasure seems to have overridden the 'wound' of a fascistic concept of selfhood.

However, just as in Chopra's 'Chthonic Colony', where the site of the wound is at once the site of the erotic, in Machado, the 'fascist' I and the other watery I are joined:

> I
> & the fascist in I
> on the dusty road
> reinventing. (p. 23)

Perhaps patriarchal violence can only be addressed when recognised within the self. And perhaps only when such internal wounding (and capacity to wound) is acknowledged can real 'reinventing' occur.

I will now turn to Canadian-born poet Lisa Robertson, who has been exploring the question of pleasure as it relates to feminist resistance for at least three decades. 'I believe my critique of devastation / Began with delight', she writes in *Magenta Soul Whip* (2005).[14] And, from *R's Boat* (2010): '*I had insisted on my body's joy and little else.*'[15] As Robertson discusses in a 2013 interview with me, her readings in feminist film criticism from the early 1980s helped her to reconsider the 'repudiation of pleasure' that she had found in some leftist political theory.[16] Film critics, such as Laura Mulvey, reclaimed 'narrative and identification from the point of view of a specifically female embodied politics, which centered on pleasure as the source of political agency'.[17] Pleasure stands in refusal to all forms of oppression, but especially to those that deny the body its desires, to those that seek to make ascetics out of all of us (hoarders and misers), and to those that insist we grow accustomed to pain and suffering inflicted, when not directly upon us, on so many near to us. Thus, Robertson's poems, with their intricate language and lush motion, offer a critique of patriarchal violence even when not announcing or describing such violence. Indeed, part of their political project, part of their insistence on freedom, is to never announce anything for long. Robertson's poems prefer mobility; they amble and stray, 'go Venus go vernal go turning go' she writes, and, 'Mostly I seek the promiscuous feeling of being alive.'[18]

'In heavy and worthy houses, I feel a violent dismay. It gets harder and harder to be female in one's life in such a house . . . I abandon the house for the forbidden book' Robinson writes in her 2012 essay collection, *Nilling* (p. 15). The 'house' here, metonymic for the heteronormative family and the enforced gender roles that such families tend to reproduce, must be 'abandoned' for the illicit pleasure of reading and writing. 'Reading, I enter a relational contract with *whatever* material, accepting its fluency and swerve' she goes on, suggesting that the literary offers a transpersonal experience of exchange, one that, in the context of this chapter, we can call erotic (p. 15).

The final poem of *Magenta Soul Whip* makes clear that for Robertson, pleasure, motion, and resistance are interwoven. In her words, they 'co-determine':

> Might there
> be a motion that is not
> itself? – Desire? Resistance?
> Chance? In my perception all three
> co-determine. In this way, I am not
> Restricted. (p. 97)

Therefore, it is fitting that this book opens by introducing the figure of the 'she-dandy', a flowing and adorned figure, sliding in and among the buildings:

> We'd be the she-dandies in incredibly voluptuous jackets ribboning back from our waists, totally lined in pure silk, also in pure humming, and we'd be heading into the buildings with ephemera like leafage or sleeves or pigments. (p. 8)

This figure gets a more thorough treatment in Robertson's 2018 essay, *Proverbs of a She-Dandy*.[19] Here Robertson explores Baudelaire's depiction of the (male) dandy and applies it to the menopausal woman. The menopausal woman, argues Robertson, holds and presents the wealth of her own autonomy. Outside of capital's demand for productivity, she is free to wander in her own pleasures:

> SHE IS THE MASTERPIECE OF THE ANCIENT SUPERIORITY OF THE IMPRODUCTIVE. SHE NEITHER BEGETS NOR WORKS, BUT DRIFTS.
>
> . . .
>
> WEALTH IS THE AUTONOMOUS EXPERIENCE OF ONE'S OWN PLEASURE, A FLAWED PLEASURE INNATE TO EMBODIMENT. MOVING EXTREMELY SLOWLY ON THE BOULEVARD, IN THE PARK, AT THE NEWS STAND, IN THE BOOKSHOP, SHE DISPLAYS HER RESISTANCE TO ALL APPROPRIATION SAVE THE POEM'S. (p. 37)

The essay makes use of the term 'resistance' more than once. Earlier, 'HER OBSOLESCENCE IS INDISPENSABLE TO HER WORK WITH RESISTANCE' (p. 31). Of course, the menopausal woman is not generally thought of as in any sense powerful. Rather, she is demoted, in our culture, to irrelevance when not openly abhorred. Robertson's radical move is to argue that it is precisely at the moment when the reproductive imperative can no longer apply that the free-moving power of the autonomous erotic body can surge.

I will finish, now, with UK poet Nat Raha, whose 'radical transfeminism' takes what she calls (from Lauren Berlant) the 'slow death' of trans women's lives as a starting point, offering in her essay 'Transfeminine Brokenness' a thorough critique of the multiple forces that impede and threaten especially trans women of colour:

> Manifestations of intermeshing forms of transphobia and transmisogyny, antiblackness, racism, xenophobia, whorephobia, femmephobia, and ableism, working in concert to create conditions of slow death, social death, and actual death for poor trans women and trans femmes/of color and/or trans sex workers are inextricable from structural economic transformations and exacerbated by the fresh governance around immigration.[20]

The response to such ongoing woundedness is, in Raha's essay, threefold. First, it must be named: 'To name the states of our brokenness: depression, hurt, trauma, fatigue/exhaustion, overwork, sadness, loneliness, stress' she begins (p. 632). Second, the limits of statist/paternalistic responses to such threats, such as equality legislation, must be acknowledged. And finally, intimate, interpersonal care, support and creativity (the eros of attachment) must be both valued and called for (p. 637).

As we turn to Raha's poems, we can find an instantiation of art as what she calls in the essay 'a powerful means for affective solidarity' (p. 637), in that her poems make visible and audible the wounds inflicted upon her and others' bodies while also reaching towards 'care' as a way to accompany, if not heal, such wounds. However, the poems are more than expressions of these agendas, for their style, their formal choices, push against legibility, demanding that, in Robertson's terms from *Nilling*, the reader 'enter a relational contract ... accepting [the poem's] fluency and swerve' (p. 15). In this sense, reading Raha demands intense attention, demands, one could say, 'care' The poems thereby draw their reader (if willing) into the community of care which they describe.

In the poem sequence 'de/compositions' from 2016, Raha takes on the 'foul / reconstruction of a nation / pinned to / weapons & trade & borders'.[21] Later in the poem, the violent effects of this State (presumably the UK after Brexit) are made evident on the bodies of the 'we' that the poem speaks for: 'our / severed years / blood of lovers un- / derfunded hospital corridors' (p. 142). But the poem also offers (in a smaller font that indicates fragility) a passage of provisional repair:

> we sew through the brightness / our
> >   sisters &
> siblings, our: slippage attentions, the
> volume in our sonic eyes painted
> , scores
> >   . . .
>
> >   our sharp &
> resolute beauty / distorsion
> on the neofash ordinary is unbroken
> lines & ignorance, jimmy
> baldwin & chalked rimbaud streets, every
> screech of fist & wardrobe, insurrectionary
> teenage dreams from sweat & pave
> // communist heels, lived your
> >   contradictions, flying
> >   false truth, the violence
> >   of yyr wills & wage relations, we
> >   work for yyr abolition continual (p. 143)

There is much to say here, too much for the space I have left. The passage begins with *making* (poesis) – the aesthetic practices implied by 'sewing' and 'painted scores'. This creative siblinghood distorts the 'ordinary' 'ignorance' of the 'neofash' (neofascism). Baldwin and Rimbaud, called upon as ancestral siblings, accompany these teenaged dreams of insurrection. The violence of (patriarchal/nationalistic) wills and (capitalist) wage relations can, in this poem, only be responded to (not healed) with the 'sharp & resolute beauty' of this siblinghood past and present, who, as the poem later announces 'stitch / a new substance of time' (p. 144).

But it is not nearly enough to offer a summary of this poem's argument. Because even more than making such meanings, the poem lives through its erotic-semiotic energies, found in the neologisms, the inventive spelling, the stray and wandering punctuation, the rejection of 'unbroken lines', and the refusal of 'normative' syntax. Reading this, feeling into it, we can discern that for Raha, such normative language (Kristeva's 'symbolic') would be tied to the 'false truth' of patriarchal power. Here we find a language animated by resistance to all forms of control, a language that shows us the continuum of patriarchal oppressions: from grammar to the 'blasted cities' of austerity, from syntax to the 'violence/violation' in streets, workplaces, and homes.

* * * *

As I was writing the final paragraphs of this chapter, my phone rang. An unfamiliar number. Because it was a local, and I was waiting for a friend, I answered. 'I want to *fuck* you', said the male voice on the other end. I hung up, skin prickling with slight fear. How did he get my number? How 'local' is he? Next a text. I read only the words 'STICK __ UP YOUR' before turning my phone over. I left the space where I had been waiting, a studio where I was alone, and went to a nearby café. When my friend and I met up, I asked her to take my phone, read the text I had not read, and block the caller. Once she had done this, we began our work: inventing a performance which will start with the following line: 'Two brothers who always, throughout their childhoods, detested one another.' This exploration of male violence will be performed by our (differently marked – she is black and I am white) women's bodies. At one point in this performance, we will place keys hanging from chains around one another's necks. We will tuck these keys between one another's breasts, touching, lightly that space.[22]

The ways in which we protect one another, create with one another, and touch one another in response to and in protest of the various and ongoing pressures of patriarchy *is* feminist poetics. Without foreclosing on our ability to be vulnerable with one another, and while still asserting our right to be angry, disgusted, outraged, and afraid, we write within this paradox. Poems can play a crucial role in helping us to navigate a feminist response to male power because of how they articulate our wounds, our very different wounds, and also for how they both articulate and instantiate our pleasures, our very different pleasures. Reading one another, entering that 'fluency and swerve' that real reading demands, is a form of erotic attachment, based as it is in pleasure, desire, and inquiry – based as it is in the desire to understand so that we can care, to care so that we can come together, and to come together so that we can continue to reimagine our world.

Notes

1 S. Ahmed, *Living a Feminist Life* (Durham, NC: Duke University Press, 2017), 22.
2 A. Lorde, *Sister Outsider: Essays and Speeches* (Berkeley: Crossing Press, 2007 [1984]), 59.
3 R. Braidotti, 'Embodiment, Sexual Difference, and the Nomadic Subject', *Hypatia*, 8:1 (Winter, 1993), 6.
4 The child is gendered male in Lacan's the 'the mirror stage'.

5 J. Kristeva, *Revolution in Poetic Language*, trans. M. Waller (New York: Columbia University Press, 1984), 48.

6 As Kelly Oliver writes, 'The semiotic is the subterranean element of meaning within signification that does not signify.' K. Oliver, 'Julia Kristeva's Feminist Revolutions', *Hypatia*, 8:3 (Summer, 1993), 96.

7 See J. Butler, 'Rethinking Vulnerability in Resistance', in J. Butler, Z. Gambetti, and L. Sabsay (eds.), *Vulnerability in Resistance* (Durham, NC: Duke University Press, 2016), 21.

8 In their introduction, J. Butler, Z. Gambetti, and L. Sabsay present 'vulnerability' as 'emerg[ing] as part of social relations, even as a feature of social relations', rather than an ontological truth for certain people or groups. See Butler, Gambetti, and Sabsay, 'Introduction', in Butler, Gambetti, and Sabsay (eds.), *Vulnerability in Resistance*, 4.

9 M. Ahiska, 'Violence Against Women in Turkey: Vulnerability, Sexuality, and Eros', in Butler, Gambetti, and Sabsa (eds.), *Vulnerability in Resistance*, 224.

10 Butler, Gambetti and Sabsay, 'Introduction', 7.

11 S. Chopra, *Queerly as the Night: Towards Post-Post-Colonialism, a Theory of Rhizomic Intelligence*, unpublished dissertation, University of Denver (2018).

12 K. Queen, *Fearful Beloved* (Argos Books, 2015), 16.

13 A. Machado, *Some Beheadings* (New York: Nightboat Books, 2018), 3.

14 L. Robertson, *Magenta Soul Whip* (Toronto: Coach House Books, 2005), 19.

15 L. Robertson, *R's Boat* (Berkeley: University of California Press, 2010), 7.

16 J. Carr, 'An Interview with Lisa Robertson', *The Volta: Evening Will Come*, 25 (January 2013), n.p.

17 Ibid.

18 L. Robertson, *Three Summers* (Toronto: Coach House Books, 2016), 42 and L. Robertson, *Nilling* (Toronto: Book Thug, 2012), 12 respectively.

19 L. Robertson, *Proverbs of a She-Dandy* (Paris/Vancouver: Morris and Helen Belkin Art Gallery, 2018).

20 N. Raha, 'Transfeminine Brokenness, Radical Transfeminism', *South Atlantic Quarterly*, 116:3 (July 2017), 635.

21 N. Raha, '"on the visions of yur futures, ruptured isles . . . "', in *Of Sirens, Body and Faultlines* (Norwich: Boiler House Press, 2019), 142.

22 This friend, the dancer/choreographer Gesel Mason, spent years developing her performance piece titled 'Sometimes You Feel Like a Ho, Sometimes You Don't: Women, Sex, and Desire,' which took Lorde's 'The Uses of the Erotic' as a starting point. See geselmason.com/women-sex-desire.

Bibliography

'Gender Pay: Fewer Than Half UK Firms Narrow Gap', *BBC News* (5 April 2019).

'The Guardian View on a Year in Feminism: 2014 was a Watershed', *The Guardian* (31 Dec 2014).

'Media Note: Anthropocene Working Group (AWG)', University of Leicester (29 August 2016).

'More Than 12 M "MeToo" Facebook Posts, Comments, Reactions in 24 Hours', *CBS News* (17 October 2017).

The People vs The NHS: Who Gets the Drugs? dir. M. Henderson, aired BBC2 (27 June 2018).

'Picador to Publish Kiran Millwood Hargrave's Debut Adult Novel' (10 April 2018), panmacmillan.com/blogs.

'Transcript: "Today" Anchor Matt Lauer Fired by NBC News', *NBC News* (29 November 2017).

Abelove, H., M. A. Barale, and D. M. Halperin, 'Introduction', in H. Abelove, M. A. Barale, and D. M. Halperin (eds.), *The Lesbian and Gay Studies Reader* (New York: Routledge, 1993), xv–xvii.

Adams, C. J. and L. Gruen, *Ecofeminism: Feminist Intersections with Other Animals and the Earth* (New York: Bloomsbury Academic, 2014).

Agustin, L., *Sex at the Margins: Migration, Labour Markets and the Rescue Industry* (London and New York: Zed Books, 2007).

Ahiska, M., 'Violence Against Women in Turkey: Vulnerability, Sexuality, and Eros' in J. Butler, Z. Gambetti and L. Sabsay (eds.), *Vulnerability in Resistance* (Durham: Duke University Press, 2016) pp. 211–235.

Ahmed, S., *Living a Feminist Life* (Durham, NC: Duke University Press, 2017).

    On Being Included: Racism and Diversity Work in Institutional Life (Durham, NC: Duke University Press, 2012).

    The Promise of Happiness (Durham, NC: Duke University Press, 2010).

    Queer Phenomenology: Orientations, Objects, Others (Durham, NC: Duke University Press, 2006).

    'Resignation is a Feminist Issue' (27 August 2016), feministkilljoys.com.

    'Robyn Wiegman, *Object Lessons*' (review), *Feminist Theory*, 13:3 (2012), 345–8.

    Willful Subjects (Durham, NC: Duke University Press, 2014).

Akwugo E. and L. Bassell, 'Minority Women, Austerity and Activism', *Race and Class*, 57:2 (2015), 86–95.

Alaimo, S., *Bodily Natures: Science, Environment and the Material Self* (Bloomington and Indianapolis: Indiana University Press, 2010).

'The Naked World: The Transcorporeal Ethics of the Protesting Body', *Women and Performance: A Journal of Feminist Theory*, 20 (2010), 15–36.

'Your Shell on Acid: Material Immersion, Anthropocene Dissolves', in R. Grusin (ed.), *Anthropocene Feminisms* (Minneapolis and London: University of Minnesota Press, 2016), 89–120.

Alderman, N., 'Dystopian Dreams: How Feminist Science Fiction Predicted the Future', *The Guardian* (25 March 2017).

Alderman, N., *The Power* (London: Penguin, 2017).

Alexander, M. J. and C. T. Mohanty (eds.), *Feminist Genealogies, Colonial Legacies, Democratic Futures* (New York: Routledge, 1997).

Alwill Leyba, C., *Girl Code: Unlocking the Secrets to Success, Sanity and Happiness for the Female Entrepreneur* (London: Penguin, 2017).

Amar, P., 'The Street, the Sponge, and the Ultra: The Queer Logics of Children's Rebellion and Political Infantilization', *GLQ*, 22:4 (2016), 569–604.

Amnesty International, 'Policy on State Obligations to Respect, Protect and Fulfil the Human Rights of Sex Workers' (2016), amnesty.org.

Amorusi, S., *#girlboss* (London: Penguin, 2014).

Atkinson, T. G., *Amazon Odyssey* (New York: Links Books, 1974).

Attwood, F., 'Pornography and Objectification', *Feminist Media Studies*, 4:1 (2007), 7–19.

Atwood, M., *The Handmaid's Tale* (New York: Houghton Mifflin Harcourt, 1986).

Baccolini, R., 'Gender and Genre in the Feminist Critical Dystopias of Katherine Burdekin, Margaret Atwood, and Octavia Butler', in M. Barr (ed.), *Future Females, the Next Generation: New Voices and Velocities in Feminist Science Fiction* (Boston: Rowman and Littlefield, 2000), 13–34.

Baccolini, R. and T. Moylan, 'Introduction: Dystopia and Histories', in R. Baccolini and T. Moylan (eds.), *Dark Horizons: Science Fiction and the Dystopian Imagination* (London: Routledge, 2003), 1–12.

Bail, H. L. and C. Giametta, 'What do Sex Workers Think About the French Prostitution Act: A Study on the Impact of the Law from 13th April 2016 Against the "Prostitution System" in France', *Synthesis* (April 2018).

Bambara Cade, T., *The Black Woman: An Anthology* (New York: Washington Square Press, 1970).

Barounis, C., 'Alison Bechdel and Crip-Feminist Autobiography', *Journal of Modern Literature*, 39:4 (2016), 139–61.

Bastani, A. *Fully Automated Luxury Communism: A Manifesto* (London: Verso Books, 2019).

Beard, M., *Women & Power: A Manifesto* (London: Profile, 2017).

Bechdel, A., *Are You My Mother? A Comic Drama* (Boston and New York: Mariner Books, 2013).

Fun Home: A Family Tragicomic (Boston and New York: Mariner Books, 2007).

Bell, R., *Sturdy Black Bridges: Visions of Black Women in Literature* (Garden City: Doubleday, 1979).

Bellafante, G., 'The False Feminism of "Fearless Girl"', *New York Times* (16 March 2017).

Bennett, J., *Vibrant Matter: A Political Ecology of Things* (Durham, NC: Duke University Press, 2010).

Berg. H., 'Sex, Work, Queerly: Identity, Authenticity and Laboured Performance', in M. Liang, K. Pilcher, and N. Smith, (eds.), *Queer Sex Work* (London and New York: Routledge, 2015), 23–32.

Berlant, L., *The Female Complaint: The Unfinished Business of Sentimentality in American Culture* (Durham, NC: Duke University Press, 2008).

Bernard, S., 'Making the Connections on Tar-sands Pollution, Racism, and Sexism', *Grist* (27 August 2015).

Bernstein, E., 'Militarized Humanitarianism Meets Carceral Feminism: The Politics of Sex, Rights, and Freedom in Contemporary Anti-trafficking Campaigns', *Signs: Journal of Women in Culture and Society*, 36:1 (2010), 45–71.

'The Sexual Politics of the New Abolitionism', *Differences*, 18:3 (2007), 128–51.

Bérubé, M., *The Secret Life of Stories* (New York: New York University Press, 2016).

Bey, M., 'The Trans*-Ness of Blackness, the Blackness of Trans*-Ness', *TSQ: Transgender Studies Quarterly*, 4:2 (2017), 275–95.

Bingham, A., 'Pin-Up Culture and Page 3 in the Popular Press', in M. Andrews and S. McNamara (eds.), *Women and the Media: Feminism and Femininity in Britain, 1900 to the Present* (New York and London: Routledge, 2014), 184–98.

Blunt, A. and A. Varley, 'Geographies of Home', *Cultural Geographies*, 11 (2004), 3–6.

Boyer, A., *A Handbook of Disappointed Fate* (Brooklyn, NY: Ugly Duckling Press, 2018).

Braidotti, R., 'Embodiment, Sexual Difference, and the Nomadic Subject', *Hypatia*, 8:1 (Winter, 1993), 1–13.

Brooks, F. (ed.), *Outskirts* (London and Exeter: Makina Books, 2017).

Brown, A. M., *Emergent Strategy* (Chicago and Edinburgh: AK Press, 2017).

Brown, E., 'California Professor, Writer of Confidential Brett Kavanaugh Letter, Speaks Out About Her Allegation of Sexual Assault', *Washington Post* (16 August 2018).

Brown, L., 'Yorick, Don't Be a Hero: Productive Motion in *Y: The Last Man*', *Image TexT: Interdisciplinary Comic Studies*, 3:1 (2006), n.p.

Brown, W., *States of Injury: Power and Freedom in Late Modernity* (Princeton: Princeton University Press, 1995).

Brownmiller, S., *In Our Time* (New York: Delta, 1999).

Butler, J., 'Against Proper Objects', *differences: A Journal of Feminist Cultural Studies*, 6:2/3 (1994), 1–26.

Bodies that Matter: On the Discursive Limits of Sex (New York: Routledge, 1993).

'Rethinking Vulnerability and Resistance', in J. Butler, Z. Gambetti, and L. Sabsay (eds.), *Vulnerability in Resistance* (Durham, NC: Duke University Press, 2016) 12–27.

Butler, J., Z. Gambetti, and L. Sabsay, 'Introduction', in J. Butler, Z. Gambetti, and L. Sabsay (eds.), *Vulnerability in Resistance* (Durham, NC: Duke University Press, 2016) 1–11.

Butler, O., *Parable of the Talents* (New York and Boston: Grand Central Publishing, 1998).

Capildeo, V., *Measures of Expatriation* (Manchester: Carcanet Press, 2016).

Carr, J., 'An Interview with Lisa Robertson', *The Volta: Evening Will Come*, 25 (January 2013), n.p.

Cart, M., *Young Adult Literature: From Romance to Realism* (New York: American Library Association, 2010).

Castillo, A., *Peel My Love Like an Onion* (New York: Anchor Books, 1999).

Cavalcanti, I., 'Articulating the Elsewhere: Utopia in Contemporary Feminist Dystopias', unpublished dissertation, University of Strathclyde, 1999.

Cecire, N., 'New at This' (21 August 2018), natalie.cecire.org.

Césaire, A., 'Letter to Maurice Thorez', *Social Text*, 28:2 (2010), 145–52.

Chapkis, W., 'Sex Workers: Interview with Wendy Chapkis', in S. Seidman, N. Fischer, and C. Meeks (eds.), *Introducing the New Sexuality Studies: Original Essays and Interviews* (London and New York: Routledge, 2007), 343–9.

Chatman, D., '"Pregnancy, Then It's Back to Business"', *Feminist Media Studies*, 15:4 (2015), 926–41.

Chávez-Garcia, M., *States of Delinquency: Race and Science in the Making of California's Juvenille Justice System* (Berkeley: University of California Press, 2012).

chávez, d. b. and r. vázquez, 'Precedence, Trans* and the Decolonial', *Angelaki*, 22:2 (2017), 39–44.

Cheng Thom, K., *Fierce Femmes and Notorious Liars: A Dangerous Trans Girl's Confabulous Memoir* (Montreal, QC: Metonymy Press, 2016).

Chira, S., 'Feminism Lost. Now What?', *New York Times* (30 December 2016).

'"You Focus on the Good": Women Who Voted for Trump in Their Own Words', *New York Times* (14 January 2017).

'Why #MeToo Took Off: Sheer Numbers Who Can Say "Me, Too"', *New York Times* (24 February 2018).

Chopra, S., *Queerly as the Night: Towards Post-Post-Colonialism, a Theory of Rhizomic Intelligence*, unpublished dissertation, The University of Denver (2018).

Chu, A. L., 'On Liking Women', *n+1 magazine*, 30 (Winter 2018).

Chute, H., *Disaster Drawn: Visual Witness, Comics, and Documentary Form* (Cambridge, MA: Belknap Press of Harvard University Press, 2016).

Clewell, T., 'Beyond Psychoanalysis: Resistance and Reparative Reading in Alison Bechdel's *Are You My Mother?*', *PMLA*, 132:1 (2017), 51–70.

Clover, J. and J. Spahr, 'Gender Abolition and Ecotone War', in R. Grusin (ed.), *Anthropocene Feminisms* (Minneapolis and London: University of Minnesota Press, 2016), 147–68.

Cobb, S., 'Is This What a Feminist Looks Like? Male Celebrity Feminists and the Postfeminist Politics of "Equality"', *Celebrity Studies*, 6:1 (2015), 136–69.

Colebrook, C., 'Stratigraphic Time, Women's Time', *Australian Journal of Feminist Studies*, 25:59 (2009), 11–16.

'We Have Always Been Post-Anthropocene', in R. Grusin (ed.), *Anthropocene Feminisms* (Minneapolis and London: University of Minnesota Press, 2016), 1–20.

Cooke, J., *Contemporary Feminist Life-Writing: The New Audacity* (Cambridge and New York: Cambridge University Press, 2020).

Coundouriotis, E., 'The Child Soldier Narrative and the Problem of Arrested Historicization', *Journal of Human Rights*, 9:2 (2010), 191–206.

Coupe, L., 'General Introduction', in L. Coupe (ed.), *The Green Studies Reader* (London and New York: Routledge, 2000), 1–8.

Cowen, D., *The Deadly Life of Logistics* (Minneapolis and London: University of Minnesota Press, 2014).

Crane. E. and L. Cheer, '$800-a-Night Escort Samantha X Defends her Lifestyle Claiming it Makes No Difference to her Two Children', *Daily Mail* (1 September 2014).

Da Silva, D. F., 'On Difference without Separability', in *Catalogue: Incerteza viva* (Sao Paolo: 32a Sao Paolo Art Biennal, 2016), 57–65.

'Towards a Black Feminist Poethics: The Quest(ion) of Blackness Towards the End of the World', *The Black Scholar*, 44:2 (2014), 81–97.

Dale, C. and R. Overell (eds.), *Orientating Feminism: Media, Activism, and Cultural Representation* (Basingstoke: Palgrave Macmillan, 2018).

Danforth, E. M., *The Miseducation of Cameron Post* (New York: Balzer + Bray, 2012).

Daring, C. B., 'Queering Our Analysis of Sex Work: Laying Capitalism Bare', in C. B. Daring et al. (eds.), *Queering Anarchism: Addressing and Undressing Power and Desire* (Chico, CA: AK Press, 2012), 185–94.

Davis, A., 'Reflections on the Black Woman's Role in the Community of Slaves', *The Black Scholar*, 3:4 (1971), 2–15.

Davis, L. J., *The End of Normal: Identity in a Biocultural Era* (Ann Arbor: University of Michigan Press, 2013).

de Beauvoir, S., *The Second Sex* (New York: Bantam Books, 1970).

de Haas, H., 'The Myth of Invasion: The Inconvenient Realities of African Migration to Europe', *Third World Quarterly*, 29:7 (2008), 1305–22.

Despentes, V., *King Kong Theory*, trans. S. Benson (New York: The Feminist Press, 2009).

Dhillon, J., *Prairie Rising: Indigenous Youth, Decolonization, and the Politics of Intervention* (Toronto: University of Toronto Press, 2016).

Dillon, S., 'Empowerment Under Threat: Naomi Alderman's *The Power*', in R. Hertel and E-M. Schmitz (eds.), *Empowering Contemporary Fiction* (Leiden: Brill, forthcoming).

'English and the Public Good', in R. Eaglestone and G. Marshall (eds.), *English: Shared Futures* (Martlesham: Boydell & Brewer, 2018), 194–201.

Dimaline, C., *The Marrow Thieves* (Manitoba: Cormorant Books, 2017).

Ditum, S., 'Never-ending Nightmare: Why Feminist Dystopias Must Stop Torturing Women', *The Guardian* (12 May 2018).

Dixon-Román, E., 'Algo-Ritmo: More-than-Human Performative Acts and the Racializing Assemblages of Algorithmic Architectures', *Cultural Studies Critical Methodologies*, 16:5 (2016), 482–90.

Dodillet S. and P. Ostergren, 'The Swedish Sex Purchase Act: Claimed Success and Documented Effects', petraostergren.com.

Doolittle, R., 'Unfounded: Why Police Dismiss 1 in 5 Sexual Assault Claims as Baseless', *The Globe and Mail* (2 February 2017).

Dotson, K., 'Tracking Epistemic Violence, Tracking Practices of Silencing', *Hypatia*, 26:2 (Spring 2011), 236–57.

Drift, M. van der, 'Nonnormative Ethics: The Ensouled Formation of Trans Bodies', in R. Pearce and I. Moon (eds.), *The Emergence of Trans* (London: Routledge, 2019).

'Radical Romanticism, Violent Cuteness, and the Destruction of the World', *Journal of Aesthetics and Culture*, 10:3 (2018), n.p.

Ducharme, J., 'Mario Batali's Sexual Misconduct Apology Came with a Cinnamon Roll Recipe', *Time* (16 December 2017).

Duncan, J. and D. Lambert, 'Landscapes of Home', in J. Duncan, N. Johnson, and R. Schein (eds.), *A Companion to Cultural Geography* (Oxford: Blackwell, 2003), 382–403.

Dworkin, A., *Heartbreak: The Political Memoir of a Feminist Militant* (New York: Basic Books, 2002).

Edinburgh Action for Trans Health, 'Trans Health Manifesto', in N. Raha et al. (eds.), *Radical Transfeminism* (Leith, 2017), 56–61.

Egoff, S., 'Beyond the Garden Wall', in Z. Sutherland (ed.), *The Arbuthnot Lectures 1970–1979* (Chicago: American Library Association, 1980).

El Shakry, O., 'Youth as Peril and Promise: The Emergence of Adolescent Psychology in Postwar Egypt', *International Journal of Middle Eastern Studies*, 43:4 (2011), 591–610.

Elfgren, S. B. and M. Strandberg, *The Circle Book 1 (The Engelsfors Trilogy)*, trans. P. Carlsson (New York: Overlook Press, 2011).

Elman, J. P., *Chronic Youth: Disability, Sexuality, and U.S. Media Cultures of Rehabilitation* (New York: New York University Press, 2014).

Eng, D., *The Feeling of Kinship: Queer Liberalism and the Racialization of Intimacy* (Durham, NC: Duke University Press, 2010).

Fahey, N., 'Beauty and the Breasts', *The Sun* (1 March 2017).

Fan, J., 'China and the Legend of Ivanka', *New Yorker* (11 April 2017).

Farrier, D., *Postcolonial Asylum: Seeking Sanctuary Before the Law* (Liverpool: Liverpool University Press, 2011).

Farrow, R., 'From Aggressive Overtures to Sexual Assault: Harvey Weinstein's Victims Tell Their Stories', *New Yorker* (23 October 2017).

'Harvey Weinstein's Army of Spies', *New Yorker* (6 November 2017).

Favaro, L., '"Just Be Confident Girls!": Confidence Chic as Neoliberal Governmentality', in A. S. Elias, R. Gill, and C. Scharff (eds.), *Aesthetic Labour: Rethinking Beauty Politics in Neoliberalism* (Basingstoke and New York: Palgrave Macmillan, 2017), 283–99.

Federici, S., *Revolution at Point Zero: Housework, Reproduction, and Feminist Struggle* (Oakland: PM Press, 2012).

Feinberg, L., *Transgender Liberation: A Movement Whose Time Has Come* (New York: World View Forum, 1992).

Felski, R., *Beyond Feminist Aesthetics: Feminist Literature and Social Change* (London: Hutchinson Radius, 1989).

Fey, T., *Bossypants* (New York: Reagan Arthur Books/Little, Brown and Co., 2011).

Finger, B., 'Matt Damon Gets It Wrong, Yet Again', *Jezebel* (23 March 2018).

Firestone, S., *The Dialectic of Sex: The Case for Feminist Revolution* (New York: Farrar, Straus, and Giroux, 1970).

Floyd, K., *The Reification of Desire: Towards a Queer Marxism* (Minneapolis: University of Minnesota Press, 2009).

Fortunati, L., *The Arcane of Reproduction: Housework, Prostitution, Labour and Capital* (New York: Autonomedia, 1995).

Frase, P., 'The Problem with (Sex) Work' (27 March 2012), peterfrase.com.

Frayne, D., *The Refusal of Work: The Theory and Practice of Resistance to Work* (London: ZED Books, 2015).

Freedman, A., 'Drawing on Modernism in Alison Bechdel's *Fun Home*', *Journal of Modern Literature*, 32:4 (2009), 125–40.

Freeman, E., 'Still After', *South Atlantic Quarterly*, 106:3 (2007), 495–500.

Gaard, G., 'Toward New EcoMasculinities, EcoGenders and EcoSexualities', in C. Adams and L. Gruen (eds.), *Ecofeminism* (London: Bloomsbury, 2015), 225–39.

Garber, M., 'They Took A Knee', *The Atlantic* (24 August 2016).

Gay, R., *Bad Feminist: Essays* (New York: Corsair, 2014).

Gessen, M., 'When Does a Watershed Become a Sex Panic?', *New Yorker* (14 November 2017).

Gill, R., 'From Sexual Objectification to Sexual Subjectification: The Resexualisation of Women's Bodies in the Media', *Feminist Media Studies*, 3:1 (2003), 100–5.

'Post-Postfeminism?: New Feminist Visibilities in Postfeminist Times', *Feminist Media Studies*, 16:4 (2016), 610–30.

Gilmore, L., *Tainted Witness: Why We Doubt What Women Say About Their Lives* (New York: Columbia University Press, 2017).

Gilson, E., 'Vulnerability, Ignorance, and Oppression', *Hypatia*, 26:2 (2011), 308–32.

Gira Grant, M., *Playing the Whore: The Work of Sex Work* (London: Verso, 2014).

Glissant, É., *Poetics of Relation*, trans. B. Wing (Minneapolis: University of Michigan Press, 1997).

Goh, A., 'Appropriating the Alien: A Critique of Xenofeminism', *Mute* (29 July 2019), metamute.org.

Gorrie, N., 'Why *The Handmaid's Tale* Is Not Dystopian for Black women – It's Real Life', *SBS* (10 July 2018), sbs.com.au.

Gossett, R., E. A. Stanley, and J. Burton (eds.), *Trap Door: Trans Cultural Production and the Politics of Visibility* (Cambridge, MA and London: MIT Press, 2017).

Graeber, D., *Bullshit Jobs: A Theory* (London: Simon & Schuster, 2018).

Green, C., 'The Droves of Academe', *Missouri Review*, 31:3 (Fall 2008), 177–88.

Gregg, M., 'Book Review: *Feminism's Queer Temporalities*', *Feminist Review*, 113 (2016), e1–e2.

Grewal, I., *Transnational America: Feminisms, Diasporas, Neoliberalisms* (Durham, NC: Duke University Press, 2005).

Grewal, I. and C. Kaplan, 'Global Identities: Theorizing Transnational Studies of Sexuality', *GLQ*, 7:4 (2001), 663–97.

Grove, R., *Green Imperialism: Colonial Expansion, Tropical Island Edens and the Origins of Environmentalism, 1600–1860* (Cambridge: Cambridge University Press, 1996).

Grusin, R., 'Introduction: Anthropocene Feminism: An Experiment in Collaborative Theorizing', in R. Grusin (ed.), *Anthropocene Feminisms* (Minneapolis and London: University of Minnesota Press, 2016), vii–xix.

Guène, F., *Kiffe Kiffe Tomorrow*, trans. S. Adams (New York: Harcourt, 2006).

Guha, R., *Environmentalism: A Global History* (London: Penguin, 2014).

Gumbs, A., C. Martens, and M. Williams (eds.), *Revolutionary Mothering: Love on the Front Lines* (Oakland: PM Press, 2016).

Gutting, G. and H. Fraser, 'A Feminism Where "Lean In" Means Leaning on Others', *New York Times* (15 October 2015).

Halisi, C. and J. Mtume, *The Quotable Karenga* (Los Angeles: Us Organization, 1967).

Hall, K. Q. (ed.), *Feminist Disability Studies* (Bloomington, IN: Bloomington University Press, 2011).

Hamad, H. and A. Taylor, 'Introduction: Feminism and Contemporary Celebrity Culture', *Celebrity Studies*, 6:1 (2015), 124–7.

Haraway, D., *Staying with the Trouble* (Durham, NC: Duke University Press, 2016).

Haraway, D., A. Tsing, N. Ishikawa, G. Scott, K. Olwig, and N. Bubandt, 'Anthropologists are Talking – About the Anthropocene', *Ethnos* (2015), 1–30.

Harding, S. (ed.), *The Feminist Standpoint Theory Reader* (London and New York: Routledge, 2004).

Hayward, E. and J. Weinstein, 'Introduction: Tranimalities in the Age of Trans* Life', *TSQ: Transgender Studies Quarterly*, 2:2 (2015), 195–208.

Heller, N., 'The Multitasking Celebrity Takes Center Stage', *New Yorker* (23 June 2016).

Hemmings, C., 'Is Gender Studies Singular? Stories of Queer/Feminist Difference and Displacement', *differences: A Journal of Feminist Cultural Studies*, 27:2 (2016), 79–102.

'The Materials of Reparation', *Feminist Theory*, 15:1 (2014), 27–30.

Why Stories Matter: The Political Grammar of Feminist Theory (Durham, NC: Duke University Press, 2011).

Henderson, M., 'The Feminine Mystique of Individualism is Powerful: Two American Feminist Memoirs in Postfeminist Times', *a/b: Auto/Biography Studies*, 23:2 (2008), 165–84.

Hernandez, J. C., 'The "Goddess" Yi Wan Ka: Ivanka Trump is a Hit in China', *New York Times* (5 April 2017).

Hesford, V., *Feeling Women's Liberation* (Durham, NC: Duke University Press, 2013).

Hess, A., 'How a Fractious Women's Movement Came to Lead the Left', *New York Times Magazine* (7 February 2017).

Hester, H. and N. Srnicek, *After Work: The Fight for Free Time* (London: Verso, 2021).

Heti, H., 'I dive under the covers', *LRB*, 35:11 (6 June 2013) 21–2.

Hill Collins, P., *Black Feminist Thought: Knowledge, Consciousness, and the Politics of Empowerment* (New York: Routledge, 2000).

From Black Power to Hip Hop: Racism, Nationalism, and Feminism (Philadelphia: Temple University Press, 2006).

'Shifting the Center: Race, Class, and Feminist Theorizing about Motherhood', in E. N. Glenn, L. R. Force, and G. Chang (eds.), *Mothering : Ideology, Experience, and Agency* (New York: Routledge, 1994), 45–65.

Hill, M. C., 'Alternative Masculine Performances in American Comics: Brian K. Vaughan and Pia Guerra's *Y: The Last Man*', *Studies in Popular Culture*, 38:2 (2016), 79–98.

Holland, S. P., *The Erotic Life of Racism* (Durham, NC: Duke University Press, 2012).

Holmes, L., *How to Start a Revolution* (New York and London: Random House, 2015).

hooks, b., *Ain't I a Woman?: Black Women and Feminism* (New York: South End Press, 1981).

'Dig Deep: Beyond *Lean In*', *Feminist Wire* (28 October 2013).

Feminist Theory: From Margin to Center (Cambridge, MA: South End Press, 1984).

'Homeplace (a site of resistance)', in J. Ritchie and K. Ronald (eds.), *Available Means: An Anthology of Women's Rhetoric(s)* (Pittsburgh: University of Pittsburgh Press, 2001), 382–90.

Yearning: Race, Gender and Cultural Politics (Boston: South End Press, 1990).

Hori, H., 'Views from Elsewhere: Female Shoguns in Yoshinaga Fumi's *Ōoku* and their Precursors in Japanese Popular Culture', *Japanese Studies*, 32:1 (2012), 77–95.

Hsu, C., 'Antidepressants Found in Fish Brains in Great Lakes Region', *University of Buffalo News Centre* (31 August 2017).

Huschke, S. et al., 'Research into Prostitution in Northern Ireland', Belfast Department of Justice (2014).

Irving, D., 'Elusive Subjects: Notes on the Relationship between Critical Political Economy and Trans Studies' in A. Enke (ed.), *Transfeminist Perspectives* (Philadelphia: Temple University Press, 2012), 153–69.

'Normalized Transgressions: Legitimising the Transsexual Body as Productive', *Radical History Review*, 100 (Winter 2008), 38–60.

IVillage, 'So, is 'High Class Call Girl' Really the Perfect Job for a Busy Mum?' *Mamamia* (1 September 2014).

Jackson, J. M., 'It's Even Harder to Watch *The Handmaid's Tale* When You Know Black Women's History', *Water Cooler Convos* (12 June 2017), watercooler convos.com.

Jacobsson, P., 'A Swedish Sex Worker on the Criminalisation of Clients' (30 August 2011), youtube.com.

Jagose, A., 'Feminism's Queer Theory', *Feminism & Psychology*, 19:2 (2009), 157–74.

Jameson, F., *Archaeologies of the Future: The Desire Called Utopia and Other Science Fictions* (London: Verso, 2007).

Jeffreys, E. and J. Fawkes, 'Staging Decriminalisation: Sex Worker Performance and HIV', in A. Campbell and D. Gint (eds.), *Viral Dramaturgies* (Basingstoke: Palgrave Macmillan, 2018), 69–90.

July, M., *The First Bad Man* (Edinburgh: Canongate Books, 2015).

Kafer, A., *Feminist Queer Crip* (Bloomington: Indiana University Press, 2013).

Kaling, M., *Why Not Me?* (New York: Random House, 2015).

Kang, N. and S. Torres-Saillant, *The Once and Future Muse: The Poetry and Poetics of Rhina P. Espaillat* (Pittsburgh: University of Pittsburgh Press, 2018).

Kantor, J., R. Abrams, and M. Haberman, 'Ivanka Trump's West Wing Agenda', *New York Times* (2 May 2017).

Keeler, E. M., 'C'est Pas Moi: On Kate Zambreno's "Heroines"', *LA Review of Books* (16 December 2012).

Keller, J. and J. Ringrose, '"But then Feminism Goes Out the Window!": Exploring Teenage Girls' Response to Celebrity Feminism', *Celebrity Studies*, 6:1 (2015), 132–5.

Keller, J. and M. Ryan, 'Introduction: Mapping Emergent Feminisms', in J. Keller and M. Ryan (eds.), *Emergent Feminisms: Complicating a Postfeminist Media Culture* (New York and London: Routledge, 2010), 1–21.

Keneally, M., 'List of Trump's Accusers and their Allegations of Sexual Misconduct', *ABC News* (25 June 2019).

Kennedy, T. A., *Historicizing Post-Discourses: Postfeminism and Postracialism in United States Culture* (Albany: SUNY Press, 2017).

Khalili, L., 'Heroic and Tragic Pasts: Mnemonic Narratives in the Palestinian Refugee Camps', *Critical Sociology*, 33:4 (2007), 731–59.

Khng, D. L., 'Philosophising Gender Politics in *Y: The Last Man*', *Journal of Graphic Novels and Comics*, 7:2 (2016), 167–77.

Kirino, N., *Real World*, trans. P. Gabriel (New York: Vintage, 2009).

Klein, N., 'Capitalism Killed Our Climate Momentum, Not "Human Nature"', *The Intercept* (3 August 2018).

Knox, B., 'Tearing Down the Whorearchy from the Inside', *Jezebel* (7 February 2014).

Koffman, O. and R. Gill, '"The Revolution Will Be Led by a 12-year-old-girl": Girl Power and Global Biopolitics', *Feminist Review*, 105 (2013), 83–102.

Kraus, C., *Aliens and Anorexia* (South Pasadena: Semiotexte, 2000).

I Love Dick (Los Angeles: Semiotexte, 2006 [1997]).

Kristeva, J., *Revolution in Poetic Language*, trans. M. Waller (New York: Columbia University Press, 1984).

Krüsi, A. et al., 'Criminalisation of Clients: Reproducing Vulnerabilities for Violence and Poor Health Among Street-based Sex workers in Canada: A Qualitative Study', *BMJ Open*, 4:6 (2014), e005191.

Laboria Cubonkis, 'Xeno-feminism: A Politics for Alienation', laboriacubonks .net.

Landsberg, A. et al., 'Criminalizing Sex Work Clients and Rushed Negotiations Among Sex Workers Who Use Drugs in a Canadian Setting', *Journal of Urban Health*, 94:4 (2017), 563–71.

Last Rescue in Siam, dir. Empower Foundation (Chang Mai: Bad Girls Film, 2012), youtube.com.

Leaning, J., S. Barterls, and H. Mowafi, 'Sexual Violence during War and Forced Migration', in S. Forbes and M. J. Tirman (eds.), *Women, Migration and Conflict: Breaking a Deadly Cycle* (London: Springer, 2009), 173–99.

Leigh, C., *Unrepentant Whore: The Collected Writings of Scarlet Harlot* (San Francisco: Last Gasp, 2002).

Leonard, S., *Wife Inc.: The Business of Marriage in the Twenty-First Century* (New York: NYU Press, 2018).

Lerer, S., *Children's Literature: A Reader's History, from Aesop to Harry Potter* (Chicago: Chicago University Press, 2009).

Levy, D., *Swimming Home* (Sheffield: And Other Stories, 2011).

Levy, J. and P. Jakobsson, 'Abolitionist Feminism as Patriarchal Control: Swedish Understandings of Prostitution and Trafficking', *Dialectical Anthropology*, 37:2 (June 2013), 333–40.

Live Nude Girls Unite!, dirs. V. Funari and J. Query (Brooklyn: First Run/Icarus Films/Query Productions, 2000).

Lorde, A., *Sister Outsider: Essays and Speeches* (Berkeley: Crossing Press, 2007 [1984]).

Lugones, M., *Pilgrimages/Peregrinajes: Theorizing Coalition against Multiple Oppressions* (Lanham, MD: Rowman and Littlefield, 2003).

Luiselli, V., *Tell Me How It Ends: An Essay in Forty Questions* (London: 4th Estate, 2017).

Lumby, C., *Bad Girls: The Media, Sex and Feminism in the 90s* (Sydney: Allen and Unwin, 1997).

Mac, J. and M. Smith, *Revolting Prostitutes: The Fight for Sex Workers' Rights* (London: Verso, 2018).

Machado, A., *Some Beheadings* (New York: Nightboat Books, 2018).

Mafe, D. A., '"We Don't Need Another Hero": Agent 355 as an Original Black Female Hero in *Y: The Last Man*', *African American Review*, 48:1–2 (2015), 33–48.

Mamadouh, V., 'The Scaling of the "Invasion": A Geopolitics of Immigration Narratives in France and The Netherlands', *Geopolitics*, 17:2 (2012), 377–401.

Manne, K., 'Brett Kavanaugh and America's "Himpathy" Reckoning', *New York Times* (26 June 2018).

Down Girl: The Logic of Misogyny (New York and Oxford: Oxford University Press, 2017).

Marchetta, M., *Jellicoe Road* (New York: Harper, 2010).

Marchetti, G., 'Lean in or Bend Over? Postfeminism, Neoliberalism, and Hong Kong's *Wonder Women*', in J. Keller and M. Ryan (eds.), *Emergent Feminisms: Complicating a Postfeminist Media Culture* (New York and London: Routledge, 2010), 193–210.

Martin, B., 'Sexualities Without Genders and Other Queer Utopias', *Diacritics*, 24:2/3 (1994), 104–21.

Marx, K., *Capital: A Critique of Political Economy*, Vol. 1, trans. S. Moore and E. Aveling, (ed.) F. Engels (Moscow: Progress Publishers, 1887).

Maxwell, F. W., *Girlcott* (New York: Blouse and Skirt Books, 2017).

McBean, S., *Feminism's Queer Temporalities* (London and New York: Routledge, 2016).

McCarthy, J. J. et al., *Climate Change 2001: Impacts, Adaptation, Vulnerability* (Cambridge: Cambridge University Press, 2001).

McCarthy, T., 'A Whirlwind Week: Trump's First 14 Official Presidential Actions', *The Guardian* (27 January 2017).

McClain, D., *We Live For the We: The Political Power of Black Motherhood* (New York: Bold Type Books, 2019).

McRobbie, A., *The Aftermath of Feminism: Gender, Culture and Social Change* (London: Sage, 2009).

McRuer, R., *Crip Theory: Cultural Signs of Queerness and Disability* (New York and London: New York University Press, 2006).

McRuer, R. and M. L. Johnson, 'Cripistemologies: Introduction', *Journal of Literary & Cultural Disability Studies*, 8:2 (2014), 127–47.

'Proliferating Cripistemologies: A Virtual Roundtable', *Journal of Literary and Cultural Disability Studies*, 8:2 (2014), 149–69.

Melamed, J., 'The Spirit of Neoliberalism: From Racial Liberalism to Neoliberal Multiculturalism', *Social Text*, 24:4 (2006), 1–24.

Merteuil, M., 'Sex Work Against Work', *Viewpoint Magazine* (31 October 2015).

Milner, A., *Locating Science Fiction* (Liverpool: Liverpool University Press, 2012).

Mintz, S., *Hurt and Pain: Literature and the Suffering Body* (London: Bloomsbury, 2013).

Mitchell, K., '"Feral with Vulnerability": On *The Argonauts*', *Angelaki*, 23:1 (2018), 194–8.

Mohanty, C. T., *Feminism Without Borders: Decolonizing Theory, Practicing Solidarity* (Durham, NC: Duke University Press, 2003).

Molina, N., *Fit to Be Citizens?: Public Health and Race in Los Angeles, 1879–1939* (Berkeley: University of California Press, 2006).

Moran, C., *How to Be a Woman* (London: Ebury Press, 2011).

Moraru, C., 'The Forster Connection or, Cosmopolitanism Redux: Zadie Smith's *On Beauty, Howards End*, and the Schlegels', *The Comparatist*, 35 (May 2011), 133–47.

Morrison, E., 'YA Dystopias Teach Children to Submit to the Free Market, Not Fight Authority', *The Guardian* (1 September 2014).

Mountz, A. and N. Hiemstra, 'Chaos and Crisis: Dissecting the Spatiotemporal Logics of Contemporary Migrations and State Practices', *Annals of the Association of American Geographers*, 104:4 (2014), 382–90.

Moylan, T., *Scraps of the Untainted Sky: Science Fiction, Utopia, Dystopia* (Boulder: West View Press, 2000).

Moynihan, D. P., *The Negro Family: The Case For National Action* (Washington: US Department of Labor, 1965).

Muñoz, J. E., *Cruising Utopia: The Then and There of Queer Futurity* (New York: New York University Press, 2009).

Murphy, M., *The Economization of Life* (Durham, NC: Duke University Press, 2017).

'The Girl: Mergers of Feminism and Finance in Neoliberal Times', *The Scholar and Feminist Online*, 11.1–11.2 (2012–13), n.p.

Ndlovu, V., *Waste Not Your Tears* (Harare, Zimbabwe: Weaver Press, 2018).

Nederveen P., 'Hybridity, So What? The Anti-Hybridity Backlash and the Riddles of Recognition', *Theory, Culture & Society*, 18:2–3 (2001), 219–45.

Negra, D., 'Claiming Feminism: Commentary, Autobiography and Advice Literature for Women in the Recession', *Journal of Gender Studies*, 23:3 (2014), 275–86.

Negra, D. and Y. Tasker, 'Introduction: Gender and Recessionary Culture', in D. Negra and Y. Tasker (eds.), *Gendering the Recession: Media and Culture in an Age of Austerity* (Durham, NC: Duke University Press, 2014), 1–30.

Network of Sex Work Projects, 'Consensus Statement: On Sex Work, Human Rights and the Law' (2013), nswp.org.

'Sex Workers Demonstrate Economic and Social Empowerment', Regional Report: Asia and the Pacific (2014), nswp.org.

Nevins, J., *Operation Gatekeeper and Beyond* (New York: Routledge: 2010).

Ngai, S., *Ugly Feelings* (Cambridge, MA and London: Harvard University Press, 2005).

Ngozi Adichie, C., *We Should All Be Feminists* (London: Fourth Estate, 2014).

Nikoleris, L., 'Oestrogen in Birth Control Pills has a Negative Impact on Fish', *Lund University* (3 March 2016).

O'Neill, R., *Seduction: Men, Masculinity and Mediated Intimacy* (London: Polity, 2018).

O'Reilly, A., 'Ain't I a Feminist?: Matricentric Feminism, Feminist Mamas, and Why Mothers Need a Feminist Movement/Theory of Their Own' (2014), mommuseum.org.

    Matricentric Feminism: Theory, Activism, Practice (Bradford: Demeter Press, 2016).

O'Toole, E., *Girls Will be Girls: Dressing Up, Playing Parts and Daring to Act Differently* (London: Orion Publishing, 2015).

Okafor, N., *Akata Witch* (New York: Viking, 2011).

Oliver, K., 'Julia Kristeva's Feminist Revolutions', *Hypatia*, 8:3 (Summer, 1993), 94–114.

Oppenheim, M., 'Hungarian Prime Minister Viktor Orban Bans Gender Studies Programmes', *Independent* (24 October 2018).

Parisi, L. and T. Terranova, 'Heat-Death: Emergence and Control in Genetic Engineering and Artificial Life', *CTheory*, 5 (2005), n.p.

Pearl, M. B., 'Theory and the Everyday', *Angelaki*, 23:1 (2018), 199–203.

Pendleton, E., 'Love For Sale: Queering Heterosexuality', in J. Nagle (ed.), *Whores and Other Feminists* (Routledge 1997), 73–82.

Penny, L., *Unspeakable Things: Sex, Lies and Revolution* (London: Bloomsbury, 2014).

Phipps, A., *The Politics of the Body: Gender in a Neoliberal and Neoconservative Age* (Cambridge: Polity Press, 2014).

Plumwood, V., *Feminism and the Mastery of Nature* (London: Routledge, 1993).

Poehler, A., *Yes Please* (New York: Harper Collins, 2014).

Popescu, G., *Bordering and Ordering the Twenty-First Century* (Plymouth: Rowman & Littlefield, 2012).

Povinelli, E. A. and G. Chauncey (eds.), 'Thinking Sexuality Transnationally', special issue of *GLQ*, 5:4 (1999).

Preciado, P. B., *Testo Junkie: Sex, Drugs, and Biopolitics in the Pharmacopornographic Era*, trans. B. Benderson (New York: Feminist Press, 2013).

Preece, S., 'DWP Forced to Admit More Than 111,000 Deaths', *Welfare Weekly* (13 August 2018), welfareweekly.com.

Probyn, E., 'New Traditionalism and Post-Feminism: TV Does the Home', *Screen*, 31:2 (1990), 147–59.

Projansky, S., *Watching Rape: Film and Television in Postfeminist Culture* (New York: New York University Press, 2001).

Prostitutes of New York, 'Statement on the Dignity of Sex Workers' (2005), nswp.org.

Prostitutes War Group, 'Pro-Festo of the Prostitutes War Group' (2017), prostituteswargroup.wordpress.com.

Puar, J. K., *Terrorist Assemblages: Homonationalism in Queer Times* (Durham, NC: Duke University Press, 2007).

Puig de la Bellacasa, M., 'Nothing Comes Without Its World': Thinking With Care', *The Sociological Review*, 60:2 (2012), 197–216.

Pussy Riot, 'Make America Great Again' (26 October 2017), youtube.com.

Queen, K., *Fearful Beloved* (New York: Argos Books, 2015).

Raha, N., 'The Limits of Trans Liberalism' (21 September 2015), versobooks.com /blogs/.

"'on the vision of yur futures, ruptures isles …'", *Of Sirens, Body & Faultlines* (Norwich: Boiler House Press, 2018), 142–4.

'Transfeminine Brokenness, Radical Transfeminism', *South Atlantic Quarterly*, 116:3 (July 2017), 632–46.

Reily, K., 'Alabama's Abortion Ban is Designed to Challenge *Roe v. Wade* at the Supreme Court. Here's What Happens Next', *Time* (15 May 2019), *Time .com*.

Renninger, B., '"Are you a *Feminist*?": Celebrity, Publicity, and the Making of a PR-Friendly Feminism', in J. Keller and M. Ryan (eds.), *Emergent Feminisms: Complicating a Postfeminist Media Culture* (New York and London: Routledge, 2010), 42–56.

Richards, J. C., 'Women, Weepies, and the Fault in Our Stars', *Post45: Contemporaries* (10 February 2014), post45.research.yale.edu.

Rivers, N., *Postfeminism(s) and the Arrival of the Fourth Wave* (Basingstoke and New York: Palgrave Macmillan, 2017).

Robbins, R., *Literary Feminisms* (Basingstoke: Macmillan, 2000).

Roberts, D., *Killing the Black Body: Race, Reproduction and the Meaning of Liberty* (New York: Pantheon Books, 1997).

Robertson, L., *Magenta Soul Whip* (Toronto: Coach House Books, 2005).
Nilling (Toronto: Book Thug, 2012).
Proverbs of a She-Dandy (Paris and Vancouver: Morris and Helen Belkin Art Gallery, 2018).
R's Boat (Berkeley: University of California Press, 2010).
Three Summers (Toronto: Coach House Books, 2016).

Rooney, E. (ed.), *The Cambridge Companion to Feminist Literary Theory* (Cambridge: Cambridge University Press, 2012).

Rottenberg, C., 'The Neoliberal Feminist Subject', *Los Angeles Review of Books* (7 January 2018).
'The Rise of Neoliberal Feminism', *Cultural Studies*, 28:3 (2014), 418–37.

Rowbotham, S., *Promise of a Dream* (New York: Verso, 2001).

Rowell, R., *Carry On* (New York: St Martin's Press, 2015).

Rubin, G., 'Thinking Sex: Notes for a Radical Theory of the Politics of Sexuality' [1984], in H. Abelove, M. A. Barale, and D. M. Halperin (eds.), *The Lesbian and Gay Studies Reader* (New York and London: Routledge, 1993), 3–44.

Salkey, A., *Riot*, illustrated by W. Papes (Oxford: Oxford University Press, 1967).

Samuels, E., 'Judith Butler's Body Theory and the Question of Disability', in K. Q. Hall (ed.), *Feminist Disability Studies* (Bloomington: Indiana University Press, 2011), 48–66.

Sandberg, S., *Lean In: Women, Work and the Will to Lead* (New York: Alfred A. Knopf, 2013)

Sargent, L. T., 'The Three Faces of Utopianism Revisited', *Utopian Studies*, 5:1 (1994), 1–37.

Scarlet Alliance, 'Principles for Model Sex Work Legislation' (Redfern: Sydney, 2014), scarletalliance.org.

Schalk, S., *Bodyminds Reimagined: (Dis)ability, Race, and Gender in Black Women's Speculative Fiction* (Durham, NC: Duke University Press, 2008).

Schneiderman, J., 'The Anthropocene Controversy', in R. Grusin (ed.), *Anthropocene Feminisms* (Minneapolis and London: University of Minnesota Press, 2016), 169–96.

Schumer, A., *The Girl With the Lower Back Tattoo* (New York: Gallery Books, 2016).

Sciolino, E., 'Violent Youths Threaten to Hijack Demonstrations in Paris', *New York Times* (30 March 2006).

Sedgwick, E. K., *Epistemology of the Closet* (Berkeley and Los Angeles: University of California Press, 1990).

'Paranoid Reading and Reparative Reading; or, You're So Paranoid, You Probably Think This Essay is About You', in E. K. Sedgwick (ed.), *Novel Gazing: Queer Readings in Fiction* (Durham, NC: Duke University Press, 1997), 1–37.

Segal, L., *Making Trouble: Life and Politics* (London: Serpent's Tail, 2007).

'Who Do You Think You Are? Feminist Memoir Writing', *New Formations*, 67 (2009), 120–33.

Selvadurai, S., *Swimming in the Monsoon Sea* (Toronto, Ontario: Tundra Books, 2007).

Sharafeddine, F., *The Servant*, trans. F. Sharafeddine (Toronto, Ontario: Groundwood Books, 2013).

Shire, W., *Teaching My Mother How to Give Birth* (London: Flipped Eye, 2011).

Shiva, V., 'The New Nature', *Boston Review* (11 January 2016).

Silman, A., 'The Most Traumatizing Moments from *The Handmaid's Tale* Season Premiere', *The Cut* (25 April 2018), thecut.com.

Sincero, J., *You Are a Badass: How to Stop Doubting Your Greatness and Start Living an Awesome Life* (London: Hachette, 2016).

Smith, H., 'Shocking Images of Drowned Syrian Boy Show Tragic Plight of Refugees', *The Guardian* (2 September 2015).

Smith, Z., *On Beauty* (London: Hamish Hamilton, 2005).

Solanas, V., *Scum Manifesto* (London and New York: Verso Books, 2015).

Southgate, M., 'An Unnatural Woman', in C. Berry (ed.), *Rise Up Singing: Black Woman Writers on Motherhood* (New York: Broadway Books, 2004), 114–19.

Spade, D., *Normal Life: Administrative Violence, Critical Trans Politics, and the Limits of the Law* (Durham, NC: Duke University Press, 2015).

Spillers, H. J., 'Mama's Baby, Papa's Maybe: An American Grammar Book', *Diacritics*, 17:2 (1987), 65–81.

Srnicek, N. and A. Williams, *Inventing the Future: Postcapitalism and a World Without Work* (London and Brooklyn: Verso, 2015).

Stern, A. M., *Eugenic Nation: Faults and Frontiers of Better Breeding in Modern America* (Berkeley: University of California Press, 2005).

Stockton, K. B., 'The Queer Child Now and its Paradoxical Global Effects', *GLQ*, 22:4 (2016), 505–39.

Stryker, S., *Transgender History* (Berkeley: Seal Press, 2008).

Stryker, S. and S. Whittle, *The Transgender Studies Reader* (London and New York: Routledge, 2006).

Suvin, D., *Metamorphoses of Science Fiction: On the Poetics and History of a Literary Genre* (New Haven and London: Yale University Press, 1979).

Takami, K., *Battle Royale*, trans. Y. Oniki (San Francisco: Viz Media, 2009).

Tasker Y. and D. Negra, 'Introduction: Feminist Politics and Postfeminist Culture', in Y. Tasker and D. Negra (eds.), *Interrogating Postfeminism: Gender and the Politics of Popular Culture* (Durham, NC: Duke University Press, 2007), 1–26.

Taylor, A., *Celebrity and the Feminist Blockbuster* (London: Springer/Palgrave Macmillan, 2016).

Taylor, K.-Y., *How We Get Free: Black Feminism and the Combahee River Collective* (Chicago: Haymarket Books, 2012).

Teller, J., *Nothing*, trans. M. Aiken (New York: Atheneum, 2010).

Thomas, A., *The Hate U Give* (New York: Balzer + Bray, 2017).

Thompson, C., 'The *New* Afro in a Postfeminist Media Culture: Rachel Dolezal, Beyoncé's "Formation," and the Politics of Choice', in J. Keller and M. Ryan (eds.), *Emergent Feminisms: Complicating a Postfeminist Media Culture* (New York and London: Routledge, 2010), 161–75.

Trilling, D., 'Five Myths About the Refugee Crisis', *The Guardian* (5 June 2018).

Trump, I., *The Trump Card: Playing to Win in Work and Life* (New York: Touchstone/Simon & Schuster, 2009).

Women Who Work: Rewriting the Rules for Success (New York: Portfolio/ Penguin, 2017).

Tsing, A., 'Salvage Accumulation', *Cultural Anthropology* (30 March 2015).

Turtschaninoff, M., *Maresi*, trans. A. Prime (New York: Amulet Books, 2017).

US Department of Justice, Civil Rights Division, 'Investigation of the Baltimore City Police Department' (10 August 2016).

Vermette, K., S. B. Henderson, and D. Taciuk, *Pemmican Wars: A Girl Called Echo*, Vol. 1. (Winnipeg, Manitoba: Highwater Press, 2017).

Vettese, T., 'Sexism in the Academy: Women's Narrowing Path to Tenure', *n+1*, 35 (Spring 2019), nplusonemag.com.

Walker, A., *In Search of Our Mothers' Gardens: Womanist Prose* (New York: Harcourt, 1983).

Wall-Kimmerer, R., *Braiding Sweetgrass: Indigenous Wisdom, Scientific Knowledge, and the Teachings of Plants* (Minneapolis: Milkweed Editions, 2013).

Wang, J., *Carceral Capitalism* (Cambridge, MA and London: MIT Press, 2018).

Watson, M. A., 'Female Circumcision from Africa to the Americas: Slavery to the Present', *The Social Science Journal*, 42:3 (2005), 421–37.

Weed, E., 'Introduction', in E. Weed and N. Schor (eds.), *Feminism Meets Queer Theory* (Bloomington and Indianapolis, IN: Indiana University Press, 1997), vii–xiii.

Weeks, K., *The Problem with Work: Feminism, Marxism, Antiwork Politics, and Postwork Imaginaries* (Durham, NC: Duke University Press, 2011).

Weheliye, A. G., *Habeas Viscus: Racializing Assemblages, Biopolitics, and Black Feminist Theories of the Human* (Durham, NC: Duke University Press, 2014).

Weidhase, N., '"Beyoncé Feminism" and the Contestation of the Black Body', *Celebrity Studies*, 6:1 (2015), 128–31.

Weisenburger, S., *Modern Medea: A Family Story of Slavery and Child-Murder from the Old South* (New York: Hill and Wang, 1998).

Wekker, G., *White Innocence: Paradoxes of Colonialism and Race* (Durham, NC: Duke University Press, 2016).

Wendell, S., *The Rejected Body* (New York: Routledge, 1996).

Wiegman, R., *Object Lessons* (Durham, NC: Duke University Press, 2012).

'On Being in Time with Feminism', *MLQ: Modern Language Quarterly*, 65:1 (2004), 161–76.

'The Times We're In: Queer Feminist Criticism and the Reparative "Turn"', *Feminist Theory*, 15:1 (2014), 4–25.

Williams, M., *This is How We Survive: Revolutionary Mothering, War, and Exile in the 21st Century* (Oakland: PM Press, 2019).

Wilson Gilmore, R., 'Fatal Couplings of Power and Difference: Notes on Racism and Geography', *The Professional Geographer*, 54:1 (2002), 15–24.

Golden Gulag: Prisons, Surplus, Crisis, and Opposition in Globalizing California (Berkeley and London: University of California Press, 2007).

Winkiel, L., *Modernism, Race, and Manifestos* (Cambridge and New York: Cambridge University Press, 2008).

Wolkowitz, C. et al. (eds.), *Body/Sex/Work: Intimate, Embodied and Sexualised Labour* (Basingstoke: Palgrave Macmillan, 2013).

Wynes, S. and K. Nicholas, 'The Climate Mitigation Gap', *Environmental Research Letters*, 12:7 (July 2017).

Yaeger, P., 'Beyond the Fragments', *NOVEL: A Forum on Fiction*, 23:2 (Winter, 1990), 203–8.

Zambreno, K., *Heroines* (South Pasadena: Semiotexte, 2012).

Zetter, R., 'More Labels, Fewer Refugees: Remaking the Refugee Label in an Era of Globalization', *Journal of Refugee Studies*, 20:2 (2007), 172–92.

Zieminski, N., 'Actress Emma Watson Says Revealing Photo Does Not Undermine Feminism', *Reuters* (5 March 2017).

Zylinksa, J., *Minimal Ethics for the Anthropocene* (Ann Arbor: Open Humanities Press, 2014).

Index

9/11, 29

abjection, 149
ableism, 99, 101, 103
abortion, 2–3, 122, 170, 197, 199
academia, 9, 141, 213
activism, 8, 25–6, 36–8, 69, 72, 77, 82, 89, 99, 113, 119, 123, 136, 171, 211–12, 214, 220
Adams, Carol, 123
agency, 4, 13, 17, 21, 89, 104, 124–6, 145, 171, 182, 191, 230
Agustin, Laura, 76
Ahiska, Meltem, 225, 228
Ahmed, Sara, 4, 10, 40, 130, 195–6, 199, 222
Alaimo, Stacey, 120, 124–6
Alderman, Naomi, 172, 175–9
Alexander, Jacqui, 183
Allen, Woody, 26
Amar, Paul, 191
ambivalence, 5, 43, 48, 50–2
anger, 36, 52, 91, 171, 210
anorexia, 200, 210, 216–17
anti-capitalism, 123, 195
anti-normativity, 13, 15–6, 21
Arruzza, Cinzia, 147
asylum, 56, 64, 198
Atkinson, Ti-Grace, 137
Atwood, Margaret
    The Handmaid's Tale, 2, 112, 170, 177
    The Handmaid's Tale (TV series), 170
austerity, 2, 13, 18, 151, 190, 234
autobiography, 100, 104–5, 218
autonomism, Italian, 143

Baccolini, Rafaella, 171, 177
Baraka, Imamu Amiri, 46
Barounis, Cynthia, 107
Bates, Laura, 85
Beard, Mary, 174, 207
Bechdel, Alison, 100, 104–7, 111
Bennett, Jane, 124–5

Berg, Heather, 73
Berlant, Lauren, 201–2, 232
Bernstein, Elizabeth, 76
Bérubé, Michael, 107
Bey, Marquis, 16, 20
Beyoncé, 83, 85–6, 203
Black Lives Matter, 2, 26, 29, 31, 38, 42, 44, 120
Blasey Ford, Christine, 36
borders, 5, 13–15, 17–18, 20, 42, 74, 182, 190, 229, 233
Braidotti, Rosi, 124, 223
Brenner, Johanna, 145
Brexit, 18, 22, 233
Brown, Michael, 36
Brown, Wendy, 186
Brownmiller, Susan, 210, 215
Burke, Tarana, 5, 10, 25, 29, 38
Butler, Judith, 132, 135, 202, 225
Butler, Octavia, 100, 108–11

Capildeo, Vahni, 55, 63–7
Castillo, Ana, 100–4, 111
celebrity, 25–6, 29, 36
Chapkis, Wendy, 71
Cheng Thom, Kai, 192
childcare, 70, 195
Chira, Susan, 99
Chodorow, Nancy, 49
Chopra, Serena, 222, 226–8, 230
chora, the, 223
climate change, 109, 115–6, 122, 195
Clinton, Hilary, 38, 91
Clover, Joshua, 117
Colebrook, Claire, 117, 135
colonisation, 121
commodity, 75, 146
contraception, 122
Conway, Kellyanne, 93
crisis, financial (2007–8), 2, 87, 143
Cullors, Patrisse, 10, 44

Cvetkovich, Ann, 138
Cyrus, Miley, 86, 99

Dalla Costa, Mariarosa, 144
Daring, C. B., 74
Davis, Angela, 44, 49
de Beauvoir, Simone, 49, 102, 135, 214
deportation, 61, 66, 74, 76
Despentes, Virginie, 201
detention, 55, 198
Dhillon, Jaskiron, 188
dignity, 71–2
Disability March, 99–100
dispossession, 13, 15–6, 47, 48
Ditum, Sarah, 170–2
diversity, 10, 14–5, 18, 199
Dotson, Kristie, 27
Dunn, Danielle, 50, 52
Dworkin, Andrea, 209, 211–12, 214

Edinburgh Action for Trans Health, 195, 197, 199
Egoff, Sheila, 185
El Shakry, Omnia, 189
Ellis, Carson, 31
embodiment, 103, 105, 147, 215, 231
empathy, 26, 29, 109, 118, 174, 212, 214–19
empire, 27, 116, 121
Endnotes collective, 145, 148
Engels, Friedrich, 147
ethics, 13, 16, 18, 21, 122–3, 125, 215

Farrier, David, 64
Farrow, Ronan, 33
Favaro, Laura, 91
Federici, Silvia, 78, 144, 146
Felski, Rita, 208, 219
female circumcision, 172
Femen, 88
femininity, 50, 78, 83, 86, 126, 174, 200–1, 219
feminism, bad forms of
    anti-sex work, 3, 73–7
    anti-trans, 3
    commodity, 88
    lean in, 3, 83, 85, 92, 121
    liberal, 148
    neoliberal, 3, 87, 92, 94
    state, 3, 13
feminism, fourth-wave, 86–8
feminism, second-wave, 48, 169, 194, 199, 209
Ferguson, Sue, 147
Ferreira da Silva, Denise, 16
Firestone, Shulamith, 152, 195
Fortunati, Leopoldina, 78, 144
Foucault, Michel, 149
Frase, Peter, 72

Fraser, Nancy, 86
Freedman, Ariela, 104, 107
Freeman, Elizabeth, 134, 138
Friedan, Betty, 49

Gambetti, Zeynep, 225
Garland-Thomson, Rosemary, 111
Garza, Alicia, 10, 44
gaslighting, 27, 34
Gay, Roxanne, 199–200, 203–5
gender
    abolition, 117, 198
    binary, 16, 20, 23, 117, 132, 139
    pay gap, 2, 89
    studies, 2, 129–30
    violence, 19
Gill, Rosalind, 84–5
Gilmore, Leigh, 202, 209
Gilson, Erinn, 215
Gira Grant, Melissa, 70
Greer, Germaine, 202
Gregg, Melissa, 133
Grewal, Inderpal, 4, 182–3
Grosz, Elizabeth, 135
Gruen, Lori, 123
Guène, Faïza, 185–6
Gumbs, Alexis Pauline, 44

Haraway, Donna, 115, 118–9, 122, 124
Harding, Sandra, 115
Heller, Nathan, 90
Hemmings, Clare, 137, 139, 209–10, 215, 218
Henderson, Margaret, 210–11
Hesford, Victoria, 134
Hess, Amanda, 99
Hester, Helen, 195–7
heteronormativity, 21, 135, 139, 224
heteropatriarchy, 5, 50
heterosexuality, 46, 132, 139
Heti, Sheila, 218
Hiemstra, Nancy, 57
Hill Collins, Patricia, 4, 43–5
Hill, Anita, 39
HIV, 17, 74, 80–1, 185, 245
homonormativity, 21
homophobia, 20, 101
hooks, bell, 43–4, 48–9, 83
hybridity, 58

incarceration, 18–9
incels, 85
interdependence, 100, 106, 110, 124
International Labour Organisation, 70
intersectionality, 102, 129, 146, 152, 203

Irigaray, Luce, 135
Islamophobia, 14

Jackson, Jenn M., 172
Jagose, Annamarie, 134–5, 138
Jakobsson, Pye, 76
Jameson, Fredric, 178
Jenner, Caitlyn, 14, 16
Johnson, Merri Lisa, 100

Kafer, Alison, 99
Kapernick, Colin, 36
Kaplan, Caren, 182
Karenga, Maulana, 46
Katsarova, Rada, 143
Kavanaugh, Brett, 36
Keller, Jessalynn, 85, 87
killjoy, feminist, 196
Kirino, Natsuo, 190
Klein, Naomi, 122
Knox, Belle, 73
Koutonin, Mawuna Remarque, 65
Kraus, Chris, 210, 216–8
Kristeva, Julia, 223, 227, 233

Laboucan-Massimo, Melina, 121
labour, reproduction, 70
labour, reproductive, 2, 52, 78, 150–1
Lady Gaga, 99
Laslett, Barbara, 145
Leigh, Carol, 70
Leonard, Suzanne, 92
lesbianism, 102, 105, 137
Levy, Jay, 76
liberalism, 13–4, 21, 43
Lorde, Audre, 4, 42, 44, 51, 222, 224, 227–8, 235
love, 42–3, 50, 52, 101, 103–4, 107, 129, 133, 214, 229
Love, Heather, 138
Lugones, María, 16
Luiselli, Valeria, 55, 58–61, 63, 65–6

Mac, Juno, 73
Machado, Aditi, 222, 228–30
Manne, Kate, 27
Manning, Francesca, 150
marginalisation, 15, 18–9
Martens, China, 44
Martin, Biddy, 133
Marx, Karl, 75, 79, 144–7
McClain, Dani, 44
McRuer, Robert, 100
menopause, 231
menstruation, 121

Merteuil, Morgane, 78
MeToo, 1–4, 85, 120, 222, 239
migration, 151
Milano, Alyssa, 26
Milner, Andrew, 171
misogyny, 20, 51, 53, 84–5, 90, 121, 196, 200
Mohanty, Chandra Talpade, 55, 57, 63, 183
Moran, Caitlin, 85, 194, 199–200, 202–4
Morrison, Toni, 43
Mountz, Alison, 57
Moylan, Tom, 171, 176–7
Moynihan Report, the, 45–7
Mulvey, Laura, 230
Murphy, Michelle, 183

Nash, Jennifer, 4, 129–30, 134
Nassar, Larry, 29
nature, 72, 100, 118, 122–3, 126, 173, 178
Negra, Diane, 87
Nelson, Maggie, 215
neoliberalism, 52, 84, 86, 90, 94, 182–3, 202, 204
Nevins, Joseph, 55
new materialism, 124–5
Newns, Lucinda, 64
Ngai, Sianne, 200
Ngozi Adichie, Chimamanda, 199–200, 202–3
non-binary, 25
non-normativity, 48, 105, 111, 122
normativity, 13, 108, 151
norms, 15–6, 107, 119, 174, 182

Okafor, Nnedi, 187–8
ontology, 123, 125, 147, 149–50
O'Reilly, Andrea, 43
O'Toole, Emer, 199–200, 202–3

pain, 36, 66–7, 100–2, 107, 109–11, 172, 226, 230
Passante Elman, Julia, 183–4
Pearl, Monica B., 215
Pendleton, Eva, 78
Penny, Laurie, 199–203
people, indigenous, 27, 38, 74, 119, 121, 124, 127, 188–9
Perkins Gilman, Charlotte, 175
Peterson, Jordan, 85
Piercy, Marge, 100, 171
Plumwood, Val, 118
Polanski, Roman, 26
police. *See* violence
politics
    communist, 145
    far-right, 2, 14, 195
    socialist, 145
pollution, 120
Popescu, Gabriel, 57

poverty, 45, 56, 109, 121, 145, 188
precarity, 15, 17, 19, 21, 69, 73, 78, 91, 145, 190, 198
Preciado, Paul, 16
privilege, 4, 57, 73, 76, 84–7, 89–93, 138, 200

Queen, Khadijah, 222, 227–9

racialisation, 5, 18, 44, 57, 61, 63, 147, 149, 186
Raha, Nat, 222, 232–4
rape, 25, 28, 34, 37–8, 47, 177–8, 191, 206, 212,
    226, 228
reproduction, 44, 47, 79, 174–5, 177, 195
reproduction, social, 50, 70, 122, 182
Rich, Adrienne, 49, 99
rights, 119
    abortion, 2
    gender, 113
    human, 71, 183
    queer, 74
    reproductive, 43, 113, 120, 122, 177
    sex workers', 74
    trans, 120
    women's, 2, 99
riots, 186
Rivers, Nicola, 85–8
Robertson, Lisa, 222, 230–2
Rottenberg, Catherine, 87, 92
Rowbotham, Sheila, 208, 214–15
Rubin, Gayle, 130–2, 135, 139
Ryan, Maureen, 85, 87

Sabsay, Letitia, 225
Sakhawat Hossain, Begum Rokeya, 175
Sandberg, Sheryl, 83, 92
Sargent, Pamela, 175
Savage, Dan, 13
Schalk, Sami, 100, 109
Scher, Paula, 34
Schneiderman, Jill, 115
Sedgwick, Eve Kosofsky, 130–3, 135, 138–9
Segal, Lynne, 208–9, 212–14
segregation, 46, 49
sexism, 1, 101
shame, 37, 210, 226
Shire, Warsan, 55, 61–3
Shiva, Vandana, 117–8
Silman, Anna, 170–1
slavery, 27, 43, 45–7, 49, 75, 108, 111, 116, 120, 143,
    172, 179
Smith, Molly, 73
Solanas, Valerie, 195
solidarity, 4, 21, 73, 77, 120, 196, 199, 210, 214–15,
    219–20, 232
Southgate, Martha, 41–3, 51–2
Spahr, Juliana, 117

Spillers, Hortense, 44, 47
Spivak, Gayatri, 135
stereotypes, 176, 178
sterilisation, 17, 44, 172, 198
Stryker, Susan, 141
suicide, 41, 52
Summers, Lawrence, 183
Suvin, Darko, 172–4, 177
Swift, Taylor, 86

Takami, Koushun, 190
Tasker, Yvonne, 87
Taylor, Anthea, 85, 89
Teller, Janne, 190–1
Tepper, Sheri S., 175
Thomas, Clarence, 39
Tometi, Opal, 10, 44
Tower Sargent, Lyman, 171
transcorporeality, 125–6
transfeminism, 4, 13, 16–8, 20–1, 232
trauma, 5, 8, 27, 36–7, 64, 232
Trilling, Daniel, 56, 60
Trump, Donald, 1–2, 34, 38, 60–1, 90–2, 170
Trump, Ivanka, 6, 83–94
Tsing, Anna, 123
Turtschaninoff, Maria, 188

United Nations, 70

Vaughan, Brian K., 175
Vermette, Katherena, 189
violence
    anti-trans, 19
    domestic, 2, 19, 145, 186, 188
    gender, 127, 178
    male, 234
    patriarchal, 233
    police, 26, 29, 31, 36, 42–3, 74, 185–6
    racial, 48
    sexual, 62–3, 66, 222
    slow, 126
Vogel, Lise, 144, 146–7
vulnerability, 26, 31, 38, 61, 76, 78, 99, 145, 187,
    191, 215–16, 223, 225, 228

Wages Against Housework, 78–9
Wages for Housework, 78, 117, 152
Walker, Alice, 51–2
Wall-Kimmerer, Robin, 124
Watson, Emma, 6, 83, 86, 88–90, 203
Weed, Elizabeth, 132
Weeks, Kathi, 72, 78, 194–5
Weil, Simone, 216
Weinstein, Harvey, 25–6, 33, 36–7, 39
Wendell, Susan, 99–100

white supremacy, 45, 52, 116
whiteness, 16, 19, 48, 65, 73, 76, 87–8, 119
Wiegman, Robyn, 129–30, 136–40
Williams, Mai'a, 44
Wilson, Darren, 36
Winkiel, Laura, 194
Women's Liberation Movement, 213–4
Women's March, 2, 34, 36, 38, 99, 170
women's rights, 173
World Health Organisation, 70

xenofeminism, 195–6, 199
xenophobia, 14

Yoshinaga, Fumi, 175

Zambreno, Kate, 210, 215, 217–20
Zetter, Roger, 56
Zylinksa, Joanna, 125–6

CPSIA information can be obtained
at www.ICGtesting.com
Printed in the USA
LVHW080843201221
706703LV00002B/71